The Rise and Self-Destruction of the Greatest Football Team in History

The Chicago Bears and Super Bowl XX

✷

John Mullin

TRIUMPH
BOOKS
CHICAGO

Library of Congress Cataloging-in-Publication Data

Mullin, John, 1947–
    The rise and self-destruction of the greatest football team in history : the Chicago Bears and Super Bowl XX / John Mullin.
        p. cm.
    Includes index.
    ISBN-13: 978-1-57243-790-6
    ISBN-10: 1-57243-790-1
    1. Chicago Bears (Football team) 2. Super Bowl (20th : 1986 : New Orleans, La.) I. Title.

GV956.C5M85 2005
796.332'64'0977311—dc22
                                                                    2005043959

This book is available in quantity at special discounts for your group or organization. For further information, contact:

Triumph Books
542 S. Dearborn St.
Suite 750
Chicago, IL 60605
(312) 939-3330
Fax (312) 663-3557

Printed in U.S.A.
ISBN-13: 978-1-57243-790-6
ISBN-10: 1-57243-790-1
Design by Robert Wyszkowski; page production by Patricia Frey
Photos courtesy of Jonathan Daniel

"Good morning. My name is Mike Ditka.
I'm the new head coach of the Chicago Bears.
My goal is to go to the Super Bowl and win it."
—*Mike Ditka, 1982, opening remarks*
at Bears first minicamp

———————————————

"It is hard to erase 17 years [with the Bears].
Nothing much else to say but
'Thank you, I appreciate it.' But this, too, shall pass."
—*Mike Ditka, 1993, final words*
at his firing press conference

CONTENTS

FOREWORD by John Madden. vii

PREFACE xi

ACKNOWLEDGMENTS xiii

INTRODUCTION: Perspectives xv

CHAPTER 1: Roots of Greatness. 1

CHAPTER 2: Da Coach 17

CHAPTER 3: 1984—The Year They Knew. 31

CHAPTER 4: Shaky Start. 43

CHAPTER 5: The Birth of Mad Mac. 55

CHAPTER 6: Settling Scores 67

CHAPTER 7: Fridge. 77

CHAPTER 8: Manure and Woofing 87

CHAPTER 9: Monday Night in Miami 101

CHAPTER 10: "The Super Bowl Shuffle" 109

CHAPTER 11: On Final Approach 117

CHAPTER 12: The Playoffs—Now Everybody Believed. 127

CHAPTER 13: The Craziest Week of Them All 139

CHAPTER 14: A Game Like No Other 153

CHAPTER 15: Living the Big Crazy 165

CHAPTER 16: Starting to Unravel 179

CHAPTER 17: Final Growls 193

CHAPTER 18: Da Super Fans, Da Bears, Da Coach 209

CHAPTER 19: Farewell 219

EPILOGUE: Where Are They Now? 223

APPENDIX 1: The Roster 231

APPENDIX 2: The Starters 233

INDEX 235

FOREWORD

"The whole thing was right out of central casting."
—*John Madden*

I ALWAYS SAY THAT IN ALL THE YEARS I've been in broadcasting, that 1985 season was the most fun year I ever saw, not only for broadcasting, but for the whole NFL. For the country, really. The Bears had been down, and there were a lot of people who were dormant Bears fans, so when the Bears finally got good, they could all come out. You went to Chicago and everybody was a Bears fan. It went across everything, whether you were old, young, man, woman. Everyone was a Bears fan.

Pat Summerall and I broadcast seven or eight Bears games that year, and we never saw a touchdown scored against them. They were the most dominant team I have ever seen. If anyone asks me about the most dominant defense of all time, I say "the '85 Bears." I don't know that there was anyone better. Ever.

The reason they were so good for football was that they made it a game. It was fun. Walter Payton was one of the all-time great players. Jim McMahon was fun to cover. They had a tremendous offensive line. They had Willie Gault and all that speed. And then that defense: Hampton, Dent, Marshall, Singletary, Wilson, Fencik—all of them were great players. And then you put in Mike Ditka as the coach and Buddy Ryan as the defensive coach. I mean, the whole thing was right out of central casting.

Halfway through that season Pat and I told the network to put us on the Bears. It was one of those things where you just wanted to be there. It was a special year, they were special, and you wanted to be there to document it. At one time the feeling at the network was, "When in doubt, do Dallas," when the Cowboys were good. When the Giants were good, "When in doubt, do New York." Pat and I felt, "When in doubt, do the Chicago Bears." Any chance you get. This was a team that earned the national exposure and they were great with it, like nobody before or since.

I had dinner with John Robinson, then the Rams coach, the night before the NFC Championship Game against the Bears. John was, and still is, very optimistic. He thinks he's going to win everything and score 50 points. In the course of having dinner, I mentioned the point that, in all their games Pat and I had done, we'd never seen a team score a touchdown against the Bears.

"Well, I didn't need to hear that right now," Robinson said. And then he went out and didn't score a touchdown either. He had Eric Dickerson coming off a 248-yard game the week before in the playoff game against Dallas. I knew he didn't have a chance.

There were so many times you remember with them. It was a time when the players were loose, having fun, enjoying everything that was going on and that they did. It was always something, something somebody was wearing, saying, or doing.

We were in Chicago when Walter was going to tie or break some record—he was always doing that anyway, it seemed like—and everybody was looking for Walter after practice. No one could find him: "I just saw him," "Think he's down the hall," "Don't know where he is," "Try the weight room." No Walter.

Finally I went out to my bus and was talking with Willie Yarborough, my driver, and mentioned that no one could find Walter.

"Oh hell, he was right out here on the bus with me, watching *Soul Train*," Willie said.

Walter was just relaxing, telling Willie about when he, Walter, was a *Soul Train* dancer. He told Willie, "I should have won that," referring to some competition. "The girl I was with just wasn't good enough."

Then, typical Walter, he said, "You know, she's probably someplace right now saying the same thing about me."

That was the whole thing. Here was a guy, breaking a major record, and he's out watching TV, talking about it with my drivers.

There was so much special. And maybe the best part, for me and for a lot of people all over Chicago and the country, was that you were living it and you knew it was special while you were living through it.

All America liked the Bears. They were America's Team. Everybody was ready for that. And I think there's just something that's good and that America likes about Chicago. America needed them. The NFL needed them. Chicago. The Chicago Bears. George Halas. The tradition. There's something right there. You want to jump in on it and hang onto it.

And they gave us that. They certainly brought all Chicago together. I spent a lot of time in Chicago then, and no matter where you went, all anybody talked about was the Bears. It didn't make any difference who you were, where you were. It brought the whole city together. It even brought a lot of the country together.

America loves to pull for the underdog. And really, these were the big, bad guys, but they were still the underdogs. It had been a long time since they'd had things go their way. Then they got good and they'd been an underdog so long, they were the Monsters of the Midway again, the Big Bad Bears, but they were a fun thing. They were your big brothers.

The guys just went on and on and on and on. That was part of it too: there was some Bear for everyone. There was McMahon for the renegades. There was Payton, the all-time great player. The Fridge for all the fun-loving big guys. There was Singletary for the disciplined guys, and Fencik for the Ivy Leaguers, the intellectuals. Whatever you wanted, they had it for you.

There was Ditka, Buddy Ryan . . . what else do you want? It was there. It was like a smorgasbord, a buffet.

They reminded me a lot of some of the Raiders teams we had. But we never had that dominant defense.

That '85 Bears defense was the most dominant thing I've ever seen. Even the Steelers; I went against those Steelers. These guys were more dominant than the Steelers.

Women started watching football and enjoying it because of this team. And again, it was because there was something for everyone. There wasn't just one guy. There were lots of people who loved McMahon, any of them.

I don't know that I ever really thought it was "over." They weren't the same in 1984, and they weren't the same in 1986. You could just see that. Still, I was always surprised that it lasted only one year. You would have thought it would have gotten them through another year or two, except things just happened to them.

But they were the real deals. We did my second "All-Madden Team" as a show from the locker room there, and McMahon came in wearing sunglasses and a buffalo head, a bears head or something. He had his daughter with him. He was that type of guy. I had a golf tournament to raise money for the school I went to in California, Cal Poly. McMahon just came and played. No call. No appearance fees. Just showed up and played in the tournament to help out. That was why he was McMahon.

That was the kind of guy so many of them were. Those players were really part of the city. Chicago was part of those players, but those players were part of the city too. They were around town, they had their shows, their appearances, and did things. And not all "money" things either. They all made some money I'm sure, but they did so many things that were pretty good. Sometimes McMahon or whoever it was would just tell the school or wherever he was appearing that his "fee" was a six-pack of Moosehead.

And something I really appreciated and respected about the fans: even when the Bears were bad, the fans still filled that place. The Bears prided themselves on defense and being tough, like Chicago. "You may have beat us, but we knocked out some guys."

People everywhere really took their side on the outrageous stuff. Americans like being a little different. They like being rebels. They like rebels. That's what this whole bunch was. They had fun, and they made it fun for everybody else too.

In my entire career in football, it was never like that before and has never been like that since. That was a magical year. There will never be anything like it—or them—again.

—*John Madden*

PREFACE

THE ORIGINAL IDEA FOR A WORKING TITLE FOR THIS BOOK, based on the tenor of comments and regrets of so many members of the '85 Bears, was *Greatness Squandered*. Almost without exception, players believe they should have won three Super Bowls, not one.

There are still hard feelings, some bitterness. When more than two dozen of the players, along with Ditka, met at Ditka's restaurant in early 2005, the purpose was to discuss how the group would market itself to get the best possible deals for themselves for the 20th anniversary of Super Bowl XX. Some of the old jealousies and scratchiness crept back in over who did what and what it was worth. With more than a touch of irony, the 1985 Bears had come together to plan their anniversary celebration and found themselves starting to behave instead like the 1986 Bears, the ones who, along with the team's owners, started squandering the greatness they had achieved.

And yet it ultimately is a celebration. Hall of Fame defensive lineman Dan Hampton still feels the sting of what was lost. And still he finds himself, to this day, driving somewhere, sometime, and feeling his thoughts drift back to that magical time in 1985, the greatest single moment in a long, distinguished life in a sport he loved. And he is far from alone in those feelings.

Pulling together history is difficult any time because memories fade or become distorted and the mind simply loses pieces and can't remember where it put them. The difficulty in chronicling the '85 Bears, however, was that the memories were *so* vivid, the events *so* colorful, that the only real question was how far short the storytelling would fall of the story.

For help I relied on the players and others who were at the epicenter in those years. This story is, after all, theirs. In most situations their stories are part of the narrative fabric. Where it seemed that their present-day perspectives needed to stand apart from what was unfolding in those bygone years, their thoughts are set off from the story. Their memories are sometimes jaded, at times sketchy because of the frenzied pace of what unfolded. They were impressionable, talented football players, young men who forever were blessed to be part of something special, and at the same time, rendered incomplete because of human misjudgment, jealousy, and greed—their own and that of others.

For those who were just too young to remember it all, the hope is that this will provide some small window to the past that will let them say, "Oh, *now* I see what it was all about."

For those who lived through those times, the hope is that this is one final chance to remember how many times somebody was getting drinks in the kitchen only to hear the living room erupt and a buddy yell, "Hey, get in here! You *gotta* see this!"

ACKNOWLEDGMENTS

MY DEEPEST THANKS go out to all of the players and individuals who gave so generously of their time and insights over the years, without whom this project never would have been possible. At the top of the pyramid are the ones who did it all—the players themselves, both the '85 Bears and those who came before and afterward: Mike Adamle, Trace Armstrong, Richard Dent, Mike Ditka, Gary Fencik, Andy Frederick, Shaun Gayle, Dan Hampton, Jim Harbaugh, Mike Hartenstine, Jay Hilgenberg, Glen Kozlowski, Dennis McKinnon, Steve McMichael, Emery Moorehead, Jim Morrissey, Keith Ortego, William Perry, Ron Rivera, Mike Singletary, Dick Stanfel, Matt Suhey, Tom Thayer, Calvin Thomas, Keith Van Horne, Tom Waddle, Otis Wilson, and Donnell Woolford.

Thanks to various members of the Bears organization: the McCaskey family, including Brian, Pat, Tim, and much-missed patriarch Ed; Jim Christman; Clyde Emrich; Kenny Geiger; Roger Hacker; Scott Hagel; Bryan Harlan; Sharon Lehner; Bill McGrane; Bill Tobin; and Ken Valdiserri. The help of NFL officials Pete Abitante and Dick Maxwell was invaluable.

Also adding to the color of the times as well as this book were John Anderson, Hub Arkush, Chet Coppock, Chuck Davidson, Les Grobstein, Wayne Larrivee, John Madden, Joe Mantegna, Julia Meyer, Fred Mitchell, Brent Musburger, Brad Palmer, Floyd Perkins, Don Pierson, Dan Pompei, Joe Ponsetto, Steve Rosenbloom, Robert Smigel, Jim Steiner, David Tossell, Bob Vasilopulos, and Steve Zucker.

Special thanks go to my agent, Greg Dinkin, without whom this book would be just a nice idea and some stories lying around my office, and to the staff of Triumph Books. And Mom and Dad, Jenny, and Kathleen, you deserve your own private "Credits" page.

BOOKS

The following books were invaluable in researching and preparing this project:

D'Amato, Gary, and Cliff Christl. *Mudbaths & Bloodbaths: The Inside Story of the Bears-Packers Rivalry*. Madison, WI: Prairie Oak Press, 1997.

Davis, Jeff. *Papa Bear: The Life and Legacy of George Halas*. New York: McGraw-Hill, 2004.

Ditka, Mike, with Don Pierson. *Ditka: An Autobiography*. Chicago: Bonus Books, 1986.

Lamb, Kevin. *Portrait of Victory: Chicago Bears 1985*. Chicago: Chicago Review Press, 1986.

McMahon, Jim, and Bob Verdi. *McMahon! The Bear Truth About Chicago's Brashest Bear*. New York: Warner Books, Inc., 1986.

McMichael, Steve, with Phil Arvia. *Steve McMichael's Tales from the Chicago Bears Sidelines*. Champaign, IL: Sports Publishing LLC, 2004.

Mullin, John. *Tales from the Chicago Bears Sidelines: A Collection of the Greatest Stories Ever Told*. Champaign, IL: Sports Publishing LLC, 2003.

Singletary, Mike, with Armen Keteyian. *Calling the Shots*. Chicago: Contemporary Books, 1986.

INTRODUCTION
PERSPECTIVES

"In a way it was like watching a magnesium flare."
—*actor Joe Mantegna*

THIS IS THE STORY about the greatest football team of all time. More than a football team, really. It is the story of one bright, shining moment in America. The 1985 Bears *were* America. They were the team that America wanted, needed, and embraced at the time and for years afterward to this day. They were a collection of characters that reflected nothing less than the best—and the worst—of a nation, a people, an era. They were, for a brief, magical instant, a band of eccentrics and athletes who went from nobodies to rock stars, from country kids and city kids to cult figures, who took America on a wonderful, wild ride like nothing before or since.

They were the boldest, most outrageous team of all time—certainly in football history, arguably in all of sports history—and their reach went far beyond football. William Perry and Walter Payton were laughing together on the cover of the January 27, 1986, *Time* magazine. Jim McMahon gave *Rolling Stone* its March 13, 1986, "rock 'n' roll quarterback" cover. David Letterman, Johnny Carson, *Saturday Night Live*, *Good Morning America*, the *Today Show*—all lined up and waited their turns for dates with the '85 Bears.

They became bigger than life, athletes on a nickname basis with America: Fridge, Mad Mac, Coach Ditka, Mama's Boy Otis, Samurai, 'Horne, Sweetness, Jimbo, Mongo, Hilgy, L.A. Mike, Double D, the Colonel, and Silky D.

They changed sports marketing in America for all time, turning athletes into personalities that transcended even their considerable athletic accomplishments. No team ever spawned so many advertising and media figures on a local level or on such a massive scale nationally. They earned tens of millions in endorsements and appearances and did it while raising millions for charity in the process. The league consisted of 28 teams in 1985; the '85 Bears accounted for more than 20 percent of all NFL merchandise sold, and for the rest of the decade, the Bears sold more NFL merchandise than any other team. In the 19 weeks of the 1985 season alone, they appeared five times on the cover of *Sports Illustrated*.

They inspired a headband on the giant Chicago Picasso sculpture, helmets on the Art Institute's lions (which of course were stolen—this was, after all, Chicago), and jerseys with Nos. 9 (McMahon), 34 (Payton), and 72 (Perry) on the three children performing in *The Magic Flute* at the Lyric Opera. They put a chip on their shoulder, put a bull's-eye on their collective chest, and dared everyone to take their best shots.

Their coronation—the epic triumph in Super Bowl XX—drew an audience of 127 million, more than any television show, sports or other, in history. Countless millions worldwide tuned in as well, knowing little about American football but knowing that this group of Americans was not to be missed. Mike Ditka once suggested that a billion Chinese could not care less about the annual NFL showcase that was the Super Bowl. But millions of Chinese were enthralled by "Dian Bingxiang" (Electric Refrigerator) of the "Ju Xiong" (Giant Bear) team. As the *Chicago Tribune*'s Don Pierson wrote, hundreds of millions of Chinese really *did* care about this Super Bowl. When the Bears traveled to London in 1986, it was the Beatles invasion in reverse: the autograph hounds included Phil Collins, Rod Stewart, George Harrison, and Ringo Starr. The Bears' visit generated more than $4 million in marketing and related revenues, twice as much as the FA Cup Final.

The '85 Bears made a record, then turned it into a video. "The Super Bowl Shuffle" proceeded to go platinum and earn a Grammy nomination, selling millions and ranking in its time behind only Michael Jackson's "Thriller" as the highest-selling video of all time. They brought athletes running into recording studios, then and still.

They helped launch pro wrestling's boom of the eighties with their roles in Wrestlemania II. They brought "woofing" to fans across the country, and then were approached by Chevrolet for a poster titled "Junkyard Dogs." They popularized the Gatorade shower, the traditional dousing of a winning coach by his players along a sideline when victory is assured.

They were the hood ornament for America in that colorful decade, with all the excesses, shortcomings, strengths, attitudes, and flaws of the "me generation," Yuppies, *Bonfire of the Vanities*, and junk bonds. The Bears Decade began at the bottom of their division along with an America that was fighting through a near-depression and still feeling the pain of the hostage crisis in Iran. They neared the pinnacle in 1984, when Olympian Mary Lou Retton was captivating the nation, then rose all the way to the top the next year with their own ten thousand–watt personas.

America rode along with them. The Dow Jones reached a record—1,500—as the Bears were reaching their peak in December 1985, gathering speed for their playoffs. Their year was shared by Garrison Keillor's *Lake Wobegon Days*, about a happier, simpler time in America, and by Studs Terkel's *The Good War*, the stories of Americans in World War II. America wanted to feel good about itself, to have some fun. The Bears gave them that every week.

The Bears' impact was so stunning and immediate in part because of timing. Virtually every unforgettable moment played out not just amid a slate of other games across the land. Those happened when the Bears were alone on a national—even international—stage. They were at their absolute best when the stage lights were brightest.

When McMahon seized the moment and came off the bench in Minnesota to rescue the faltering Bears in the third game of the season, it was not on a Sunday. It was a special *Thursday Night Football* event, with the football world watching.

When the gap-toothed fat kid lined up at fullback, blocked for Payton, and then scored a touchdown of his own, it was not on Sunday—it was *Monday Night Football*, the most-watched single game of every week. Perry became "the Refrigerator" to America and a global audience when no one else was playing.

When they stumbled to their only loss, it was not just a defeat. It was *Monday Night Football* again, the most-watched *MNF* game in history, topping even the night of the Fridge. Balls bounced off helmets and went for Miami touchdowns. The Bears coach and his top defensive assistant fought at halftime in the locker room. The Miami team that kept the Bears from a perfect season was the franchise that 13 years earlier had itself gone undefeated all the way to a Super Bowl win.

> "In a way it was like watching a magnesium flare. The thing built up to this one moment in time and then ignited itself with this brilliance. But when it burned out, you knew deep down it wasn't going to sustain. It was going to give you something great, great heat, for that minute, but then it was going away. And you would never have that heat, that brilliance, again."
>
> *–Joe Mantegna,*
> *actor and Chicago native*

When the Bears reached the playoffs, the team from the Second City, the town with the perpetual civic inferiority complex obliterated New York and Los Angeles within the span of eight days, finishing off the Rams with Wilber Marshall's fumble return as the snow flurries began to fly on cue: "It's a Wonderful Bears Life."

Then on to their very own Super Bowl.

Just when they were at their zenith with America along for the ride, the *Challenger* space shuttle exploded, killing schoolteacher Christa McAuliffe and the crew. The Bears shared in the sorrow, and some even felt their fortunes begin imperceptibly to nose over and start down at almost that same moment. About the time that the stock market was suffering the worst one-day crash in its history, the Bears were staggering out of the 1987 strike that irreparably tore their internal fabric, coinciding with what was the end for Payton and several of the Bears' best and brightest.

The rise and self-destructing collapse of the '85 Bears was indeed the bonfire of the vanity.

And they played football. Oh, how they played the game. Like nobody before or since. The best of all time.

The '85 Bears went through a season winning 15 games, losing only 1, then put on a performance in the playoffs and Super Bowl that no team has ever approached.

They smashed the New York Giants and the Los Angeles Rams on consecutive playoff weekends, allowing just 118 yards rushing and no points—total.

During the Super Bowl week, Bears players saw fear in New England Patriots' eyes—when they were not embroiled in one of a succession of misadventures ranging from acupuncture fights with team management to whether or not McMahon had called the women of New Orleans "sluts." In a Super Bowl like no other before or since, they showed that the Patriots had reason to be afraid. New England's rushing total was seven yards.

In one six-game stretch, the Bears' *defense* scored 27 points. Opponents' offenses for the same six games scored a combined 27 points. McMahon, Payton, and the offense were scoring 143 of their own. The Bears led the league in both total and rushing defense and were third in passing defense. Fourteen of the Bears' nineteen opponents had scored 10 or fewer points. Eight different defensive players scored that year, not counting Perry on offense.

> "You will never see anything like that defense again. With the substitutions, you don't get the defensive personality that they had. Now, when it's a passing situation, a middle linebacker comes out, linemen come out. With those guys, Singletary and Wilson and the rest of them all stayed in and played every down. Can you imagine even Mike Ditka telling Otis Wilson that he wasn't fast enough to play passing downs?"
> —*Brent Musberger, CBS-TV,* former NFL Today *anchor*

And it was not strictly defense. The offense and defense combined to score 456 points; 420 of those were scored by the offense. The Bears sent nine players to the Pro Bowl after that season; four of them were on offense. For the first time the NFL wanted the highlight film of a team's season out for sale *before* the Super Bowl. The NFL knew what was coming and wanted the merchandise ready.

The Bears fell short of Super Bowls before and after 1985, but Super Bowl winners wanted no part of them. In the years from 1981 through 1991, the Bears played seven Super Bowl champions the year after those teams' triumphs. The Bears won six of those games, two over the Giants.

The argument lives forever over which team was the greatest in football history. The sixties Packers of Vince Lombardi. The seventies Pittsburgh Steelers of Chuck Noll, Terry Bradshaw, Joe Greene, and Franco Harris. The San Francisco 49ers of Bill Walsh. The nineties Dallas Cowboys that Jerry Jones put together and won three Super Bowls in four years. Now the New England Patriots of Bill Belichick.

> "If they had won two more, maybe even one more, there wouldn't even be a debate. There would be no discussion. The only teams to compare were the seventies Steelers and maybe the 1972 Dolphins, but only because they were undefeated. But for that one year, nobody comes close."
> —*Hub Arkush, publisher of Pro Football Weekly*

And the '85 Bears.

Consider: the Packers won five NFL titles, the Steelers four, the 49ers five, and the Cowboys and Patriots three.

The Bears are in that debate with one. Just one.

It was one moment in time. Only one, as it turned out. The greatest team in history won exactly one Super Bowl and never even reached another. And yet, had it been a succession of Super Bowls, while establishing a dynasty and removing any doubt in that classic argument, it might have lessened the magic of that moment.

> "Jim [McMahon] was looked at as a free spirit and a winner, and he brought so many people to the game of football, mainly young children and women. To this day, middle-aged women come up to me and tell me. 'You know, I never watched a football game before Jim McMahon and the '85 Bears.'"
> —*Steve Zucker, agent for Jim McMahon*

In that one shining year they became the best of all time. Dallas coach Tom Landry, who saw the seventies Steelers in Super Bowls of his own, said the '85 Bears defense was beyond even Pittsburgh's "Steel Curtain" defense. John Madden, whose Oakland Raiders won a Super Bowl and battled the Steelers in the playoffs four of five years in the seventies, including two consecutive AFC Championship Games, places the Bears at the top of the football pantheon.

For a bright, shining season, America was a Bears fan. A Fridge fan. A Ditka fan. A McMahon fan. And it had little to do with football. The men—or women—on the street did not know what McMahon's passing statistics were, but they sure knew what was on his headband and why he was wearing it.

When NFL commissioner Pete Rozelle fined McMahon and the Bears $5,000 for McMahon's wearing an Adidas headband in the divisional playoff against New York, McMahon responded by wearing a contraband headband in the NFC Championship Game against Los Angeles—with "Rozelle" markered on it.

The commissioner, who himself had helped build football over two decades into a rival of baseball for the honor of being America's favorite sport, sent McMahon a thank-you note. McMahon then wore a headband, among several, in the Super Bowl that called attention to juvenile diabetes and helped to raise millions to fight that dreaded disease.

> "If you asked people to name five players from any of the past 30 Super Bowls, you have a better chance at them remembering five '85 Bears than pretty much anybody else."
> —*Robert Smigel,* Saturday Night Live, creator of *"The Super Fans"*

The ripples still spread far outward from the Bears' splashes. Richard Dent, the Most Valuable Player of Super Bowl XX, took on inner-city poverty with his Make a Dent Foundation. Dent and his wife, Leslie, led a drive to raise money for children's heart surgery. Jim Covert, father of a child with spina bifida, attacked that disease and others through foundations and charitable work.

McMahon, agent Zucker, their wives, and several other couples were involved in starting a Rolls-Royce auction in the garage area of Loeber Motors, a North Shore luxury car dealership. It began with a few hundred people. Twenty years later, the now-annual event drew nearly five thousand people, all helping to raise money for the Juvenile Diabetes Foundation. Ditka, criticized for his self-promotion and quest for celebrity status, has used that status for years on behalf of Misericordia Heart of Mercy and children and adults with mental and physical disabilities. Otis Wilson has established programs for children's fitness through schools and has as his goal to work with the governor of Illinois to help the state's children.

The '85 Bears phenomenon—Fridge, Mad Mac, Da Coach—lasted long after the principals had departed the main stage. Although so much of the greatness was squandered, it never completely left those Bears—not all of the magical pixie dust that Chicago, America, and eventually England and Europe found there. In 2004, Ditka still commanded $30,000 to $50,000 as a keynote speaker and was the advertising figure for Levitra. Perry was the marketing point man for Big Ass Fans.

Saturday Night Live immortalized Da Coach and Da Bears in sketches that started almost exactly five years *after* the Super Bowl moment. In 1992, the year of Ditka's unraveling in the Minneapolis Metrodome, which he had once ridiculed as "the rollerdome," *SNL* unveiled yet another episode of "The Super Fans." Ditka appeared as a guest on *Saturday Night Live* in January 1993—four days after he was fired as head coach of his beloved Bears.

The skit: Bill Swerski's Super Fans, with George Wendt (Bob Swerski), Chris Farley (Todd O'Connor), Mike Myers (Pat Arnold), and Rob Smigel (Carl Wollarski).

The setting: Ditka's Restaurant, Chicago.

SWERSKI: Now, when we were last privileged to observe da Bears, they were playing the Giants in the postseason. The final score of that game was 31 to 3, and I shan't say who won. Pat, what happened?

ARNOLD: I think it's pretty obvious that coach Ditka had his mind on more important things.

WOLLARSKI: There was a war on, my friend.

O'CONNOR: That's right, our boyssss were overseasssss.

ARNOLD: Yeah, da Coach was probably too busy helpin' Schwarzkopf. . . .

SWERSKI: Now, what if da Bears were to enter the Indianapolis 500? Uh, what would you predict would be the outcome?

O'CONNOR: How would they compete?

SWERSKI: Well, let's say they rode together in a big bus.

WOLLARSKI: Is da Coach drivin'?

SWERSKI: Of course.

WOLLARSKI : Then I like da Bears! . . .

SWERSKI: Now, what if da Bears entered da Preakness?

SUPER FANS: Da Bears!

In the end, the very source of the '85 Bears' greatness was also their tragic flaw, that which would bring them down. In the final analysis, what made them great was their incredible personality—individually and what it became collectively. What eventually brought them down was that same personality, when the egos from team president Michael McCaskey on down went out of control and took everything else down with them. They could not be on top for very long because of their own volatility, a chemistry that began to over-heat the longer it was exposed to the spotlight. They were a sun that went supernova, then dimmed and could not be brought back.

> "When the [1987] strike was over, everything was changed. Ditka had alienated players. It's like in a marriage, if you find your wife is cheating on you, you can stay together but it'll never be the same again. And it was never the same again. It was sad. After 1985 the foundation crumbled bit by bit. The shuttle, which had Christa McAuliffe going along representing all of us who weren't astronauts, went down just days after the victory parade through Chicago. The stock market, that just could go nowhere but up, crashed in 1987, just like us, and would never be the same . . . just like us."
> *—Dan Hampton*

In the end, it was a team that blew itself apart from the inside, starting with mismanagement from the top down in ways that still anger the players who worked so hard to hand the city and franchise a Lombardi Trophy. A team whose players were reaping millions in endorsements for the likes of Coca-Cola and McDonald's and were guesting on every national and local radio and television show of any consequence, were in the locker room minutes after

"We definitely lived life to the fullest, all of us. My thing is that they put on your grave the year that you came and the year that you left. In between is the little dash, and life is what you did with your 'dash.' You met some people, you had some fun, some people helped you and you helped them, and that's your dash. That's what it's all about, filling your dash. It's gone too fast."
—*Richard Dent*

their moment of triumph, the most-watched and dominant Super Bowl in history, fighting among themselves over the free hats that were given out.

In the end, the only shots they could not overcome were their own and those of the very team ownership for whom they were making millions.

Maybe a measure of the greatness was that it took so many blows to bring it down:

• President Michael McCaskey allowing or causing the losses of Jim McMahon, Willie Gault, Wilber Marshall, and Otis Wilson and never replacing them

• Ditka losing the players because of seeming double standards, the Doug Flutie debacle, and driving a stake into the players' hearts during the 1987 strike

• The exit of Buddy Ryan, the guru of the ferocious 46 defense

• The jealousies and endorsements that cut into the friendships and single-minded attitude needed to be champions

• The injuries to McMahon

• The retirement of Payton

• The quality of a conference that contained at the same time Bill Parcells' New York Giants, Joe Gibbs' Washington Redskins, and Bill Walsh's San Francisco 49ers, so good that there was scant room for even a slight stumble

Even with all of that against them, the Bears still went 14–2 in 1986, 11–4 in 1987, and 12–4 in 1988. They still annihilated mighty Parcells and his Giants to open the 1987 season after the Giants had won the Super Bowl.

But they could not recapture the magic of 1985. They changed from being a fist to being a bunch of fingers, too many individuals worried about themselves, their endorsements, and their wives whining about who was getting what deal. They were not the first champions who rotted from the inside out, just the best. They could not handle success, either their own or each other's.

They should have won more. But oh, the one they did win. . . .

CHAPTER 1
ROOTS OF GREATNESS

"Buddy, now remember who wrote that letter for you."
—*Gary Fencik*

IN 1981 THE DETROIT LIONS ANNIHILATED the Bears 48–17 in a
Monday night game, which was especially humiliating because of how much
of the country and the NFL watched that game.

It was Jay Hilgenberg's rookie year. Even though Hilgenberg was going
to go on to be one of the NFL's great centers and go to seven Pro Bowls, he
was stuck on the bench behind starter Dan Neal. Hilgenberg had a burst of
insight.

Hilgenberg was sitting beside guard Revie Sorey on the bench watching the
humiliation. He turned to Sorey.

"Revie, we're the worst team in the NFL."

Sorey just nodded. "Yeah."

"Yeah, but Revie, I'm the worst player on the team too," Hilgenberg said.
No argument. "Yeah."

"Revie," Hilgenberg concluded, "that makes me the worst player in the NFL."
Sorey did not argue.

The Bears may have been the NFL's charter franchise, but as the seventies
drifted into the eighties, they were in tatters under the declining stewardship
of Papa Bear George Halas. In that, they were indeed America's Team.

The people and the country had been battered, beginning with the Iranian
hostage crisis to start the decade. The "Miracle on Ice" was an exquisite pick-
us-up for America in the 1980 Olympics, but it was over so fast.

Then came the economic crisis of the early Reagan years, Americans out of
work and frightened. Mount St. Helens erupted. John Lennon was murdered

in New York. An attempt to rescue the hostages in Iran failed disastrously amid a sandstorm in the desert and GIs were killed.

Reagan was shot in 1981. Two months later, so was the pope. A few months later, Egyptian president Anwar Sadat, the voice of reason and the best hope for peace in the Middle East, was killed. In December 1981 came the first reports of a disease called AIDS.

For Chicago, sports were scant refuge through the early eighties. The White Sox won their American League division by 20 games in 1983, then sputtered feebly in the playoffs and fell short of the World Series. The next year, the Cubs won their division, led 2–0 in a five-game series with the San Diego Padres, then did the unthinkable and lost the next three games to fail.

Into this run of misery—real as well as athletic—came the Bears.

WALTER PAYTON—"SWEETNESS"

The Bears had Walter Payton, the personnel masterstroke of general manager (GM) Jim Finks and superscout Bill Tobin, and had picked up defensive end Mike Hartenstine from Penn State in the second round of that same 1975 draft. They were the only '85 Bears still with the team as the calendar began a new decade.

Payton was, for so many years, what there was of the franchise.

"He was the greatest Bear of all," Ditka said flatly, musing that the Almighty appeared to have decided one day that He was finally going to do it right, make Himself the perfect football player. So he made Walter Payton.

Fred O'Connor, Payton's first running backs coach, thought, "God must have taken a chisel and said, 'I'm gonna make me a halfback.'"

Minnesota defensive back Bobby Bryant once described tackling Payton: "It's similar to roping a calf. It's hard enough to get your hands on him. And once you do, you wonder if you should have."

Twelve years after he retired, Payton still held or shared eight NFL records, including the all-time rushing mark of 16,726, since broken by Emmitt Smith.

He was the Bears' offensive hammer in 1985, nine times rushing for 100 or more yards. He led the NFL in rushing only once, in 1977, but Payton topped 1,000 yards ten times, and six times had more than 1,400.

From the small Mississippi town of Columbia and a star at predominantly black Jackson State University, Payton was a race car driver, amateur and professional. He invested in forest land and nursing homes. He owned restaurants, leased heavy equipment, and made millions as a motivational speaker. But his life was his ultimate motivational speech.

When Payton died in 1999, Dan Hampton was among those who spoke at the memorial service in Soldier Field. Hampton said he remembered a guy who played so hard on that very field and left all he had right there. Then Hampton's hands shook and his voice trembled. "I have a little girl, four years old," he said. "Ten years from now, when she asks me about the Chicago Bears, I'll tell her about a championship and I'll tell her about great teams, great teammates, and great coaches, and how great it was to be a part of it.

"But the first thing I'll tell her about," he said as his voice broke, "is Walter Payton."

How to describe Payton. . . . To borrow from drama and theater, action is character. In this case, *a* character.

Payton burst in on a serious team meeting being conducted by an NFL official on the subject of drugs. In his moustache he had sprinkled powdered sugar. "Ain' no cocaine on this team!" Payton hollered.

When Dave Duerson made the 1986 Pro Bowl, he noticed a very, very warm sensation during practice in Hawaii. Payton had managed to season Duerson's athletic supporter with liquid heat. When President Ronald Reagan called him in the locker room after Payton set the all-time rushing record, Payton took the phone and immediately assured the president, "The check's in the mail."

Fittingly, the title of his autobiography, published the year after his death, is *Never Die Easy.*

DAN HAMPTON—"DANIMAL"

In 1979 change came to the Bears in the form of Dan Hampton, who, like Payton, was the fourth overall pick of his draft. An All-American at Arkansas who would be named the NFL's defensive player of the year in 1982, he came in for a predraft visit that had included watching film with Buddy Ryan.

Ryan was sitting alone in a darkened room at Bears headquarters when Hampton was brought downstairs to meet him. The defensive coordinator was playing a reel of film that showed former Notre Dame All-American Alan Page, now a Minnesota Supreme Court justice, then a Vikings defensive tackle. Page had been one of the quickest defensive linemen in the history of the NFL but was then well past the prime of a career that he would finish playing with the Bears.

Ryan told Hampton, 6'5", 270 pounds, he hoped the Bears would draft the big Arkansas All-American. He also told Hampton he thought he could coach him to play like Page, whom Ryan had coached while on the Vikings staff.

"Danimal," as Hampton came to be called, would finish his own career with a dozen knee surgeries and no two fingers that point in exactly the same direction. He also would become, as Ryan predicted, the NFL's 1982 Most Valuable Player, selected by *Pro Football Weekly*.

Hampton lived and played on the edge. He picked up a five-foot alligator once for the experience. He and Steve McMichael terrorized biker bars. He performed in a six-man band with Payton and four other Chicago athletes, Hampton on lead and rhythm guitar and singing, to raise money for charity.

The Bears worked out in minicamps at an old school building, where the bottom floor was about three stories high and windows were broken out everywhere, with cardboard taped up all over them. The locker rooms had 14-foot ceilings, and the practice field was 40 yards by 50. Hampton took one look around and thought, "This is pro football? In Arkansas we had a beautiful place."

Hampton's hope was to be drafted elsewhere, preferably by the Miami Dolphins. The first morning of the draft, director of administration Bill

McGrane called him. The draft started at 9:00 and it was about 9:05. McGrane said, "Dan, this is Bill McGrane and we've—"

"Shut up, Marty, and get off the phone," Hampton hollered, figuring it was Marty Mitchum, his old running buddy back at the dorm at Arkansas. "I'm waiting for an important call."

Hampton hung up on McGrane twice. The third time, McGrane yelled right away, "Do not hang up! This is Bill McGrane of the Chicago Bears."

It was anything but instant success for the future Hall of Famer. When he came to training camp, Hampton could take guard Revie Sorey, push him back three yards, and throw him off to the side. Ryan started calling him "Super-Rook."

In the first preseason game, however, against the New York Jets, Hampton went head-to-head with Marvin Powell, the Jets' All-Pro tackle and a USC All-American like future Bear Keith Van Horne. Powell clamped his hands on Hampton, and Super-Rook could not get him off.

After that game, Buddy went over to Hampton. "You ain't no 'Super-Rook,'" Ryan said. "You're just 'Big Rook.'"

The nickname stuck, making Hampton one of the few Ryan ever honored with more than just calling him by number. And keeping Ryan's respect was one of the strongest drives within the team.

Hampton began 1980 playing exceptionally for the first three games. Then the Bears went to Pittsburgh to face the defending Super Bowl champions. Terry Bradshaw and the offense rolled over Hampton and the Bears 38–3, with the Steelers linemen pushing Hampton around wherever they wanted to put him. He was reduced to a blocking dummy.

On the plane home Hampton went by Ryan, who was uncharacteristically quiet amid the team's customary beer drinking and all-too-frequent feeling that they had gotten their butts whipped but it was no big deal.

The next morning Ryan was puffy-eyed in the meeting room, and players knew he had been up all night. After the special-teams meeting for the entire team, Ryan pulled the divider across the room and it was just the defense, the coaches, and Ryan.

"Let me tell you guys something," Ryan began. "As a defensive coordinator, I look for ways they can match up. I know we don't have 11 great players to match up with the world champions. But the way I look at it, if I got four or five guys I can count on week in and week out to always be there, always be as good as you can be, and if I can get three or four other guys to show up and have a great day that one day, play over their heads, they can do anything we want to do."

Then he turned and looked straight at Hampton.

"Big Rook," he said, "I expected you to always be one of those core guys, to always be there and fight your ass off. Well, you looked like shit. You didn't do nothing but embarrass yourself. And you know what? If you want in, you've got to sell it all out. You gotta be there every week."

Ryan had tears in his eyes. He turned the light off, sat down, and started the film. Players usually went out after the meeting, but that afternoon Hampton went home and did some painting in the garage of the house he had bought. But he had tears in his own eyes and could not see to paint. That night he could not sleep, and the next day Ryan's words continued to eat at him and jar his soul. Hampton made a vow that never again would he ever have Buddy Ryan tell him he had let Ryan down. It meant that much to Hampton.

STEVE McMICHAEL—"MONGO" AND "MING"

Steve McMichael's arrival was inauspicious. He'd slipped to the third round of the 1980 draft because of a knee injury but got enough of a signing bonus from the New England Patriots to put money down on a Cadillac for himself. He rarely got off the bench in his rookie season, however, and was cut at the end of training camp in 1981.

But not before beginning his NFL reputation as a crazy. He threw his helmet at a coach and eventually was told by coach Ron Erhardt that he was part of the NFL's "criminal element," which was somewhat true. He and some pals would go to restaurants, get drunk, and throw food at each other, *Animal House* style. His chief antagonist was Fritz Shurmur, the New

England defensive coordinator and someone he would run across again at just the right moment to suit McMichael.

The Bears called; they wanted to take a look at him, not as a defensive tackle but as a backup center. That tryout lasted as long as it took the Bears to find out that he could not long-snap. His first stint with the Bears ended in his release.

But in October, defensive tackle Brad Shearer, an All-American at Texas while McMichael was there, was hurting from a bad knee of his own. Finks called and offered McMichael another contract.

Hampton went with Shearer to pick McMichael up at the airport.

"Who is this guy?" Hampton asked.

"McMichael, a guy I played with at Texas," Shearer said. "He's a wild man."

They picked McMichael up at O'Hare—McMichael and his burnt-orange garment bag with a Texas "UT" on it and three suitcases that were some sort of imitation cheetah skin. Within a week or so, Shearer's knee was so bad that the Bears gave him some severance pay and cut him. The door was open for McMichael.

McMichael had gone through his money and was about to go through the big white Cadillac too. About a week after the Bears cut Shearer, all of that cheetah-skin luggage turned up in the foyer at Halas Hall. Creditors had located him, sent people up from Texas, and repossessed McMichael's Cadillac. They passed on the luggage.

Hampton did more than just pick McMichael up at the airport. The two became close friends and busted up an occasional biker bar, until McMichael noticed that "some of those f***ers are carrying guns!"

For all of his fights in practice, McMichael was nicknamed "Mongo" after the Alex Karras character who knocked a horse unconscious with a punch in the movie *Blazing Saddles*. He was accorded a second moniker in "Ming" after "Ming the Merciless" from the vintage Flash Gordon series.

OTIS WILSON

Otis Wilson arrived in 1980, the first-round pick out of Louisville. He and Matt Suhey were the only rookies to make the team from that draft.

Wilson grew up in the Brownsville section of Brooklyn, two blocks away from Mike Tyson. Growing up amid switchblades, guns, pimps, and drugs, he had learned survival.

He used those skills in the NFL and in dealing with Ryan.

Through high school and college at Louisville, entire defenses had been structured for Wilson. He never paid attention to the total scheme. He did not have to. He *was* the scheme. Just make tackles.

But under Ryan, everyone was expected to know more than just their own responsibilities, some to know everyone's. And Ryan was both patient and impatient. He did not like rookies whatsoever. "We did OK, but that 55 [Wilson] killed us," Ryan said after one early eighties season.

But Wilson began to study, putting the mental side of the game on top of his amazing physical skills. He sat in Ryan's office, sometimes on the floor, watching film and enduring Ryan's legendary written tests.

"I'm out of school, Buddy," Wilson protested. "Why're you giving me these exams?"

"You need to understand the total package," Ryan kept saying. "I want you to know what everybody's doing."

To help Wilson, Ryan told veteran Bruce Herron to mentor No. 55. This was great for Wilson, who now had the perfect out. When Wilson wanted to improvise and Ryan hammered him for it, Wilson had his pat answer: "Well, Buddy, that's what Bruce told me to do."

> "Buddy had a T-shirt that his son gave him. On the front was: 'I'm sorry. I can't remember your name, but is it OK if I call you "Asshole."' Even if it wasn't OK, Buddy was going to call you that anyway, until you 'earned' your name."
> —*Otis Wilson*

BUDDY RYAN

If the players learned how to deal with Buddy Ryan, he was also the master in dealing with them. Therein lay perhaps the greatest single key to what the '85 Bears defense became.

Ryan put his players through a year or two of boot-camp treatment before he would let them have a modicum of respect. He called Mike Singletary "50" until Singletary was a Pro Bowl middle linebacker, then called him "Samurai." Ryan did not want to become too familiar with them or refer to them on a name basis because, like soldiers, they could be shot and killed or, in this situation, cut and gone. Ryan would have a hand in the termination, and he did not want to worry about someone when they were gone. At the end of the day, they were still numbers to him.

But numbers were in fact everything to Ryan. His prime directive was rushing the passer, formulated when he was with the New York Jets and coach Weeb Ewbank on the staff that won Super Bowl III with Joe Namath. Ryan heard Ewbank's constant fixation on keeping Namath protected and reasoned, from the defensive perspective, that if Ewbank was that concerned about his quarterback, that was probably where he should be attacking other teams.

"Namath doesn't get hit," Ewbank said. "If we gotta block eight, we block eight, but he doesn't get hit."

Ryan's response: "Well, that's easy. If they block eight, I'll rush nine. Because I'm going to get him. If the most important thing is to protect the quarterback, then mine is to get the quarterback."

And that became what his 46 defense was all about. Ryan kept sending blitzers until they overwhelmed the protection, and with the players he had in 1985, that happened alarmingly fast.

Ryan also understood how to reach the egos and talents he had assembled in front of him.

While watching running back O. J. Anderson run over people on film of Cardinals games, Ryan turned to Wilson. "Ooh, you better get hurt in practice this week," Ryan told his linebacker. "I don't want him running over you like that."

Ryan turned to McMichael, then in his drinking prime. "McMichael, I don't care if you go out and get drunk," Ryan said. "Just don't take any of the 'real' players with you."

Ryan's motivational efforts extended to the offense as well. He grasped early on that McMahon was the best chance for the team's success, so rather than yell at him, Ryan found ways to build him up. The offensive linemen he approached differently.

When Ditka took over as head coach, he told Ryan that he wanted to run the flex defense that had been so successful for the Dallas Cowboys when Ditka played and coached under Tom Landry.

> "He'd say to the offensive line, 'You fat asses can't block anybody in practice; how you going to do it in a game?' And Covert, Bortz, and those guys would turn into animals."
> *—Dan Hampton*

"He is the head coach," Ryan told his players. "He has the right to run whatever defense he wants. Now, *I* won't run it. I'm going to be down on my farm in Kentucky. But he can run whatever he wants."

"L.A." Mike Richardson—"L.A." for his love of the West Coast, "L.A." for "Lazy Ass" to many of his teammates—blew a coverage and afterward the media was asking what happened on the play. Richardson was nowhere to be found. Gary Fencik stood in front of his own locker, took responsibility, and said that it was his fault the Bears had been beaten on the play.

That Monday Ryan stood up in the team meeting and turned to Richardson.

"Fencik covered your ass out there," Ryan said with that tone of voice that made a chill run through everyone in the room. "But if you

> "Buddy, I guarantee you, never stayed up nights worrying about us or our personality defects. And he treated us all the same. Like shit."
> *—Dan Hampton*

ever do anything like that again, I will cut your ass on the spot."

JAY HILGENBERG—"HILGY"

Some pieces came together slowly. Suhey, drafted after Wilson in 1980, eventually inherited the job of Payton's fullback escort from Roland Harper. Tight end Emery Moorehead came in 1981, a castoff from the Denver Broncos.

Jay Hilgenberg also came in 1981 with a chip on his shoulder over not being drafted. He had been a standout at Iowa but was in a career funk early and initially told the Bears he was not sure he wanted to play for a team that did not think enough of him to draft him. Being slighted on draft day put a quiet rage in his play all through his career, although he pouted through the early years, did not work out anywhere close to the level he needed to, and did not challenge starter Dan Neal.

> "Screw the draft. I liked playing against number ones."
>
> –Jay Hilgenberg

Hilgenberg did see the field, however briefly, in 1981 and found himself against the Raiders. Defensive end Howie Long was a fellow rookie, and the two had gotten to know each other at the Blue-Gray All-Star Game. He came on to snap for the first extra point.

"Hey, Jay," Long called.

"Hey, Howie," Hilgenberg said.

Defensive tackle John Matuszak, 6'8", 300 pounds of legendary wild man "the Tooz," stood up and roared, "Hey, just snap the f***in' ball, rook!"

"Yes, sir," Hilgenberg said. The ball was snapped immediately.

Throughout his career, however, the bigger the reputation opposite him, the better.

Hilgenberg was not the only center in his family growing up in Iowa City. Younger brother Joel made the NFL as a center with the New Orleans Saints. "We're the only family that plays catch not facing each other," Hilgenberg said.

KEITH VAN HORNE—"'HORNE"

In 1981, the year of *Chariots of Fire* and *On Golden Pond*, Walter Cronkite was signing off the *CBS Evening News* for the final time. The Bears were drafting Keith Van Horne in the first round and Mike Singletary in the second, and lucking into Hilgenberg after all the rounds were completed.

Van Horne was the first major step by the Bears in building a dominant offensive line, starting at the position GM Finks considered vital in his offense.

He was also a major step in upgrading the rock music presence of the staid Bears. Guitarist Van Horne became friends with Rolling Stone Keith Richards, and when the Bears invaded England in 1986, their "groupies" not surprisingly included Rod Stewart, Eric Clapton, Phil Collins, Ringo Starr, and George Harrison at various times.

Van Horne had not expected to play his rookie year coming out of USC. But injuries forced the Bears to improvise, and the Bears threw Van Horne at left tackle, a position he had never played before and did not play very well in his first NFL season.

He also was in the role of number one pick of the Chicago Bears. He did not handle that well at all. As he struggled through the season he repeatedly heard what a bust he was and went completely into a shell, adding to the mistaken perception that the massive, easygoing Californian was simply aloof.

The press was merciless, however. When he arrived at O'Hare from California, he had not been told to wear a suit and tie. The TV cameras met him as he came off the plane, in the process creating an unfair first impression. "Look at this California kid; who does he think he is?" was the public perception, one that would haunt Van Horne for years even as he became one of the dominant right tackles in the NFL. During Van Horne's career, the Bears played against the Oakland Raiders and Hall of Fame left end Howie Long four times; they faced Reggie White, often considered the greatest defensive end in league history, and the Philadelphia Eagles three times. The Bears won six of those seven games.

GARY FENCIK

Gary Fencik had come to the Bears in 1976, the year after Payton and Hartenstine, cut by the Miami Dolphins in what coach Don Shula called "the biggest personnel mistake I ever made."

Fencik was a Yale graduate with cover-boy looks. He also had a head for business situations and not simply because of his MBA. As 1981 came to its woeful finish, it was increasingly apparent that there was going to be a coaching change and that head coach Neill Armstrong probably was not going to be back. But Ryan had begun welding the defense into something, and players were afraid he would be fired along with Armstrong.

Fencik and Page authored a letter to Halas asking Papa Bear to retain Ryan as defensive coordinator. They then protected themselves by having all the defensive players sign it. Halas showed up at the training center at Great Lakes Naval Training Center on a snowy day, and Fencik nearly threw up because Halas never came to practices. Something was up. There could be only one reason why he was there. "Oh my God, what did I do in that stupid letter?" was Fencik's thought.

Teams broke up into offense and defense, and Halas asked the defensive coaches to step away. He told everybody he had gotten that letter and then pointed a finger around the group and said, "Your coaches will be back next year."

That was when they knew that Armstrong was going to be fired. When he had a chance, Fencik sidled over closer to the defensive coaches and reminded Ryan, "Buddy, now remember who wrote that letter for you."

JIM McMAHON—"MAC"

A letter was part of Jim McMahon's welcome to Chicago. But this one was not nearly as well received by Halas.

The Bears drafted McMahon with the fifth pick of the 1982 draft. While they were negotiating with him, *E.T.: The Extraterrestrial* opened in June. Halas would soon find himself wondering if he was not dealing with his own personal E.T.

Papa Bear told McMahon he was too small, had a bad arm and knee, could not see well enough (maybe the ever-present sunglasses were the clue), and that maybe he ought to go to Canada because he was not likely to make it in the NFL. If he got $200 a game, Halas told him, he would be overpaid.

McMahon got his $200 a game. Agent Jerry Argovitz hammered out a deal for $100,000 the first year, $150,000 the second, and $190,000 plus an option year. But McMahon and Argovitz were under pressure because of a looming July 15 deadline, when the collective bargaining agreement between the league and the players association was due to expire. Tension already was rising, which would culminate in a seven-week strike later in the season, and rookies theoretically could not negotiate after that July 15 date, meaning McMahon might be forced to sit out a year.

But George Allen was heading up the Chicago Blitz of the USFL and had some conversations with Argovitz and McMahon. Nothing ever came of it, although McMahon at least felt briefly that he had some leverage.

McMahon was set to go in and sign his contract. Argovitz, however, handed Finks and Halas an addendum to the contract that stipulated that McMahon had signed the contract under "duress, distress, and coercion," referring to the July 15 deadline. Argovitz was reserving the right to sue the Bears and nullify the entire contract. Finks threw the note away. McMahon would then arrive for his inaugural press conference stepping out of the limo, shades in place, beer in hand. Welcome to the Bears.

JIMBO, THE COLONEL, AND THE 1983 DRAFT

Three months after the Vietnam Memorial was dedicated in Washington, the last episode of *M*A*S*H* aired in February 1983, watched by 106 million viewers. Michael Jackson debuted the "moonwalk" in May while performing "Billie Jean." It was Jackson's turning point and set him on a course toward music history.

At about that same time, the true turning point, the event that put the Bears on final approach to destiny, was also taking place: the 1983 draft, one of the greatest not only in Bears history but also in that of the NFL. The Bears started with Jim Covert as the sixth pick of the first round to anchor the other side of the line opposite Van Horne. Finks and his staff brought in speedy receiver Willie Gault with their second pick of the first round, then cornerback Mike Richardson, safety Dave Duerson, and guard Tom Thayer with their next picks, plus tight end Pat Dunsmore later in the fourth round. All but Dunsmore became full-time starters.

Covert was a Western Pennsylvania strongman who grew up in a town across the river from Mike Ditka's hometown of Aliquippa. His grandfather and father both worked more than 30 years in the steel mills, along with four other family members. He had been the left tackle protecting Dan Marino at

Pitt and did not allow a single sack his senior season, when Marino threw more than 400 times. Marino was selected 26th overall in that 1983 draft, by the Miami Dolphins, a selection the Bears would rue two years later.

The Bears sat out the fifth, sixth, and seventh rounds because they had traded away picks in those rounds, then struck with picks that would leave the NFL shaking its head for years afterward because anyone could have taken these players and passed: Richard Dent and Mark Bortz, both in the eighth round.

Bortz and Dent were big-time stars from small-town America. Both would go on to Pro Bowls. Dent became one of the most feared NFL pass rushers of all time and a Hall of Fame candidate. Bortz was from the small Wisconsin town of Pardeeville, a devout student of military history and one of the Bears' most feared offensive linemen.

Both Bortz and Dent were the strokes of scouting genius by Bill Tobin, who showed that imagination is an underrated part of NFL scouting.

> "Bortzie was like a cyborg. If you got in a fight with him, you'd have to kill him because he would just keep coming, like some evil machine."
> —*Dan Hampton*

Bortz was a defensive tackle at Iowa. The Bears needed an offensive guard. Tobin scouted him and persuaded the draft room to grab him. Then he went down the hall to offensive line coach Dick Stanfel. "Dick," Tobin said, "we gotcha a guard."

Dent, who never played football until his junior year of high school because he had to work, was an undersized speed rusher at Tennessee State whom only Tobin among Bears personnel staffers had seen. He was a small-school product—227 pounds, with bad teeth—but Tobin had seen few players with Dent's explosion and track on the ball. Tobin figured Dent would be a tough sell, so he began lobbying for Dent in the second round to get Dent's name in the Bears' draft mix. Finks and the group laughed that off.

When the Bears finished their fourth-round pick, the group broke for lunch in the span when the team did not have picks. When they came back, the draft was in the seventh round and Dent hadn't been picked. Finks could not resist.

"'Toby,'" Finks kidded Tobin, "that second-round defensive end. Looks like he's still on the board."

When the Bears' turn in the eighth round came, they grabbed Dent. One of the biggest pieces of the Bears' greatness of the eighties was in place. They spent $5,000 to take care of Dent's dental problems, the rotten teeth and nerve trouble that made eating an ordeal. Dent grew an inch in height and 40 pounds in weight, and the Bears had their greatest pass rusher.

Time magazine's Man of the Year for 1982 was a computer; the announcement of the award was followed closely by the discovery of the first computer virus.

In October 1983 Papa Bear Halas died, to be succeeded by grandson Michael McCaskey, who was placed in charge of running the team. McCaskey would be voted NFL Executive of the Year for the 1985 season; to the players' thinking, it was another computer and virus making the news.

Matters did not get better immediately for the Bears, but they definitely were starting to become more fun. Tight end Jay Saldi, after spending most of his career with Dallas, was with the Bears for two years, 1983 and 1984. His trademark came with him: long, long blond hair sticking out from under the back of his helmet.

Saldi had a helmet with the straps up both sides and around the back. After one play Saldi came off to the sideline and took his helmet off without unsnapping the straps; he was bald! The wig was stuck in his helmet.

Saldi saw everybody's faces and hastily pulled the helmet right back down over his ears. And he never again took his helmet off on the field.

History would unfold with the Bears returning Washington's fury in one of the rivalries that defined the decade.

CHAPTER 2

DA COACH

"He was the reason we won that Super Bowl and
the reason why we didn't win three."
—*Richard Dent*

TRYING TO INSTILL SOME SWAGGER AND WINNING tradition into a team that by 1981 had lost most of what it had of both, Halas turned to perhaps one of the more unlikely head-coaching hires in the history of his franchise or any other.

Mike Ditka. It was the same Mike Ditka who had declared in a sixties negotiation that Halas threw nickels around like manhole covers and whom Halas had unceremoniously traded to the Philadelphia Eagles shortly thereafter. It was the Mike Ditka, descended from Ukrainian parents, who came out of the western Pennsylvania steel country with the disposition and style of something heat-treated and forged in one of the steel mills near the Ditka home in Aliquippa.

It was the Mike Ditka who *made* the '85 Bears. He was their personality— or rather personalities—their driver, the sum of their contradictions, the perfect foil for McMahon, the "creator" of the Refrigerator. And the '85 Bears made Ditka. He needed conflict, needed edginess, and they gave him all he needed.

Ditka had been Halas' first-round pick in the 1961 draft and had stood up to Papa Bear more than once during his years as a Bears player. Trading Ditka, a Hall of Fame tight end, to the Eagles in 1967 for quarterback Jack Concannon began the nearly uninterrupted decline of the Bears over the next 15 years until Halas reversed his mistake.

After his playing career concluded with a Super Bowl ring as a Dallas Cowboy, Ditka joined Tom Landry's staff and began coaching special teams for the Cowboys. Ditka studied the methods and mind-set of the Dallas legend, developing an awe and respect for Landry that would exponentially heighten the stakes and tensions when the two teams met in 1985.

Before that, however, was the matter of becoming a head coach. A Bears head coach. Ditka had been thinking for several years about taking that step, with the Bears as the only place he could see himself as the top football figure. In 1981, as the Armstrong years were winding down to a dismal finish, Ditka wrote Halas a letter:

> I just want you to know that if you ever make a change in the coaching end of the organization, I just wish you would give me some consideration.
> —Mike Ditka

Halas was intrigued. The next year he brought Ditka to town and the two struck a deal around Halas' kitchen table. The ship was in the water and launched.

It was not the only epic move Halas made in 1982. That year, general manager Jim Finks determined that the Bears needed a quarterback, specifically the one who had set 56 Division I passing records: Jim McMahon.

> "Ditka was an unusual hire. He made a personal appeal to George Halas. Was he a great coach and would he beat teams on Madden Football, Joe Gibbs, Bill Walsh? No. But for a guy to get you up for a game, he was simply awesome. He knew how to put the chip you needed right on that shoulder."
> —*Gary Fencik*

MAKING THE CUT

Ditka brought the team together at his first minicamp in Arizona State's Sun Devil Stadium not long after his hiring and made it very clear that the future was not going to be simply more of the same.

"Gentlemen," he began, "good morning. My name is Mike Ditka. I'm the new head coach of the Chicago Bears. My goal is to go to the Super Bowl and win it. Some of you will be there; some of you won't."

When Halas hired Ditka to take over the Bears, it was with the idea that he also would make over the Bears. Part of that would include weeding out players he did not think fit with the program.

It was brutal for all of them, even the ones who did fit. Ditka and his wife went to a dinner spot called Me and Mrs. P's one evening where they met up with Hampton, Hartenstine, McMichael, and their wives.

Ditka bought every bottle of champagne in the place, and they drank it all. Ditka got looser and started to vent about whom he disliked and who was in trouble. "I'm getting rid of this guy," Ditka snarled more than once. "He ain't shit." Or, "This guy's no good; he's gone."

The three players now were starting to get uncomfortable, for two reasons. Some of those on Ditka's hit list were friends and teammates they had played with for years, and they did not want to hear this vitriol. After all, the team had not even had a full practice together.

> "People like Noah Jackson, Rickey Watts, they weren't disciplined football players, and Ditka required disciplined football players. And we needed discipline. Under Neill Armstrong, nice guy, it'd be, 'Oh well, we lost.' Ditka would be like, 'We lost! It's the end of the world! Somebody's not going home!'"
> *–Shaun Gayle*

And one other thing: "I'm sitting there thinking, man, I don't know if I want to know all this stuff," Hartenstine said to Hampton. "I might be on the list too."

The weeding out was immediate for some, a little slower for some others, but inexorable in every case. Rickey Watts. Alan Page. Vince Evans. Mike Phipps. Noah Jackson. Gone.

SYBIL

Ditka was a tangle of contradictions, befitting the nickname the players gave him: "Sybil," the title of a book and movie about a psychotic woman beset by multiple personality disorder.

He demanded loyalty, yet he was on the Dallas staff when he wrote to Halas about the Bears job when a fellow coach was still in that spot. While playing for the Bears, he had flirted with the Houston Oilers of the American Football League in 1966 to the point of agreeing to a contract, getting a check, and lying about it, yet he ran off punter and tight end Bob Parsons in 1983 for talking to the Chicago Blitz about a coaching position.

Parsons, one of the most consistent players at what he did, had talked to the Chicago Blitz about becoming a coach when he retired—not a player, a coach. With a few games remaining in that season, Ditka brought in another player, cut Parsons, and went up to the Metrodome to play the Vikings.

Parsons showed up for the game and sat in the upper deck as a fan. When Vikings linebacker Matt Blair blocked a Chicago punt, Parsons stood up and applauded. A fan in the upper deck had a sign, "Please pardon Parsons," and Parsons got up, walked all the way over to the man, and shook his hand.

Ditka demanded loyalty, then lost the team in 1987 when he stood behind the Spare Bears during the strike. In subsequent years he insisted that those young players be included in the media guide like the regular players.

Ditka told his players not to become consumed with commercials, appearances, and the trappings of success after the Super Bowl, and he berated them for losing focus. Then he proceeded to do more than anyone else, on his way to becoming America's pitchman. Ditka had gone bankrupt a couple of times and was determined never to feel that pain again. Some of the ads were cheesy, but he took all he could get, knowing all too well that it could vanish.

Ditka's Sybil-esque nature appeared off the field as well as on it.

Chicago sports talk legend Chet Coppock cohosted a Ditka radio show with former Bear Mike Pyle for WMAQ-AM radio in Chicago. Even though Pyle and Ditka had been cocaptains of the 1963 NFL championship team, Ditka passed up few chances to make his show partners feel uncomfortable.

The night before the Super Bowl, the group was in Ditka's suite at the hotel. Coppock, a longtime close-up observer of the Bears who has been to more than a half-century of Bears openers, had a question for Ditka.

"So, Coach," Coppock asked, alluding to the turning point of the 1985 season in the Thursday night game against the Vikings in week three, "just how vital was that block that Payton threw on Studwell in Minnesota? I think that block set the tone for this team."

Ever the contrarian, Ditka was not handing out credit, even to Payton, whom he considered the greatest Bear. "He was just doing what he's paid to do," Ditka said dismissively.

During a 1983 game, TV cameras showed McMahon getting a pain-killing injection right in his throwing hand while on the sideline. Coppock questioned the strategy of putting his quarterback at some risk.

"Well, what the hell would you have done?" Ditka shot back. "What other options did I have?"

Yet, when Coppock was abruptly fired by Channel 5 as their sports anchor, within an hour Coppock's phone rang. It was Ditka offering his sympathies and asking if there was anything he could do.

The Bears media guide cover for 1992, Ditka's final season, consisted of nine snapshots of Ditka: in a golf hat, in a Bears winter cap, with his hair permed, near eruption giving "the Look" to an offending questioner. They were all "Ditkas." It was a fitting final volume, as it turned out, for the Ditka Bears: the "Sybil cover."

A PLAYER'S COACH

In the 1983 preseason game against the Kansas City Chiefs, Emery Moorehead missed a block that resulted in lost yardage. Later, the pass on a tight-end screen went off Moorehead's hands into those of a welcoming Chief.

"You're done! You're done!" Ditka screamed at Moorehead, sending him to the bench for the rest of the game. Moorehead suffered through Monday's film session and the Tuesday off-day. On Wednesday he came in. There was Ditka.

"Emery, you didn't play that good," Ditka said. "But you're still the guy I chose to play the position. You're the guy. You're the guy I'm counting on, the offense is counting on, the team is counting on."

That was it. Ditka had broken Moorehead down, then built him back up with the message: he was mad at the play, not the player.

It was not all fury. In 1983 Ditka was so enraged after the Bears lost to Baltimore that he broke his right hand hitting a locker. Before the Denver game a week later, he declared, "Win one for Lefty." They did.

It also was not all fair either.

In 1989 the Bears faced the Packers in Green Bay. Third quarter, third-and-three, and Van Horne was called for being offside. He was not offside, he knew it, but the officials called it. With the penalty, the Bears failed to convert and were forced to punt.

As Van Horne came off to the sideline, Ditka snarled, "Son of a bitch, I'm going to kick your ass!"

Van Horne was headed toward the bench. But this threat was too much. Van Horne turned and went right at Ditka.

"Bring it on, motherf***er," the big tackle said levelly. Line coach Dick Stanfel grabbed Van Horne, one of the toughest of the Bears and a proud man who would have crushed Ditka with one punch. Van Horne had taken on benches of Packers and Cardinals protecting Payton. Now he was holding his helmet by the face mask in his right hand and this tormentor was going down. Hilgenberg grabbed Ditka and kept the two separated, possibly saving Ditka's life.

The next day in the team meeting, Ditka railed, ripping Van Horne in front of the whole team. "Dyko, you're starting next week," Ditka yelled, promoting Van Horne's backup on the spot.

The team session broke up and in the offensive line meeting, Stanfel played the film of the penalized play back and forth six times. In none of the playbacks did Van Horne jump offside.

"It was a bad call, Keith," Stanfel declared. "You weren't offside."

After the meeting, Stanfel pulled Van Horne aside. "Keith, I think you owe Mike an apology," Stanfel said. "I don't care what happened, but you don't call your head coach a motherf***er."

"I owe *him* an apology?!" Van Horne stammered.

But Van Horne wanted the incident over and told Stanfel, "I don't agree with you, but if it's the right thing to do, all right."

Van Horne went into Ditka's office and sat down. "Mike, I want to apologize," he said. "It was the heat of the moment, and I apologize."

"It's all right," Ditka said. Then he added, "The league office called and agreed it was a bad call."

Ditka had gotten the call before the team meeting and still trashed Van Horne in front of the team.

Against the Vikings in 1984, Shaun Gayle was in a quandary. Ryan wanted L.A. Mike Richardson playing; Ditka wanted Gayle. Richardson started and Ditka pulled him and sent Gayle in. Ryan pulled Gayle and sent Richardson back in. Then, with Tommy Kramer already under center, Ditka looked at Gayle on the sideline and roared, "I want you out there right now!"

"Coach," said Gayle, "they're about to run the play."

"I don't give a damn," Ditka bellowed. "Get in there for Richardson!"

Gayle ran out toward the formation. Fencik grabbed him.

"What are you doing?" he yelled. "We're going to have 12 men on the field!"

"Hey," Gayle said, "I am *not* going back there! Ditka said to get out here."

The Vikings ran the play, the flag was thrown, and the matter was settled. Back in the locker room afterward Gayle was in his locker with Fencik on one side, Todd Bell on the other, demanding an explanation. Ditka walked in and ordered, "Leave him alone; I sent him into the game."

The next day the defense was watching game film and the play came on the screen. Ryan turned the machine off, turned the lights on, and said very slowly, "I don't care if Jesus Christ himself sends you in a game. You never go in a game unless I tell you."

Right, thought Gayle. And I'll be in Atlanta by sundown the day I defy Ditka.

There were as many takes on Ditka as there were players in the locker room. Perhaps the most important, the one that was there with them in the hours and minutes before games, was Ditka the player. He had been everywhere they had been, and then some.

MOTIVATION

Ditka prided himself on his motivational powers, but he missed as many players as he inspired.

He angered Dent with his references in the media to "Robert" Dent, a gesture of disrespect that Dent did not like and that added to the core edginess between offense and defense. Dent knew how to irritate Ditka, and that was to disrupt his precious offense in practice, which Dent was more than capable of doing.

The "Robert" thing made matters personal to Dent, who knew precisely what Ditka was trying to do. Because he did not show Dent respect, Ditka got little in return from one of the foundations of the defense upon which he rested. Ditka, for all of his understanding of what players go through, did not understand some of the ones he had.

The fact was, however, Ditka could motivate. Not every guy, not always the right way. But sometimes . . .

David Tate, a rookie defensive back from Colorado in 1988, was on special teams in the first game he'd played. Most players had been stars in college and never played much special teams. So when they got to the NFL, some needed to just survive and did not always understand that; they thought they were still on scholarship. Ditka disabused them of any such notion.

The Bears were in a meeting watching film and Ditka slammed the projector down.

"David," he yelled, "if you don't learn how to play special teams, you're not starting. And you probably didn't get your degree. So you're going to be back home in Denver washing cars!"

Tate learned to play special teams and in 1990 led the Bears in special-teams tackles.

BEAUTY AND THE BEAST

Ditka had his own distinctive panache.

In 1987 he had ripped the Hubert H. Humphrey Metrodome in Minneapolis, where the Vikings play, calling it more like a "rollerdome" than a football stadium. He

> "You couldn't go to him even with the doctor and say, 'Coach, I fractured my hip in a drill and I can't go.' He said, 'Oh, I did that. Hurts too.' How many coaches can say they did that? You had to respect that. You had to respect him."
> —*Shaun Gayle*

> "Some people, thanks to Ditka, said I was taking plays off. They didn't know what the f*** I was doing. They don't know what I'm dealing with. Sometimes I'm doing a bull rush to set up another, and sometimes I'm setting up a bull rush too. You don't know what I'm working on. I can't just go flying around all day and expect my body to hold up. Pass rushing is like pitching; you throw balls, you throw strikes, you set things up."
> —*Richard Dent*

despised the artificial turf ("If cows can't eat it, we shouldn't be playing on it").

The next day Ditka did his press conference wearing roller skates and skated through the offices at Halas Hall.

Not to be outdone, the Vikings cheerleaders wore roller skates the next time Ditka brought the Bears through there.

In 1989, before the disastrous season that led up to the final fall, Ditka headed up a $2.5 million ad campaign all over the country for Budget Rent A Car's truck operation. His punch line was "Next to me, Budget's trucks are the toughest things on wheels."

Then the camera pulled back to show Ditka perched on roller skates.

He also had his breaking points.

Armor All rust proofing, billing itself as "the Protector," hired Ditka as a spokesman and dressed him in a suit of armor. Channel 2 got a tip, went to Soldier Field, and there was Ditka, in a suit of armor, on a horse. Ditka was immediately angry that he was being filmed and got down off the horse and started chasing the crew in his suit of armor. "Get the f*** outta here!" armored Ditka yelled. "Can't you leave me the f*** alone?!"

Because of his explosive and unpredictable personality, Ditka often became the story, sometimes for all the wrong reasons. Television stations camped out at Halas Hall; press conferences were not to be missed. It may have been morbid curiosity—that portion of the public that really *does* go to a NASCAR race hoping to see a crash—but it was must-see theater.

The television stations were always looking for chances to show Ditka in a different light, including when he bought a Harley-Davidson motorcycle. On a Monday when local schoolchildren were out of classes and flocking to Halas Hall, Ditka got on the Harley and the cameras rolled.

"Yeah, fine, get me on the bike, ya f***ers," Ditka ranted. "Go ahead, ya bastards. I can't do anything without you f***ers."

The camera operators reminded him, "Mike, there's kids—"

Ditka started the bike, then stopped. "I think I'm gonna go take a shit. Why don'tcha follow me inside while I take a shit."

"Mike, the kids—"

Ditka got back on the bike and left. The next day he was profusely apologetic. And he apologized to the schools. It was just his ready-fire-aim temper.

In 1986, after a 44–7 dismemberment of the Bengals in Cincinnati, Ditka came out and talked outside the locker room. A disgruntled Bengals fan started screaming at Ditka.

"The Bears will *not* go back to the Super Bowl!"

"Get him outta here! Get your mouth shut!" Ditka bellowed back at him. The guy kept yelling. "You ain't goin' nowhere! Nowhere!"

Now the press conference was in full circus mode. He made a circle with his thumb and index finger and thrust it at his tormentor. "This is your IQ, buddy—zero!" Ditka yelled.

One of the reporters tried to ask him a question. Ditka cut him off. "No, I'd rather talk to that guy," Ditka snarled. "I *know* I'm smarter than that son of a bitch."

STAYING POWER

Everyone had a Ditka story, from the state trooper who stopped him for driving under the influence of alcohol to the kids at Misericordia, for whom Ditka raised millions and gave so generously of his time.

His impact and personality continued for 20 years, long after Fridge, McMahon, and the rest had departed the stage. Even as the eighties and the Bears' greatness ebbed, Ditka was still America's huckster. At one point he was shilling for Campbell Soup's Chunky Brand, Hanes Corp., Budget Rent A Truck, American Home Products Corp.'s Dristan Decongestant, Old World Trading Co.'s Peak antifreeze, and Talman Home Federal Savings in Chicago. He also was pitching the American Express credit card and the TCBY frozen yogurt chain. He and Dick Butkus did a commercial together for a rust protector for cars—the Iron Mike image. When Levitra sought a pitchman for its wares in 2003, who better than the very symbol of tough guy?

Ditka has "outlived" his enemies, at least professionally, which may be his ultimate triumph. San Francisco's Bill Walsh, derisively dubbed "the Genius" by Ditka, is no longer in demand as a studio analyst. Ditka is. He always did say he was smarter than Walsh.

QUARTERBACK DEBACLES

For all of the Ditka legend, he may have been the worst quarterback handler in history. The problem, from the players' perspective, was that Ditka had all these ideas that he knew how to play and coach offense. But he ruined quarterbacks. Steve Fuller, who got the team through so many things when McMahon was down, never got respect from Ditka. Mike Tomczak eventually had to go into therapy. Only McMahon, to his credit, was big enough to stand up to Ditka. And poor Rusty Lisch. . . .

Backup quarterback Lisch had a little rabbit's foot that he wore on his belt in the games. Plus he could not remember any plays so he had a big band on his wrist where he wrote the plays.

Late in the 1984 season, on *Monday Night Football* against San Diego, Lisch went into the game, threw an interception, and came off the field. Ditka exploded. Lisch was very religious, a Bible reader on the planes to and from road games, but Ditka tore into him mercilessly and without letup.

> "What it felt like it came down to was Ditka doing what he wanted to do rather than necessarily what was better for the team or the right way to do it. Flutie in fact was a pretty regular guy, but the shoes that he was asked to fill—McMahon's—were too big. And McMahon didn't want him to fill them. Sometimes Mike lost sight of what the goal was."
> —*Jay Hilgenberg*

After the defense got the ball back, the offense headed back onto the field. All except Lisch. He stayed on the sideline, silent.

"I don't think I can go back in after the way you talked to me," Lisch said.

Ditka sputtered and then his whole demeanor changed. A nice Sybil appeared.

"I was just kidding, Rusty," Ditka said. "I want you to play. C'mon, kid."

Ditka did not suffer slights lightly, perceived or real. He was vilified in and out of the locker room for his handling of the Doug Flutie situation in 1986, when he brought in an alternative quarterback because of McMahon's injuries and then gave him what players considered special treatment that included Thanksgiving dinner at Ditka's house. Two years later, the Bears were lit up by Flutie in a 30–7 thumping in New England. Ditka gloated.

"The next time anybody questions my judgment of talent," he said, "just think about it, gang."

Fittingly, Ditka's time in Chicago began with a quarterback "problem"— McMahon was drafted the year Ditka was hired—and ended with one—the Harbaugh audible in the Metrodome.

Ditka's demise in 1992 began when he lost all control and raged at Jim Harbaugh in front of the team, television, and the Minnesota Metrodome after Harbaugh called an audible he should not have. The Bears were still winning 20–7 after that, but they would lose that game 21–20. After that, Michael McCaskey had the beginnings of the pretext he needed to fire Ditka. Claiming that with free agency coming, nobody would ever come play for a seeming schizoid, and citing incidents like the one in Minnesota, McCaskey waited until the end of the season and then fired Ditka, a decision he'd waited a long time to make.

McCaskey had been a ballboy at Bears training camp in Rensselaer, Indiana, while Ditka was a player. According to Bears lore, Ditka occasionally grabbed the young McCaskey by the feet and hung him upside down over a dorm toilet. It is unlikely that McCaskey could ever look at Ditka without seeing himself hanging inverted over a dorm toilet, which doubtless did little for Ditka's job security.

Ditka's brand of football was basic Chicago. That was the idea when Halas brought him back to town. Ditka challenged the Bears during the 1985 training camp to put a chip on their shoulders and keep it there. When it slipped from time to time, he put it back.

"The main thing was," Ditka said, "I tried to put us in a role of underdog, the outcast, the team nobody liked. I know it wasn't true, but this was one of the ways I had to deal with them."

Whatever Ditka's foibles and rough edges, without him, 1985 would never have come to pass as it did for the Bears. Time has at once softened and clarified his perspectives. When the players gathered in 2004 to plan a strategy for marketing themselves in the 20th anniversary year of Super Bowl XX, Ditka said that whatever he made from anniversary activities was going into the players' pool.

"Without you guys," Ditka said, "none of this ever happens for me."

CHAPTER 3
1984—THE YEAR THEY KNEW

"Howie Long told me he hadn't been beaten
up that bad since grade school."
—Keith Van Horne

NINETEEN EIGHTY-FOUR. FOR SO LONG this year belonged to George Orwell and his apocalyptic novel about the future of the future. By the end of this 1984, however, the future belonged to the Bears. They became Big Brother.

Nineteen eighty-four. In May the average home price in the United States topped $100,000 for the first time. Two months later the Russians retaliated against the U.S. boycott of the 1980 Olympics in Moscow with a boycott of their own. They stayed away from the Los Angeles Games, but in the end, those belonged to Mary Lou Retton anyhow.

It was in this year that the Bears would begin their dominance, establishing in their own minds how broad the realm of the possible really was. Events unfolded through this year and season that proved to be the precursors of all that would happen a year later. The first shots in the brutal Mike Ditka–Forrest Gregg feud were fired. The Bears would annihilate the two teams from the previous Super Bowl—including the Los Angeles Raiders in a game so violent that one announcer, an NFL Hall of Fame lineman, termed it "frightening"—and in the process come to believe they themselves were destined for a Super Bowl, exactly as Mike Ditka had predicted. And they in turn would be destroyed by the 49ers in a game that would start the hunger for 1985 and also would include a gesture of perceived disrespect that would lead ultimately to the international phenomenon known as "the Refrigerator."

Ditka at the time was smoldering over being denied a contract extension by Michael McCaskey. The Bears had come out of 1983 with an 8–8 record, winning five of their last six games and narrowly missing the playoffs in only Ditka's second season—because of a loss in Green Bay.

But the reality was that Halas, not McCaskey, had hired Ditka. Ditka was not McCaskey's guy in any respect whatsoever. Halas had died in November, and with that went Ditka's security.

The Bears did go ahead with one significant move, however, planning to take their training camp to Platteville, Wisconsin, from Lake Forest, Illinois. They would "camp" there through 2001, and if players did not always like being away from home, the fact was that Platteville was a beautiful place to be and work—small town, nice pubs—and the Bears over time claimed it as their own.

About the time those developments were taking place, Wilber Marshall was arriving as the number one draft choice in a Bears draft that included Ron Rivera in the second round and Shaun Gayle in the tenth. Rivera was a linebacker from the University of California who would be hired as the team's defensive coordinator two decades later. Gayle, a defensive back with the assassin's mentality of Fencik, would replace Fencik in 1987 and would develop into one of the best pure tacklers in Bears history—with a dose of Ditka motivation.

During a game against the Chargers, Gayle was playing bump-and-run at corner and starting to cramp badly.

"I can't bump-and-run," Gayle pleaded. "I gotta play off a little bit."

No, Ryan said, Gayle needed to be up on the line of scrimmage. Gayle went back out and was beaten for the second-longest pass completion in Chargers history, an 88-yarder from Ed Luther to Bobby Duckworth for a touchdown. Gayle walked toward the sideline, trying to avoid Ditka, who shuffled over to intercept him.

"I heard things I never heard before," Gayle said.

WILBER MARSHALL—"PIT BULL"

Wilber Marshall was a special pick. He had been a frightening impact player at Florida who came in with an attitude that angered some. Marshall thought he was a superstar, a stud, and the rest of the locker room ought to feel lucky to have him. He'd come to the right place. He got the right coach.

Ryan broke him down to a buck private even though he was so much better physically than anyone the Bears had at that moment, easily beating out Jerry Muckensturm, who had a dead nerve in his shoulder. Knowing Marshall was an Academic All-American, Ryan got under his hide by addressing him as "Stupid." But then, slowly but surely, when Marshall started doing what he was supposed to, Ryan rewarded him with recognition that was not easily earned.

Quickly, Marshall figured out, as Wilson and others had, that Ryan was not impressed at all with college clippings or stats and did not respect someone unless they respected what he was trying to do and was part of the team. That was the key to Ryan as a great coach and leader of men.

Marshall was in the right spot at exactly the right time. He came out of Florida in the middle of a bidding war between the NFL and the United States Football League, one that saw Herschel Walker, Steve Young, and others follow the money into the fledgling league. Marshall parlayed that into a four-year deal worth $1.6 million, far eclipsing both Singletary and Wilson as well as most of the defense. It was the size of Marshall's deal that set Al Harris on the ill-fated course of his own holdout in 1985.

Marshall, nicknamed "Pit Bull" by teammates, had a brooding style that not everybody could handle. Washington and Houston, where he went after leaving the Bears, could not deal with him. One of the greats on one of the greatest defenses in history, Marshall was nothing more than an average player after leaving in 1987; he got hurt and was never challenged to overcome everything the way Ryan had challenged him.

But that was off in the future. In 1984, things were happening closer to home.

Hilgenberg, still offended at not being drafted when he came out of Iowa, had inherited the center spot from Dan Neal. He had spent three years feeling sorry for himself for the draft snub, but in 1984 he suddenly got serious about himself and his career and began to work with the weights, adding physical strength to the intelligence and leverage skills from his wrestling background.

Beginning with the next season, Hilgenberg would represent the Bears in seven straight Pro Bowls.

Over on the defense, Jim Osborne went out of the starting lineup at defensive tackle, and Hampton moved from right end inside to tackle, making room for Dent.

Dent had spent his rookie season studying Hartenstine and learning technique on how to use his hands to complement his innate speed. Dent finished 1983 with three sacks; he set the franchise record in 1984 with 17½. Dent also picked up a case of NFL attitude from Hartenstine.

> "I broke my thumb and could only play special teams one year. Somebody asked me why would I do that. But I felt like, hey, I had a chance to hit somebody from Detroit or Green Bay. I don't care. If I can't hit 'em 50 times, I'll just hit 'em 5."
> —*Mike Hartenstine*

DITKA VS. GREGG

One of the NFL's elite border wars also was now entering a new, vicious phase, one that would help define the Ditka regime.

Forrest Gregg had taken over from Bart Starr as the Packers coach in 1984. Ironically, the Bears had done in Starr with their 23–21 win in the final game of 1983, creating the job vacancy for Gregg. Gregg had been a Hall of Fame right tackle with Starr on the Lombardi teams that had been the scourge of Ditka the player. Now Gregg wanted to infuse a Lombardi attitude in the lethargic team he had taken over. On August 11, 1984, there the Bears were for him.

It was the second of four exhibition games for each team. Green Bay went ahead 14–0 in the first half, and the Bears answered with a field goal late in the second quarter. With one minute 12 seconds to play, Gregg called a timeout. Ditka seethed: preseason protocol dictated running a couple plays at that point and just heading into the locker room.

The situation was exacerbated by the game's being played at County Stadium in Milwaukee, where the logistics of a baseball arena determined that both benches were placed on the same side of the field, not on opposite sides.

"Why the hell are you calling timeout?" Ditka roared. "This is an exhibition game! Let's just go in!"

"I need to work on my passing game," Gregg shot back.

Ditka exploded: "You sorry son of a bitch!"

"Suck my cock, Ditka," Gregg suggested.

Halftime did nothing to quell the fury that was building. Ditka blew up at Ryan for a blitz call that the Packers beat. Ryan responded by throwing down his headset at one point and going at Ditka as hard as Gregg had.

All this for an exhibition game, which not coincidentally was the last preseason game ever between the two teams. It was, however, far from the last serious incident between them.

A month later the teams faced each other in the regular season. McMahon played with a broken right hand but did not survive the first quarter. His already aching back became too sore after a hit that McMahon considered a dirty, cheap shot. The culprit: a relative unknown named Charles Martin, a defensive lineman who would find himself at the epicenter of a Bears-Packers problem two years later. Martin's 1986 transgression would, in the minds of all Bears fans, alter the history of the franchise and do more than any single thing to deny the Bears a second straight Super Bowl.

Back in 1984, the game proved memorable for a reason having nothing to do with Martin or McMahon, Ditka, or Gregg. An interception by Leslie Frazier not only swung momentum in the Bears' favor but also was perhaps the first true step toward the team's believing it had the promise of something special.

Frazier was defending Pro Bowl wide receiver John Jefferson. A pass arrived, and Frazier, in a move that would be replicated in the 1985 opener against Tampa Bay, jumped over the top of Jefferson to make an interception. He was immediately flagged for pass interference. Jefferson walked over to the official.

"No, he never touched me," Jefferson said. And the referee picked the flag up. No penalty.

PURE VIOLENCE: NOVEMBER 4, 1984—LOS ANGELES RAIDERS, SOLDIER FIELD

While the events of 1984 redefined the Bears-Packers rivalry and injected it with an element of thuggery that would endure through Gregg's four years as head coach, it was the Raiders game that removed any doubt in the Bears' minds about what they could do. It also removed any doubt in the Raiders' minds.

The Bears came into that November 4 game following wins at Tampa and at home against Minnesota, standing at 6–3 overall. The Raiders were the defending Super Bowl champions, having destroyed the Washington Redskins 38–9 in what would be the last AFC Super Bowl win for more than a decade. They were the NFL's swashbucklers, the badasses of the league.

And they were crushed. Hall of Fame defensive end Howie Long said afterward that he had not been beaten up that badly since he was in grade school. Van Horne and the rest of the Chicago offense broke him down along with the rest of the supposed bad boys. Hall of Fame defensive tackle and TV analyst Merlin Olsen said several days afterward that what he saw in the Raiders game frightened him.

Not surprisingly, quarterbacks were being knocked out of the game, sometimes more than once. Marc Wilson was beaten up and forced to the locker room with a fractured arm. David Humm then suffered a knee injury and was done, leaving at that point only punter Ray Guy to get under center because the Raiders were going without a true third quarterback.

Guy wanted no part of that, and at first he was nowhere to be found. Raiders told the Bears later that Guy had gone into the locker room and told Wilson to get his tail back out there because Guy, accustomed to standing the customary 13 yards behind center, was in no mood to get any closer than that to the seething mass of destruction that was the Bears.

Eventually Guy was spotted over at the end of the bench on a 70-degree day with a rain cape over his head. The game was stopped for six minutes so the Raiders could tape Wilson up and get him back into the game just to hand off and avoid getting killed.

But Raiders quarterbacks were not the only ones taking savage hits. McMahon scrambled out of the pocket in the first half, went down, and was speared in the back by defensive lineman Bill Pickel. McMahon was in agony. He had been hit in the kidney area helmet-first, and his ribs lacerated his kidney in several places and tore off part of it.

McMahon kept playing but was having trouble talking and at halftime told doctors he could not breathe. Still, back out he went; he tried to call a play but was ordered off by members of his offensive line. He went in and made a trip to the bathroom where nothing but blood came out, and

> "Beating the Raiders was the big game in '84 because they were the champs. And they were scared to death, man, they were scared to death."
> *–Emery Moorehead*

strength coach Clyde Emrich called for an ambulance. McMahon was finished, for the day and for the season.

While McMahon was fighting through pain off the field, his mates were administering some of their own on it. The final score was 17–6, and afterward, defensive end Lyle Alzado came up to Wilson and the defense.

"You just kicked our asses," said Alzado, who was no stranger to asskickings, having administered enough of his own. "You deserve it. You kicked our asses."

Indeed, the ass-kicking was complete. Alzado and Long had been demolished, not by the defense, but by the offense. To Hilgenberg it was big because the Bears could measure themselves against the best. He would say later that it was the most physical game he was ever in.

Fear was setting in among opponents, for good reason. The week before the Raiders game the defense had set a franchise record with 11 sacks in the 16–7 win over Minnesota. The Bears beat up veteran Archie Manning, who was winding down his distinguished career with the Vikings, so badly that after one Manning trip to the Metrodome turf, Wilson just stood over him. "Don't get up, man," Wilson said. "Don't even get up. You need to stay down till they take you out of the game."

The season would end December 16 with 12 sacks at Detroit, a mark that still stands, along with the 72 sacks for the season, as the record for the franchise.

That month, Michael Jackson released "Thriller," which became the top-selling video of all time. Less than a year later, "The Super Bowl Shuffle" would make a run at Jackson's record.

The headiness from the turnaround year was tempered by a looming situation that could bring the entire rebuilt edifice crashing down: Ditka's contract. After the Bears beat Detroit 16–14 on November 18, Ditka said on a radio appearance that there was a good chance he would not be back as coach in 1985. The man who had hired him—Halas—was dead, and McCaskey's strength was not decision making. He and Ditka did not talk about Ditka's contract for the first time until the off-week before the Washington playoff game, and McCaskey announced a new contract just before the San Francisco game, which made it more of a distraction than a positive. But at least Ditka had a future in Chicago.

And the Bears were about to take another giant step, one that they themselves almost could not believe.

DECEMBER 30, 1984–WASHINGTON REDSKINS, RFK STADIUM

Ditka's Bears had won the NFC Central Division for the first time ever but were obligated to go on the road to face the annual-powerhouse Washington Redskins at RFK Stadium. It would be the Redskins who would knock the Bears out in the first rounds of playoffs in 1986 and 1987 in Soldier Field. But this day belonged to the Bears. They would deliver the knockout.

At the start of the second quarter, Redskins running back Joe Washington took a pass slanting across the middle. Todd Bell met Washington with a tackle that sent Washington one way and the ball another and was so violent that some Bears were afraid at that instant that the blow had killed the Redskins running

> "When Todd Bell hit Joe Washington, that was the turning point," Wilson said. "I felt sorry for Joe. He just lay there and I picked up the ball and ran about 10 yards. That's when we thought we could be something. That was when it started: 'Let me get one now!' It was like a snowball effect."
> —*Otis Wilson*

back. Fencik considered waving the para-
medics onto the field.

The hit jolted both teams. Prior to that,
the Bears were intimidated, not so much
by the Washington Redskins team itself,

> **"They couldn't do *anything.* You know, we are really, *really* good. And we were kicking their *ass!*"**
> **—Gary Fencik**

but by the moment. It was a big moment, and they were still a young team
that had not had the success yet.

But in the fourth quarter, the defense walked onto the field with the
Redskins owning the ball in the Bears' end of the field four straight times. The
Redskins got nothing, not even a first down.

For the first time, even more so than after the Raiders game, players looked
at each other with a dawning realization.

Gault caught a Fuller pass and simply ran away from cornerback Darrell
Green, the perennial winner of the NFL's fastest-man competition. Payton
completed a halfback pass to Pat Dunsmore. John Riggins may have been on
his way to the Hall of Fame, but he was not getting there through the Bears'
defense: he had 21 carries for just 50 yards. Theismann was sacked seven
times. The numbers show that Washington outgained the Bears 336 to 310,
but Payton ran for 104 yards. The Bears had arrived.

Or so they thought. They had lost both McMahon and Frazier in the
Raiders game, and there were limits to how high the offense and defense
could rise to offset those losses.

JANUARY 6, 1985–SAN FRANCISCO 49ERS, CANDLESTICK PARK

If Washington showed the Bears they belonged, the NFC Championship
Game showed them where they did not belong. But the lead-up to the game
was a preview of the personality the Bears were about to turn loose on the
unsuspecting NFL.

Ditka rode from Santa Rosa, California, to the press conference in San
Francisco with Bears PR director Ken Valdiserri in a limo. They brought along
something to drink—a number of bottles of California's finest. Forty-niners
coach Bill Walsh was on the dais first for the national media press conference,

his customary stiff, reserved self issuing the customary coach-speak.

Ditka came in, illustrated the effects of quality vintages on his media moments, and had the press corps in hysterics.

On the way back, Ditka and Valdiserri finished what was left of the wine. They met Jeannie Morris, wife of former Ditka teammate Johnny Morris, and Bob Vasilopolous from Channel 2 at a desig-

> "He was closer to a player than to a coach, a hard-living guy. He was one of them down deep. Ditka's explosions on the sideline were not those of a coach; they were those of a frustrated player. He was one of them back in the beginning."
> *—Bobby Vasilopolous, Channel 2 producer*

nated restaurant. A woman selling roses came by; Ditka bought all of them and gave them to Morris. "Here, Jeannie," Ditka burbled. "Your old man wouldn't buy these for ya."

Ditka and the group continued drinking; Ditka picked up the meal tab for everyone, then passed out. The next day, Saturday, he was coaching and getting his team ready for Sunday and the 49ers.

But for all of the pregame color, the 49ers, on the cusp of their dynasty, handed the first of several demoralizing eighties playoff losses to the Bears. They more than doubled the Bears' yardage (387–186), sacked Fuller eight times, and even handed Payton the indignity of being sacked attempting a pass. Only one Bears wide receiver—Dennis McKinnon—caught a pass. It did not matter that the Bears sacked Joe Montana three times. The Bears were humiliated 23–0. The 49ers added to the moment by telling tackle Jim Covert, "Next time bring your offense."

Walsh, whom Ditka would deride with the sarcastic "genius" designation for years, tipped the first domino that would culminate in the history of the era. He inserted 280-pound guard Guy McIntyre as a blocking back, creating his so-called "Angus Backfield," leading for Wendell Tyler or Roger Craig late in the game, a gesture that Ditka, ever on the lookout for perceived slights to constructively heighten antagonism, would seize on the following season and make "the Refrigerator" part of the decade's history.

The McIntyre move did not particularly incense the Bears players. They were being thoroughly whipped at the time, and the 49ers were having fun, something the Bears could more than understand even if it was at their expense. The Bears were not moving the ball, they were making mistakes, and nothing was going right.

The game was just 6–0 at halftime, but the 23–0 final was indicative of where the Bears stood compared to the league's best. "The playoff game against Washington was big for us, but then to get beaten so bad by the 49ers. . . . We could say we came this far, but look at how much more we had to go," Fencik said.

That loss was nothing less than a launching point. They were so close to the Super Bowl that Ditka had told them on his first day as coach that they would reach and win. On the plane ride home, McMahon sat across the aisle from Singletary and, although he had not played because of his kidney injury, apologized for the offense's performance and complimented the defense. Covert leaned in and told Singletary that it all would get done and done right.

No one could have imagined just how right it would all be.

CHAPTER 4
SHAKY START

"There was always something that changed the game.
Then we just started feeding like dogs on raw meat."
—*Otis Wilson*

NINETEEN EIGHTY-FIVE WAS GOING TO BE DIFFERENT. A Super Bowl was responsible for getting all of that started.

Ronald Reagan was sworn in for his second term as president, and that was supposed to be done, according to the Constitution, on January 20. But because that date fell on Super Bowl Sunday, Reagan was sworn in a second time on Monday, the 21st, so Americans could watch—the game *and* the swearing-in. Washington may be lacking in feel for Americans on some points, but the Beltway was inhabited by enough Redskins fans to know that in a ratings taffy-pull, inaugurations have no prayer opposite Super Bowls.

The Bears had decided on their plane ride back from San Francisco that they were going to do more than watch the next Super Bowl. The off-season was never really "off" for a group that was determined to make its own run at history—literally, in some cases.

Gayle had broken his leg in the December 9 game against Green Bay, and trainer Fred Caito told Gayle to run with Olympic speedster Gault as part of Gayle's rehabilitation in the spring of 1985.

"Are you kidding?" Gayle laughed.

"No, I'm not," Caito said.

So they took off running in the woods around Lake Forest. An hour or so later, Gayle got back to Halas Hall. Gault had already showered and gone.

"How'd you do?" Caito asked, referring to Gayle's leg.

"I can tell you honestly, Fred," Gayle insisted, "that I never lost sight of him completely. Honest."

In April, New Coke appeared in what was either one of the great marketing gaffes or one of the great inspirations of all time. It sparked a global debate over whether the new beverage was a step up or down from the old. Coke resolved the question with an equally celebrated "comeback" of "Classic Coke" that would coincide generally with the international explosion of classic Bears.

The first Live Aid concert for African famine relief was performed in Philadelphia, with another in London. Tina Turner, Mick Jagger, Phil Collins, Bob Dylan, Paul McCartney, U2, Joan Baez—celebrities were lining up to be associated with the relief effort, and some of them would be Bears "groupies" by the end of the year.

Back in Chicago, WGN radio sponsored a Bears function at Soldier Field in June. New play-by-play man Wayne Larrivee was part of the event and noticed something he had never seen before. He went home and confided in his wife that he had seen a team that he knew, without question, was going to win the Super Bowl.

> "These guys are the most focused group of people I had ever been around, and that includes the Bulls championship teams of [Michael] Jordan. I have never seen a group of people so focused on one goal. It was guaranteed that they were going to win the Super Bowl."
> —*Wayne Larrivee*

CAMP COMBAT

About that time, the Bears were heading for their second Platteville training camp. More or less. The team headed out for the southwestern Wisconsin hamlet. Players cleaned out lockers at Halas Hall and either took the bus with the rookies or drove their own cars or trucks.

McMichael, still not completely recovered from his repossessed Cadillac, had a beat-up Bronco with a front seat broken at a bizarre angle. He pulled up in front of Halas Hall to get things from his locker, left the Bronco running, and went inside. Ken Margerum and one of the offensive linemen carjacked the heap and drove away—all the way to Platteville, 180 miles from Halas Hall.

It was a stunt that McMichael could appreciate. He and Hampton became Platteville legends with their vocal rendition of "Up Against the Wall Redneck Mother" in the Second Street bars, while McMahon arrived at camp not in McMichael's Bronco but in a limo, wearing sunglasses and finishing off a beer.

Not all things were fun, however. For various reasons, an animosity was growing between the two sides of the ball, spawned in part by Ditka's burgeoning problems with Ryan and vice versa. The offense did not want to go live with the defense; no one did. But Ditka and Ryan lived for confrontation, and Ditka, a member of the 1963 Bears championship team that won despite open hostility between units, was more than happy with a simmering rage all around. After all, he had one himself.

The situation was not as bad as people once said about the Boston Red Sox — 25 guys going to dinner in 25 separate cabs. Or as bad as the 1963 Bears team, where the defense trotted off the field after stopping one opponent, and defensive end Ed O'Bradovich just snarled at the offense, "Just try and hold 'em, all right?"

The two units in 1985 were not close off the field. Thayer hung out with Hampton on occasion, but Thayer, the Notre Damer from Chicago's tough south suburb of Joliet, struck teammates as always the politician, always trying to ingratiate himself with somebody. And why not? He had to go against Hampton, McMichael, and Perry every day.

Ditka relished the nine-on-seven sessions of training camp that were exclusively running plays and where the expectation, as the defense saw it, was to almost let themselves be blocked so the hole could develop, the receiver could get open, and the quarterback had time to throw. But running at anything more than half speed, the defense could foul up the plays.

> "I know for me my biggest fears were afternoon training-camp practices against Ming because I couldn't block him and they knew we were going to throw every time in 'team' drill. I was scared to death of those practices. I remember Dick [Stanfel, line coach] saying, 'Tommy, he's going through you like shit through a goose.' It was brutal."
> —Tom Thayer

Ditka regularly started fuming and ranting because, beginning in 1985 and for years to follow, there would be eight thousand to ten thousand people watching practices up close from the gentle hillsides that started only yards behind the players on the sidelines. The defense typically cooperated—to a point. But Dent, Hampton, Marshall, McMichael, and Wilson were not the types to let Tom Thayer or anyone else knock them off the ball in front of a crowd.

Gradually egos came into play. Ditka became irate.

"OK, that's it," he stormed. "You f*** with us, we're going to start cutting you. We'll make it live." That would mean that the backs like Suhey and the linemen would start cut-blocking, going low to make the defensive players slow to protect their knees.

"Fine, let's make it live," Dent taunted back. "Let's make it *all* live!"

For the offense, it was not good news.

> "Ditka saying, 'OK, let's make it live,' was like your dad saying, 'OK, here comes the belt.' Your dad may be downstairs, you jack your brother a good one when you're supposed to go to sleep, and your dad yells, 'Here comes the belt!'"
> *—Tom Thayer*

The practices went on like that, even into the season: bloodletting on Wednesdays and Thursdays, if the coaches thought they had played badly in the game. If the defense gave up 10 points, Ryan and the players would be angry and throwing people around. "F*** you, *make* it live!" was their attitude. And the combat was making them better.

What was also happening, amid the crashing and make-it-lives, was that one of the NFL's greatest offensive lines, with Bortz, Covert, and Hilgenberg going to Pro Bowls and Van Horne who should have, was going every day against one of history's great defenses—line, linebackers, defensive backs. Dent said that after he'd gone against Covert every day in practice, what problem was he going to have with anybody on Sunday? Hilgenberg said simply that the games were easy after practicing against Hampton, McMichael, and even Perry, a rookie whose understanding of the defense and his assignments had not caught up to his strength.

There was also a singular purpose that was never far below the surface.

The San Francisco game may have been on Bears minds every day between January 6, 1985, and the start of training camp and games, but it was not the only thing.

CONTRACT CHANGES

Dent; Singletary; safety Todd Bell, who had delivered the memorable hit in the Washington playoff win; and defensive end and linebacker Al Harris were contract impasses with Jerry Vainisi, who succeeded Jim Finks as general manager, and ultimately McCaskey. All four were potentially going to be out of the defensive picture they so defined. It was not until early August that Dent broke down and settled for $90,000 a season, not much of a raise from the $70,000 he'd played for in 1984 when he set the franchise sack record.

Singletary and his wife, Kim, were to the point of putting their house up for sale and moving back to Houston; the problem there was Singletary felt lied to by Vainisi and McCaskey's suggesting that he could possibly redo his deal, then hiding behind "team policy" that the Bears did not renegotiate existing contracts. The Bears wanted to lock Singletary up for six years; he wanted the deal trimmed to four. But the bigger issue was honoring one's word, and Singletary was in no mood to play for people who he felt did not honor theirs.

McCaskey finally relented and agreed to four years. Singletary made it to training

> "In that '85 camp, Buddy threw me in at free safety, first time ever. Ditka yells, 'Give the quarterback a "look."'' So the ball is snapped, I start running, way to my left, then way to my right, making motion all over the place. I'm huffing and puffing, and the ball hadn't been thrown. So then they put Fencik in. Gary just turns, runs straight back, the ball is thrown right to him; he intercepted it. I realized right then, there was great value in knowledge."
> —*Shaun Gayle*

> "Mike Singletary gets up the first day of camp and says, 'I refuse to go home early this year!' We heard that and we knew what was going on. We were going to make it; everybody had the same goal."
> —*Emery Moorehead*

camp August 22, joining Dent. But Bell and Harris never came to terms, sat out the season, and never made it to a Super Bowl.

Other changes were to cost some people their only shots at a Super Bowl. Bears broadcasts had been done on WBBM for seven years beginning in 1978, with Joe McConnell doing play-by-play and sportscaster Brad "the Professor" Palmer providing color. After 1984 the broadcasts moved to WGN, and with that change came a new broadcast team.

At the center was Larrivee, who had done Kansas City Chiefs broadcasts for seven years and was highly respected nationally. But the move angered many because McConnell had a following and Larrivee was unknown in Chicago. McConnell had called classic games like the one in which Payton broke Jim Brown's rushing record and the Washington game in 1984, and listeners just were not sure if they liked the change.

The main "Voice of the Bears" was not the only switch. Television had been successful with three men in the booth, but the format had never been tried successfully on radio. WGN gambled. The station brought in Jim Hart, longtime star with the Cardinals and a Southern Illinois University alum, to do color with Larrivee. Hart was a "name," but not many knew he was a local guy.

Then came the masterstroke.

Dick Butkus, considered by so many—certainly by Chicagoans—to be the greatest linebacker and perhaps the greatest single defensive player in the history of the game, was put in with Larrivee and Hart. Butkus was Chicago-born, a star at Chicago Vocational High School, All-American at the University of Illinois, and installed in the Hall of Fame in 1979. The move created a buzz of its own around the Bears.

The broadcasting became part of the story. Larrivee was precise and detailed in his play calling without being pedantic. He never yelled. His voice would go up in the excitement, and he had all the pitch but never came across as a screamer. And every single play call contained personnel adjustments, what formation they were in, and what the down and distance were. Few realized they were seeing the whole picture because Larrivee was so fluid.

And the mesh with Hart and Butkus was perfect. Butkus may have sued the Bears over the handling of his career-ending knee injuries (he won), but he was a Chicago Bears fan who just happened to know the game as well as anyone alive.

WGN became a growing part of the Bears' impact, with programming changes, players doing phone-ins with hosts, and sports coverage orchestrated by Chuck Swirsky, an unabashed Chicago sports fan himself. The impact was heightened because the Bears were unfolding at a time when FM radios in cars were not the standard equipment they are now. There was no all-sports talk radio at the time, and WGN simply was where most of the action was.

The Bears wobbled through a 1–3 preseason that included defeats by Indianapolis and Dallas, the latter a brutal game marred by fights that earned Bears and Cowboys a combined $20,000 in fines. Singletary was not there; neither were Bell or Harris.

SEPTEMBER 8, 1985—TAMPA BAY BUCCANEERS, SOLDIER FIELD

In five of the first seven games of the season, the Bears came from behind to win, three times from being down in the third quarter. Even Washington and Green Bay led 7–0 before the sky—and the Bears, both offense and defense—fell on them.

> "We struggled the early part of the year, then got on a roll. The first four weeks are all about getting your things together. In the last eight weeks, it was all together."
> —*Richard Dent*

With heat reaching 130 degrees on the artificial turf, Tampa Bay got the Bears down 28–17 on opening day, with neither the offense nor the defense looking like anything special. Then in the third quarter came what Ditka would later call the biggest single play of the season.

Tampa Bay quarterback Steve DeBerg dropped to pass; Dent sensed a change in Tampa left tackle George Yarno's weight shift and drifted into the flat to the defense's right side. Frazier, in deep zone coverage, saw DeBerg set quickly in three steps, knew the throw was coming at that instant, and broke before the ball was in the air. DeBerg threw and Dent leaped, tipping the pass. Frazier made the acrobatic interception and returned it 29 yards for a touchdown. The dam had burst.

> "I remember Leslie Frazier's interception the first game of the year, against Tampa Bay. He came right over the top of the guy and made the play, doesn't touch him and makes an incredible interception. We were getting it handed to us that day."
> —*Keith Van Horne*

The Bears had not come from 14 points behind to win a game since 1980. Yet a lot of the media had missed the turning point of the game and season because they were watching baseball. They had turned over to watch Pete Rose tie Ty Cobb with hit number 4,191 at Wrigley Field, and they never saw the end of the 38–28 victory.

The offense ran 34 times and passed 34, with McMahon completing a career-high 23. Payton got 120 yards on 17 carries.

But James Wilder had run all over Ryan's defense for 166 yards, and people were whispering that the defense was not the same without Bell and Harris, both 1984 starters.

That was true. It was not the same defense. It was about to become frighteningly better.

THE "46"

Few defenses in NFL history have terrorized the league the way the "46" did. The defense had gotten its name from the number of former safety Doug Plank who, ironically, was gone at the end of Ditka's first year.

The 46 defense was becoming more than offenses could handle, with six defenders (four of whom would be voted to the Pro Bowl) up on the line, Marshall over the tight end, usually to the right, and Wilson outside of him. Ryan put no one directly over the right tackle, typically the offense's biggest lineman who also typically works better with somebody directly opposite him but not as well when he has to go find somebody—especially if that some-body was Marshall or Wilson, one of whom was usually blitzing and both of whom were too much for any tight end one-on-one.

Much of the damage came from the defensive end who shifted down inside nose-up on the center. Usually it was Hampton rather than Dent. Hampton was a former Pro Bowl tackle and could dominate inside as well as on the edges; Dent was better in space and coming from the quarter-back's left, usually the blind side. Much was predicated on the blitzing of Marshall and Wilson and on Hampton. He could not be blocked to either side, and if he was just single-blocked, he had to hit the quarterback within two seconds. Hampton considered himself unblockable with a single block. There were not many technique moves involved inside: a surge rush from a horde of dominating physical athletes and then hit the quarterback.

Dent believed in a rule of three: all great defenses had three great pass rushers or the equivalent of them coming from somewhere. The "Fearsome Foursome" of the sixties Los Angeles Rams had Rosey Grier, Deacon Jones, Lamar Lundy, and Merlin Olsen. The "Purple People Eaters" brought Carl Eller, Jim Marshall, and Page from the seventies Vikings. The "Steel Curtain" had Mean Joe Greene, L. C. Greenwood, and Dwight White for the pressure from the seventies Steelers.

The Bears were far beyond any of those. They had three rush linemen in Dent, Hampton, and McMichael. They also had three linebackers and two safeties who brought terror to the pocket. Twelve different Bears had at least a share in a quarterback sack in 1985 and 1986.

With Hartenstine at end and Hampton at tackle, the Bears had an entire front four of rush threats. Eventually Hartenstine's job was handed to Perry, which gave the defense more against the run.

SEPTEMBER 15, 1985—NEW ENGLAND PATRIOTS, SOLDIER FIELD

That month the *Titanic* was finally located in the depths of the Atlantic Ocean. The discovery took some attention away from the young season, but anyone who looked away too long missed something in Chicago.

> "There was always something that changed the game. Then we just started feeding like dogs on raw meat."
> —*Otis Wilson*

The New England Patriots were in Bears territory less than 30 seconds of the entire game: two snaps from the 49-yard line late in the first half and a 90-yard pass-and-run from quarterback Tony Eason to running back Craig James in the fourth quarter. Eason was sacked six times and threw three interceptions, and the 16 runs netted a total of 27 yards in what was a preview of Super Bowl XX.

Ryan called the New England game the defense's best game, which was good timing. McMahon's upper back was in traction, and Payton rebruised some ribs and carried only 11 times for 39 yards.

Singletary had three sacks and an interception. But he played an even bigger role in establishing an element of intimidation that went to the core of an opponent. Singletary simply studied so much and so well that he knew from the smallest "tells" what his foe was about to do.

What Singletary had seen from New England was that as the Patriots broke their huddle, Eason unconsciously looked for a split second in the direction the play was to be run. Singletary kept studying; a particular backfield shift also told him the Patriots were about to run a draw.

Singletary saw the shift and screamed "Draw!" Eason froze. One of the offensive linemen turned his head and growled at Eason, "Well, are you gonna change the play or what?"

Singletary's "Samurai" was settling in, a nickname coined because of the noises he made on the field. Against the Patriots, he loosed a Samurai scream on a pass toward Craig James and broke early on the ball. James heard it in time to knock the ball down, costing Singletary a second interception. "For once I should have been quiet," Singletary said.

Singletary had a premonition. He told his wife, Kim, that this was the team they would play in the Super Bowl. He and the Bears also knew that if they broke quarterback Tony Eason, they had the Pats. And they knew they could break him.

The 20–7 defeat of New England was a statement game, a foreshadowing of what was to come to pass four months later.

After the game, however, the power struggle between Ditka and Ryan escalated. Ditka and personnel chief Tobin, who'd drafted Perry out of Clemson in the first round, wanted Perry playing. Ryan, who had neither time nor patience to spend on rookies, particularly ones whose work ethics he questioned, did not want to move Hampton out of the tackle spot inside.

Perry eventually got the starting job and history along with it. First, however, there was some business to be done in Minnesota.

Chapter 5

THE BIRTH OF MAD MAC

Ditka: "Why'd you throw it to Willie?"
McMahon: "Because he was open."

JIM McMAHON HAD NOT ATTRACTED much notice outside Chicago, not really even that much outside the Bears themselves. He had missed the end of the 1984 season, the Bears were 1–3 in the preseason, and he had not been a dominant force in 1985—yet.

But something was happening, something so big that it would affect the very core of the Bears. They had not exactly swept anyone away yet, neither Tampa Bay nor New England, although the first stirrings were indeed there.

What was quietly forming inside the locker room was an unshakable faith in McMahon, something the Chicago Bears had not felt for a quarterback since Sid Luckman in the forties. The offense believed that when McMahon was in the huddle, they were going to win. They bonded with his attitude. He helped matters by joining the offensive-line dinners on Thursday nights, picking up the check when it was his turn, and starting a celebratory tradition of head-butting his linemen after touchdowns, which were going to become dramatically more frequent.

The first time Jim Finks saw him, Finks said, "This guy knows how to play. He knows how to play, where to put the ball, knows the game."

McMahon was hurt in the Raiders game the year before, and more than just the offense felt that if McMahon had been healthy, they would have beaten San Francisco and gone on to win that 1985 Super Bowl. Payton was still great, and other members of the offense were becoming factors. But what Montana was for the 49ers, McMahon was for the Bears.

SEPTEMBER 19, 1985—MINNESOTA VIKINGS, HHH METRODOME, MINNEAPOLIS

The Bears faced a short week after beating New England, which was always a problem for preparation and even more so when the game was away. The 2–0 starts for both teams only raised the tension going into a crucial divisional game.

Singletary got into several fights with teammates in practice before the Minnesota game; he went home and told his wife, Kim, "This is the biggest game of our lives."

Thursday night was a transplanted *Monday Night Football*, which meant it was the only game on and therefore the entire football-watching world would be tuned in. Ditka, McMahon, and the Bears had the stage all to themselves.

Edginess existed between the Bears and the Vikings. The Minnesota franchise was founded in 1961, and in its first NFL game, the expansion team pushed around the venerable Bears in a 37–13 embarrassment of Chicago. The Vikings had tremendous talent all through the eighties and were annually upset at how many Bears were voted to Pro Bowls when they thought they were every bit as good as the Bears were.

Minnesota coach Bud Grant also did not particularly like Ditka or how he had gotten the job through Halas. "It's not what you know, it's who you know," Grant said. Ditka remembered insults, slights, and perceived slights, and if there were not any, he manufactured them.

The Bears found out that Bud Grant had criticized one Minnesota opponent over its players' sloppy appearance and demeanor during the national anthem. Grant praised his Vikings and called for ABC to show the anthem live, telling his players that they would stand with feet together and at attention. Like a bunch of schoolkids, the Bears thought.

Before the Bears took the field, Ditka told them, "You will stand there with your feet together, helmet under your left arm, right hand over your heart. We'll fix them. Now let's see who has more class."

The national anthem was announced, and the Bears snapped their hands over their hearts and came to attention. They continued to do it that way the rest of the season, Ditka's personal one-up of Grant.

"McMahon was more old-school training camp stuff, whether shaving his head, coming out with high-tops, just fun stuff. It wasn't just Ditka he'd have had problems with. Anybody who tried to pull authority on him would have been in for a fight. Jim was going to be Jim, and I think Ditka was probably good for him. He held everybody up to a higher standard. When you're playing football and you'd have pain that might take someone out of a game, you'd push yourself beyond the limits. There were times when he felt the play he wanted was going to be better than the play that was called. But he understood the offense as well as anyone could have, and he understood defenses. He was the type of guy who could be a great quarterback without watching tons and tons of tape."
—*Tom Thayer*

It would fall to McMahon to do the real damage, however.

McMahon had a bad back and an infected leg and excused himself from practice leading up to the game. Then he spent most of Wednesday's prep day in the Dome sitting in stands with his idol, Joe Namath. Some thought he should have been on the field with the team. Others knew it was just basic McMahon, all part of the package.

McMahon spent two nights in traction with his back problem and had a leg infection from a turf burn as well. Still, when Ditka told him he was not starting, McMahon was livid. There were tales of furniture being thrown. McMahon had never played on national TV, having been out of the 1984 playoff games against Washington and San Francisco because of the lacerated kidney suffered from the hit in the Raiders game. And this game, like so many of the Bears' epics of 1985, was on national TV, the only game on.

McMahon started the game sulking at the end of the bench. Pouting or not, there was not much to be upbeat about in any case.

The Bears scored first on a 24-yard field goal by Kevin Butler. Minnesota tied it when Jan Stenerud converted from 25 yards, leaving the score 3–3 after the first quarter. But neither offense seemed able to close the deal, and for a third time a drive stalled in the red zone, and Butler put the Bears ahead 6–3 with a kick from the 9.

Then Minnesota quarterback Tommy Kramer began to heat up. He gave the Vikings back the lead with a 14-yard pass to Anthony Carter, and Minnesota went in at halftime with a 10–6 lead and Kramer on his way to 436 passing yards. The second half began with the Bears stopped again inside the Minnesota 20 and Butler connecting on a 34-yard boot through the uprights. Kramer answered with a nine-yard scoring pass, and the Bears were officially in trouble. Fuller completed 13 of 18 passes, but the team was missing something.

The Bears in fact were angry at each other, even within the offensive and defensive units. Hampton was sniping at the defensive backs for not stopping Minnesota receivers. Frazier shot back at Hampton that the linemen and linebackers ought to worry more about getting after Kramer themselves.

With the Bears trailing 17–9 in the third quarter and the offense stalled, McMahon began pestering Ditka to let him in, regardless of whether or not McMahon had practiced in the days before the game. The Bears needed something. Then the TV announcers reported there was activity down on the Bears' sideline.

ENTER: McMAHON

With seven minutes 32 seconds to play in the third quarter, that something the Bears needed was in Ditka's ear on the sideline, and there was no doubt where this was going to end up. Ditka and McMahon exchanged words, and McMahon trotted out onto the field and into a place in history.

McMahon came onto the field like a gunfighter coming into a saloon knowing he is the baddest of the bad in the place. The first thing he did, of course, was curse out the offense when he got to the huddle.

The offensive players registered shock initially because Fuller had not been injured. McMahon's comment, when he was done cussing out the group, was simple: "We're going to go down that field and get six."

Ditka's last order to McMahon was a conservative play call. "Get your ass in there," Ditka said, "and throw a screen pass."

McMahon called the screen pass. But events conspired for a different outcome.

McMahon took the snap and started to drop back. Then he stumbled and nearly went down. Over on defense, the Vikings knew McMahon was not very mobile, particularly with the problem of his infected leg. So they blitzed what they anticipated would be a stationary quarterback and in the process left their defensive backs exactly where McMahon wanted them: alone.

McMahon's linemen picked up most of the blitzing defense, but linebacker Scott Studwell came free up the middle while Hilgenberg was occupied. Studwell was running full out and had McMahon in his sights. Just before he could reach McMahon, Payton stopped him cold with a classic block that saved the game as well as McMahon's health. Had Studwell driven McMahon down into the artificial turf, McMahon would have been back out of the game and possibly the season.

Meanwhile, far down the field, Gault was running flat out with his world-class speed, and McMahon knew that if the Vikings were blitzing, Gault would be in single coverage. McMahon unloaded as far as he could heave a football. Gault took it in stride and finished for a 70-yard touchdown that had shocked the Vikings and brought fans rushing back from kitchens and bathrooms all over the country to see what had happened.

Afterward McMahon said, "Willie's going to be wide open at some point, and I'm going to throw him a pass. There's only a 50 percent chance he's going to catch it, but he'll be wide open and they have to cover him."

At the moment, however, he had Ditka to deal with. No problem.

"What'd you call?" Ditka demanded as McMahon reached the sideline.

McMahon said he had called the screen pass.

"Then why'd you throw it to Willie?" Ditka said.

Vintage McMahon: "Because he was open."

Suddenly the defense came alive as well. An interception gave the ball to McMahon and his suddenly rejuvenated offensive teammates at the Minnesota 25. After that, the Vikings never had a chance.

McMahon ran a bootleg. His first two receivers, Payton in the flat and Moorehead crossing over the middle, were covered. McMahon reacted instantly for his own personal target of choice, the end zone. There McKinnon was getting behind the defense that was reacting to the short patterns of Payton and Moorehead. McMahon, rolling to his left, fired on the run. McKinnon made the catch and suddenly a 17–9 hole was a 23–17 Bears lead.

The defense was snarling now and shut Kramer and the Vikings down again. McMahon missed Gault on a 68-yard deep strike—Gault outran this one—but seconds later found McKinnon again for a 43-yard touchdown. The legend of Mad Mac was set, right down to the spoof of Mel Gibson's "Mad Max" film character. McMahon was photographed for a poster in military gear, bullet bandolier, helmet, and a cigar.

Some players remain convinced that Ditka figured the Minnesota game was lost back when it stood 17–9. He sent McMahon in because he just wanted to get McMahon out of his ear.

McMahon's own genius and experiences worked against him with Ditka. The Bears offense had nowhere near the sophistication and forward thinking as the one he had played under at Brigham Young. His coach at BYU was LaVell Edwards, the guru credited with creating many of the intricacies and concepts that would come to be known as the "West Coast offense" when disciples like Bill Walsh and Mike Holmgren spread the Edwards gospel.

Edwards sent all the plays in from the sideline, but McMahon had the freedom to change the plays. Ditka and offensive coordinator Ed Hughes were neither as flexible nor as creative. The Bears were elementary, brought on by years of having Payton to rely on. Ditka had been a tight end; sometimes his play calling and game planning reflected his own experiences and perspectives.

On the other hand, when McMahon improvised on the touchdown passes to Gault and McKinnon, he was just doing what he had always done.

Lost in the Minnesota madness was a change taking place in front of McMahon. Thayer was a backup when the season started and did not play a down in the first two games, sitting behind Kurt Becker. So removed from playing was Thayer that he dallied and caught the last bus over to the Metrodome. He arrived so close to game time that he did not get his ankles taped.

But Becker suffered a knee injury in the first half that would take him out of the starting lineup for good. Line coach Dick Stanfel came down to where Thayer was sitting—no tape, low-cut shoes, just watching the game.

"You're in at guard!" Stanfel said. "Becker hurt his knee."

Thayer went in and promptly turned an untaped ankle severely on his second play. At halftime, Thayer headed for the training room, put on high-tops, got his ankles taped, and made it back for the second half. With McMahon in control and the defense now in charge of the Minnesota offense, the Bears moved to 3–0 with their 33–24 victory.

Mc-MANIA

The next morning, a marketing and media typhoon descended on McMahon, whose business and contract were taken care of by agent and friend Steve Zucker. The two were suddenly in the middle of something that threatened to go rapidly out of control. McMahon and Zucker had talked even before that game, and McMahon was absolutely sure that they would win it all that year. The Bears were on their way, and so was McMahon.

On Friday morning Zucker called up Rick Fisdale, one of his oldest friends and head of advertising giant Leo Burnett.

"What should I do?" Zucker wondered.

"Whatever you do," Fisdale cautioned, "don't do any commercials now."

"Why not?" Zucker asked, startled and confused.

"Because whatever you're offered now," Fisdale predicted, "it's going to multiply by 10."

Fisdale was right, and Zucker took the advice. The only commercial McMahon did was with Perry for Diet Coke, in October, after Perry had his first moment of fame.

And that was all they did, off the field. McMahon and Zucker just sat and waited, even though they were awash in phone calls and mail. Zucker had been a criminal trial lawyer, and his last client in criminal law, at the end of 1983, was *Hustler* publisher Larry Flynt. Then he met McMahon and began his career as an agent.

Zucker did not represent the quarterback when McMahon first came out of BYU. He knew Fisdale, who was a fraternity brother of Jerry Argovitz at the University of Texas. Argovitz and Zucker became friends, Argovitz going on to become a dentist, then getting involved in real estate, then becoming a sports agent. One of his clients was McMahon.

Argovitz did McMahon's first Bears contract. Like too many dealings between players and George Halas, it was contentious.

A year after doing the McMahon contract, Argovitz bought the Houston Gamblers of the United States Football League. McMahon went to see Zucker, whom he had met on occasion previously.

"You know, Jerry can't be my agent anymore because of owning this new team," McMahon said. "I'd like you to do it."

"I don't know how to do that," Zucker said.

"That's OK," McMahon said. "I trust you."

So began one of the most important relationships that would affect this era in sports and pop culture. They started with nothing more than a handshake and were still on a handshake basis 20 years later.

The night in June 1984 when Zucker did his first McMahon contract, McMahon and his wife, Nancy, were at the home of Zucker and his wife, Shelley. McMahon raised a point.

"You know, we never talked about your fee," he said to Zucker.

Zucker laughed. "You mean I'm going to get paid for this?"

McMahon set a generous percentage, which he always paid Zucker, and that was it.

McMahon was pleased with both the results and the relationship. He talked about Zucker among teammates, and at one point Zucker represented more than a dozen of the Bears through 1985–1987: Hilgenberg, Bortz, Van Horne, McKinnon, Wilson, Gayle, Duerson, Dent (as an attorney), Butler, McMichael, and Ken Margerum.

What Zucker and McMahon, along with the other members of the Bears organization, were doing was nothing less than changing sports marketing in America. McMahon was emerging as more than a football player. He and

Zucker were leading the way toward the Bears being personalities, not simply faces and names to link to products.

The two shared more than just product deals and contracts. As the season ended and McMahon Inc. began to roll, Zucker went with McMahon and other clients to appearances. For Zucker it was like being with a rock star. For an opening at the Brickyard Mall on Chicago's west side during the 1986 season, the crowd surpassed twenty thousand.

Even the didn't-happens were memorable. *Sports Illustrated* came to Zucker with a subscription deal. The decision was whether to use McMahon or Joe Montana in a commercial.

At one point during the negotiations, Zucker stammered, in all seriousness, "Why would you want Joe Montana?! He's passé. McMahon, that's the guy you have to have." At the time it seemed absurd that Montana was mentioned in the same breath as McMahon.

And *SI* agreed. It did in fact take McMahon over Montana. The commercial never got past test-marketing, but would have netted McMahon about 50 cents per subscription.

In 1987, he was on course for a *Newsweek* cover, but a loss the weekend prior killed the deal.

At the end of the Super Bowl and all its accompanying sideshows, most involving McMahon, he was the hottest marketing property in the country. He was on the cover of *Rolling Stone* and on the national talk shows. For all of his intractability with the media, he was an advertiser's delight. Kraft Miracle Whip, paint pellets, Honda scooters, Revo sunglasses—he always did things on first takes and the deals were all substantial, national.

McMahon did not take every endorsement opportunity that came his way. He had a philosophy under which he said, "I will not do a commercial for a product I do not use or believe in." McMahon was also willing to say no and walk away.

McMahon and Zucker turned down several fast-food deals because they could really only do one, and that was going to be Taco Bell because that was McMahon. He loved Taco Bell, so he and Zucker did that instead of some of the hamburger deals. The first Taco Bell spot was filmed right after the Super Bowl, at the University of Southern California library.

When McMahon, then in his early twenties, began working with Zucker, he told his agent exactly what he wanted: "I want to make enough money to where I never have to work again if I don't want to after football." Zucker took care of that. The millions McMahon pulled in from endorsements and appearances were more than the amount made by all five Super Bowl quarterbacks immediately before him.

MAC APPEAL

As the Bears established themselves as winners, the national infatuation was with McMahon's outspokenness and the perception that he said exactly what was on his mind, like it or not. Americans like their rebels. And he was able to back that attitude and personality up with winning on the field.

> "To this day, middle-aged women come up to me and tell me, 'You know, I never watched a football game before Jim McMahon and the '85 Bears.'"
> *—Steve Zucker*

McMahon was looked at as a free spirit and a winner, and he brought new fans to the game of football, mainly young children and women.

McMahon's relationship with the media was strained at best, contemptuous at heart, hostile at worst. The only individuals with whom McMahon feuded on the magnitude of Ditka—for whom he had a core respect as a fellow player—were ones with pens and microphones.

Bill McGrane, the team's director of administration, got on a bus to ride to a game and McMahon invited him to sit next to him. McMahon had his hair combed and everything and looked perfectly normal, with a lunch box his wife had packed for him.

"We're talking here and you're the most normal guy," McGrane said.

"Well," McMahon said with a smile, "I don't have anybody to irritate."

> "McMahon was a prick. He called Walter 'Wally' and all that but he didn't give a shit about Walter. He didn't care about anybody but McMahon."
> *—Hub Arkush,*
> Pro Football Weekly

McMahon's expressed attitude was that of Norm Van Brocklin, the Hall of Fame quarterback and later coach of the Atlanta Falcons. When Van Brocklin was dying of brain cancer, *Atlanta Journal* columnist Furman Bisher went to see him.

"You know," the Dutchman told Bisher, "I wish they had a brain transplant. I'd ask for a sportswriter's because I'd know it had never been used."

McMahon's dislike for the media was reciprocal.

But inside the locker room, inside the huddle, was a different world.

Most of the offense loved McMahon, or at least loved going to work with him. McMahon, not Payton, was the leader of the offense. He took chances, put himself on the line, stood up to Ditka for himself and for them, changed plays, and made them work for touchdowns.

> "I don't know why Dan hates McMahon so much. Once you get to know Jim, he's cool. He's cocky, but he's got some brains between his ears. To me he was the quarterback who didn't have the physical abilities to do a lot of things but had the mental ability to do anything. He was able to read things the way I thought I could on defense, and that's the kind of guy you want. I'd rather go to war with a guy like that rather than a guy who goes by the book or worries about somebody being mad at him. It's Sunday; it's your day. You've got rules, but it's your day. If I have to worry about that fine line when I play, I'm never going to be shit, and Jim didn't worry about that line. That's the man you're looking for in sports."
> *—Richard Dent*

Tight end Emery Moorehead said there were 44 guys who liked Jim and one who did not: Hampton. Teammates suspected that the ill feelings were rooted in things said and done during the 1982 strike. Others thought the problem was simple jealousy; Hampton at that point of his Hall of Fame career was arguably the single best player on the team, but McMahon and subsequently Perry were harvesting the biggest shares of endorsement and appearance money along with Ditka. And when Hampton felt McMahon was putting himself ahead of the team, whether he was or not, the rift deepened.

Football is basic, McMahon reasoned. Somebody has to be somewhere at some point in time. He read the defense on the other side of the line of scrimmage and knew where to attack and where he wanted his personnel, and as long as everybody was on the same page, it worked.

McMahon showed the world how well it worked on that *Thursday Night Football* game in Minneapolis. McMahon and the Bears grabbed America and shook it awake. As so often was the case for the Bears then, nothing would ever be the same.

Chapter 6

SETTLING SCORES

"People liked John Wayne to walk into a bar and announce,
'Whiskey for my men and beer for my horses.' That was us."

—Dan Hampton

WASHINGTON CAME TO SOLDIER FIELD on September 29. The Redskins
and Joe Theismann were the darlings of an East Coast media that saw the sports
universe rotating slowly on a New York–Dallas–Washington axis. Washington
won a Super Bowl under coach Joe Gibbs, and the Redskins had some leftover
bad taste from the 1984 playoff game that had seen Theismann and his offense
do nothing with four possessions in Bears territory in the fourth quarter.

Once again, the Bears were going to make a statement when it would have
the greatest possible impact.

The Bears were 3–0, one of the only two undefeated teams at that point, but
they had needed big comebacks to win two of the three. When they fell
behind Washington 10–0, a smattering of boos accompanied the beginning of
the second quarter in Soldier Field.

Not surprising. The upset of the Redskins that was the high point of the
previous season looked like a mirage after the visitors outgained the Bears
141 yards to 2 in the first quarter. "Well, we're 4–0, but I'll guarantee you
it's not because of anyone in this group," Ryan said after the Bears had
recovered to savage Washington 45–10. "Don't let anybody blow smoke up
your butt. Understand what the situation is." The 46 defense was suddenly
back to what Ryan had once dubbed "our Swiss cheese defense—it's got
holes in it and it stinks."

In the first quarter, McMahon threw four passes and completed only one,
and that one was to a Redskin. The offense was still too much Payton-left-
Payton-right to most of the NFL, which was content to put eight defenders up

within a couple yards of scrimmage and dare McMahon and the Bears to pass and prove that what happened in Minnesota was to be believed.

The Bears were missing two offensive linemen, and Payton gained all of six yards in seven carries. They finished with their fewest first downs, rushing yards, and passing yards of the season. And still they scored 45 points on a team that would win multiple Super Bowls in the eighties.

Washington defensive end Dexter Manley, who Ditka one day would claim had "the IQ of a grapefruit," was among the NFL's best pass rushers. The Bears were without Covert. Backup Andy Frederick came off the bench and made Manley disappear.

RAW SPEED

After Washington took its 10–0 lead, the Bears exploded.

Gault took the ensuing Washington kickoff at the 1-yard line, squeezed through a hole at the 20, picked up blocks by Gayle and Dennis Gentry, and was gone. Just . . . gone. Ninety-nine yards. The game was over.

Against Tampa Bay it had been Frazier who seized the moment and an interception. In Minnesota it had been McMahon. Now it was Gault, to many the least likely Bear to make the turnaround play.

It was not an ability issue. At the University of Tennessee, when Gault walked back to his goal line to await a kickoff, the entire crowd of 107,000 rose in anticipation. He had run a 9.2 in the 100-yard dash. With the ball, he was a bird in flight.

Defensive backs were discovering that it was one thing to cover receivers who run great routes or have fantastic hands. But it was quite another altogether when it was someone who can beat them deep—at will, anytime he wanted to. And there was nothing they could do about it.

Watching Bears game film, players noticed that Gault had the unprecedented ability to take a cornerback and a safety "out of frame." Not just deep—out of the frame to the point where the defensive players were not on the screen anymore, anywhere. If all else failed, the Bears reasoned, the other guys did not have an Olympic sprinter on their side of the ball.

In the first round of the 1983 draft after the Bears had taken Covert, they selected Gault. The speed receiver had a number of nicknames. The one most repeated, however, was "Hollywood." Gault had acting ambitions and seemed at times less committed to football than to his extra-football career. He spent considerable time on his appearance and wardrobe and networking with producers and executives in show business. Gault would go on to enjoy a respectable career in film and television, including appearances on *The West Wing* and *The Pretender*.

Gault was a novelty in several respects. He was the first prominent athlete who ate healthy before his time, eschewing red meat and seeking out fruits and vegetables.

> "Theismann was scared to death. He was terrified."
> —*Otis Wilson*

Gault caught 40 passes his rookie season. He grabbed 34 in 1984. The total fell to 33 in 1985. He was losing respect in the locker room with a group that respected toughness and had not seen much of it from Hollywood.

But Gault was changing the face of his sport. He was creating a niche unlike any other with his speed. The Bears had a play called Big Ben in which Gault simply took off running, stopped for an instant, then took off again with a move and speed no defensive player could match. McMahon then just heaved the ball as far as he could.

Gault also was part of the mystique of the team. His greatest games were in the Super Bowl and on the Thursday night game in Minnesota. Like the entire team, the bigger the stage, the better Gault played.

The Washington game was another big stage.

The Gault return started the Bears toward 31 second-quarter points, a franchise record. After that runback, the defense went on the attack, as it had after McMahon's passes in Minnesota. The Redskins netted a total of one yard from their next three possessions while the Bears were scoring three touchdowns. The height of indignity for Theismann was shanking a punt out of bounds for exactly one yard. Theismann likened the experience of playing against the Bears defense to being on a freeway without a car.

The Bears did not particularly dislike Theismann. They just saw him as a media creation who made a career behind "the Hogs," his offensive line, and giving the ball to John Riggins. His name had been pronounced THEES-man until 1968 when the Notre Dame PR machine had the pronunciation changed to THIZE-man to rhyme with Heisman. As a talker he may have fit right in with the Bears in one respect. "Nobody in the game of football should be called a genius," Theismann once uttered. "A genius is somebody like Norman Einstein."

Theismann's career came to a sickening end in week 11 when Giants linebacker Lawrence Taylor landed on Theismann's left leg in one of the grisliest injuries ever filmed. Not even the Bears would have wished that on Theismann.

Ditka added a twist in the Washington game. He had McMahon hand off to Payton, then go the other direction. Payton then threw to McMahon for a 13-yard touchdown. Everything was working as the Bears scored 45 straight points for a 45–10 win to end September.

The city was starting to embrace the team. McMichael gave Singletary a couple of tickets to a wrestling extravaganza at the Rosemont Horizon, so Singletary and Dan Rains went. Hulk Hogan was there. When Singletary and Rains walked in, the arena erupted.

"Samurai! Samurai!" Fans were crowding around for autographs, giving the pair a standing ovation; eventually security guards had to rescue the two linebackers. It was only the beginning.

OCTOBER 6, 1985—TAMPA BAY BUCCANEERS, TAMPA STADIUM

October started with the Tampa Bay rematch, and the game began as badly as the first game with the Bucs had. Into the third quarter, with McMahon playing poorly, the Bears fell behind 12–0 and still trailed 12–3 in the third quarter.

This time it was Duerson with an interception. The Bears' rookie safety grabbed a Steve DeBerg pass that the offense turned into a touchdown pass to McKinnon. But it would be another McMahon move that got the Bears over the top, another instance of McMahon tugging in a different direction from his head coach.

With four minutes remaining, the Bears still led only 20–19. They faced third-and-three at their 24. Old Bears wisdom was to run Payton, and if that did not work, punt, let the defense take over, and close it out. That was Ditka's call.

McMahon argued for a slant to Moorehead, who was on his way to the best game by a Bears tight end since Ditka 20 years earlier. The coach relented, and McMahon got the first down with an eight-yard completion to Moorehead.

Three plays later, down to the two-minute warning, the Bears were in control. Second-and-11 at the Chicago 41. Run some clock and take the win.

McMahon thought otherwise. He knew Tampa Bay, knew the Bucs would blitz. Ditka, for all of his smashmouth impulse, agreed to a try for a dagger strike to Gault. Tampa Bay blitzed, McMahon threw, and Gault took it to the 11. Payton then finished the issue with his second touchdown run of the day.

The final 27–19 score was less the story, however, than the cementing and evolution of the character of the Bears. The Frazier interception in the first Tampa Bay game was a savior. McMahon's heroics in Minnesota were out of desperation.

The plays of Duerson, McMahon, McMichael (fumble recovery), and others against Tampa Bay were different. In the days before the game, Wilson talked about

> "Our defense was fun to watch and scary to watch. I wouldn't have wanted to play against them. That's why we were able to run the ball so well, practicing against those guys. Plus, [laughs] we did have Walter Payton, after all."
> —*Keith Van Horne*

the Bucs as a tough opponent until he remembered they had not won a game this season.

"So it shouldn't be much of a problem," Wilson conceded. The swagger was building.

And not just on the defense. McMahon and the rest of the offense believed that every touchdown was worth 14 points because of how difficult it was to score on the Bears defense. If the Bears had a 10-point lead going into the second half, the game was over.

The offense was the top-scoring in the NFL, and the defense of Ryan was proving unblockable. They had the best running back in football and the best pass rush in history. There was growing reason for the swagger.

Even Ditka, for all of his chip-on-the-shoulder worry, got it. "I just know that when I try to play it close to the vest, that's when they don't play good football," Ditka said. "When I let Jim wheel and deal back there and give him a lot of leeway, he plays better. He thrives on it."

OCTOBER 13, 1985—SAN FRANCISCO 49ERS, CANDLESTICK PARK

The Bears were 5–0, and people were throwing $5,000 at players just to show up for an hour of handshakes.

But another day of reckoning was upon them.

The loss to the San Francisco 49ers in the NFC Championship Game ended their 1984 hopes and at the same time lit a fire in the Bears. Seeing the 49ers go on to the Super Bowl and trample the Miami Dolphins and quarterback Dan Marino convinced them that they could at least see the top of the mountain even if they were not quite ready to make the ascent.

This game, at San Francisco in the same stadium where the championship game had been played, was a statement game for every member of the organization, starting with Ditka. The 49ers were the last team to beat the Bears. Their coach, Bill Walsh, was being accorded the mantle of genius for his West Coast offense, which Ditka pointed out was like most schemes, working remarkably well when Joe Montana, Roger Craig, and Jerry Rice ran them.

On Wednesday before the San Francisco game, Perry was working after practice with Singletary, simulating an offensive lineman or fullback lead-blocking. Ditka came by, working on a cigar, and watched. He asked Perry if he thought the rookie could run with the ball.

Perry's head nearly shook loose nodding. Ditka just walked away, but he had seen what he wanted.

The next day, Perry began being called down to the offense's end of the field late in practice. Hampton did not like it; neither did most of the defense, who knew Perry did not know what he was doing on his own side of the ball, let alone whatever else Ditka had him doing.

The Bears had measured themselves in 1984 against the Raiders, the defending Super Bowl champs that season. They had twice mauled the Washington Redskins, another Super Bowl winner. The 49ers were next.

The 49ers and their fans had taunted the Bears on the way off the field after the playoff loss. Ditka's pregame comments to the team were not Knute Rockne–esque; they were way beyond that.

"We gotta make some war out there today!" Ditka said, starting to pace. "We gotta play with dedication and purpose on both sides of the ball! This is the one! This is the one we've waited all year for!"

Ditka's face was reddening, and his voice was rising.

"It's going to be man-on-man, hand-to-hand combat out there! A war! If you beat the man across from you, we're going to win!"

The Bears beat man after man in red uniforms. This time they remembered to bring an offense. And it was far from the one that San Francisco so easily shut down the last time. Of the first 20 plays, 15 were passes. The Bears threw for 115 yards in the first quarter alone and scored the first four times they had the ball.

The lead went to 16–0 before San Francisco returned an interception and added a field goal for a 16–10 halftime score. It was deceiving and about to get completely out of hand.

In the second half, the Walsh-Montana offense gained all of 45 yards against a Bears defense that came into the game ranked only 12th in yards allowed. The 49ers finished with just 11 first downs and 183 total yards, then all-time lows for a Walsh team.

McMichael had utterly dominated Pro Bowl guard Randy Cross while Hampton was caving in the rest of the San Francisco middle. The passing offense of choice for the 49ers was for Montana to release the ball quickly. But Frazier and Richardson were jamming his receivers at the line, forcing him to wait an instant longer to unload. It was time he did not have. Seven times Montana went down, the most he would ever be sacked in one game.

It was another in the succession of furies unleashed by the 46 defense. It was an eight-man front but like no other before it or since. Eight-man fronts, with a safety moved up into the tackle-to-tackle "box" and close to the line, were typically designed to stop rushing attacks. This one was different; it was an attack all its own, built around Ryan's simple axiom that all defense begins with destroying the quarterback. If the offense blocked with five, Ryan sent six. If seven stayed in to block, Ryan sent eight. Behind the front were the two cornerbacks and one safety.

The talent level and the variations within the scheme were proving to make it overwhelming against offenses that had not caught onto it and did not have the talent to deal with it. The defense had a dozen formations and 80 specific pass coverages, which meant that the quarterback did not know who was blitzing, the linemen did not know whom to block, and the backs were over-matched even when they could figure out their assignment in the space of two seconds.

Hampton dropped down from end to head-up on the center, McMichael and Perry were over the guards, and no interior three blockers could handle those three one-on-one. Dent stayed outside and was one-on-one with the left tackle, and the former eighth-round pick was then the NFL's best pass rusher.

In Singletary, Marshall, and Wilson the Bears had linebackers too fast for linemen and too strong for ends and backs to block. Ryan's "AFCs"—automatic fronts and coverages—were studied over and over so that the entire defense reacted as one to every change the offense made, often before the offensive players were finished shifting. Ryan did not sit in standard 4-3, 3-4, or other defensive alignments; he had the best players in the NFL playing faster and smarter than anything since the seventies Steelers, and this system was at another level up from the "Steel Curtain."

The Bears broke their form on offense in a way that would take them to yet another level as well. Instead of Ditka's standard run-to-set-up-the-pass approach, the Bears had come out throwing and only then turned Payton and the line loose. Payton's 24 carries and 132 yards were both highs for his season up to that point.

With the score 19–10 early in the fourth quarter, Payton carried the ball on 9 of 13 plays on one drive, finishing with a 17-yard run that made the final 26–10 statement.

Almost.

ENTER THE REFRIGERATOR

On the Bears' final two offensive plays, Ditka was ready to give Walsh his answer for the Guy McIntyre gambit in the playoffs. Into the huddle came Perry.

> "That was the biggest win of the year. He avenged the loss the previous year, does it out there, uses Perry for the first time, sacked Montana seven times, Walter ran all over them. I think Mike knew they had something special after that game."
> *–Ken Valdiserri*

"Gimme da ball, gimme da ball," Perry yelled, delivering the play.

Once the laughing died down, McMahon did exactly that. Twice Perry carried, each time for two yards. The 49ers were incensed. The Bears did not care.

So began the legend of the Refrigerator.

The flight home was all fun for a change. The Bears were 6–0 for the first time since 1942, and the confidence was building. So was the alcohol consumption.

Ditka headed up Interstate 294 from O'Hare Airport after midnight along with the rest of the caravan. But a state trooper pulled him over for speeding, improper lane usage, and driving under the influence. He was handcuffed by an officer looking to make a name for himself—that or he was a Packers or 49ers fan.

Ditka was humiliated. He quit drinking until after the Giants game in the playoffs. He also was hit with a $300 fine and a sentence of 12 months of court supervision.

The incident cost him no respect from his players, however. They just wondered how Ditka was the only one who got nabbed.

CHAPTER 7

FRIDGE

"I was big when I was little."
—*William "Refrigerator" Perry*

DITKA'S ENCOUNTER WITH THE STATE POLICE diverted some attention from football matters, but only briefly. The '85 Bears were about to become international news.

William Perry was in the game for the final two plays, ran twice, and gained two yards on each run. But the impact was far greater than yardage.

"Refrigerator Mania" started in the week leading up to the Green Bay game, which already had more than enough animus of its own with the Ditka-Gregg problems mixed into an always-charged rivalry. The musings started: if Ditka used Perry to settle a score with Walsh, what was he prepared to do with the big rookie when it came to Gregg and the "Red Bay" Packers?

There was method to Ditka's ploy, however, well beyond just issuing an insult. The Bears were not very good at closing in the red zone yet, and Perry, an awesome athlete underneath the extra bulk and jokes, was the ultimate goal-line force. Ditka had played enough offense himself to know it.

He also now had another way of getting Perry playing despite the resistance of Ryan, who still refused to force what he called "the fat kid" and "wasted draft choice" into the lineup. Ryan suggested that Perry was more exciting on offense than he was on defense, so offense "must be easier." The little stints of offense were having the effect of motivating Perry, who suddenly was having more fun than ever and actually working at practice.

As the Green Bay week went along, Perry headed down toward the offensive end of the field more frequently.

FRIDGE

Perry could take a joke, which was a good thing. If the kidding and insults hurt, he rarely showed it. Hampton dubbed Perry "Biscuit" on the observation that Perry was a biscuit short of 350. He also called Perry "Mudslide," which was not as kind. Hampton kidded that "Fridge went home one weekend and the chicken population went down by a third."

It was difficult not to like Perry. He was funny without trying to be. He had a gap-toothed smile and did not bother with the cosmetic of putting in his false right front tooth just for the cameras. When Ditka gave the team time off to go Christmas shopping downtown, Perry came up with the idea to wear his tooth so people would not recognize him.

He preferred Coors Light beer because it came in a can that crushed easily. Perry popped the top, held the can ready to drink, then crushed it and shot the entire contents into his mouth. Beer was his idea of a diet food because it filled him up so he did not eat so much, and the next day he sweated it out at practice and so did not gain any weight. Fridgian logic.

He was particularly excited when Keystone came out with a light beer that had six fewer calories per can.

Perry weighed 13½ pounds at birth, the 10th of Hollie and Inez Perry's 12 children. His paternal grandfather stood 7' tall and weighed 300 pounds. Perry weighed 220 pounds in seventh grade and 315 as a freshman at Clemson, where teammate Ray Brown followed Perry into an elevator and observed that Perry looked like "a refrigerator" from the back. Posters of Perry were hot sellers even while he was at Clemson.

> "Fridge could've killed me anytime he chose to. He was a great teammate, never trying to hurt you, but he was quicker off the ball than anybody I ever saw. The strength he had in his legs was just beyond belief. He could've been as great as he wanted to be."
> *–Jay Hilgenberg*

Perry never achieved superstar status in the NFL on the field, but he was a dominant lineman in college. He never quite put the pedal down all the way in the NFL, certainly not in practice, which did him little good with Ryan. But he was appreciated over on the Bears offense nonetheless.

Ryan was asked how Perry looked to him on film.

"It depends," Ryan said, "on what speed you run the projector."

But Perry was perfect for the Bears. He was the big guy with a sense of humor who played a violent game in front of millions with the visible enthusiasm of a kid. Perry was America's big kid brother.

The eighties found America's obsession with fitness growing at a dizzying pace as working out, jogging shoes, health clubs, and warm-up suits reached the level of status symbols. Into a nation immersing itself into mass narcissism came Perry, the smiling counterpoint to all of that who celebrated exactly who and what he was. He had a sense of wonder that conveyed an unspoken "Can you believe this?" and America smiled right along with him. He had a 22-inch neck and wore a size-58 coat. He ate his breakfast cereal out of a mixing bowl and quaffed 48 cans of beer after games and to wash down three or four chickens for dinner. He also could dunk a basketball from a standing jump.

Perry, even more than McMahon at that point, drove the Bears' national popularity engine. Carson, Letterman, *Today*—all the shows wanted Perry. His size, which became NFL-normal, was an abnormality then. That, his personality, the way Ditka used him, Ditka's personality, and the exposure that had come with *Monday Night Football* all converged in an individual unlike any the NFL or sports in general had ever seen.

He had a simple way of looking at life, something else that America loved in its heroes. Perry bought a coat and had it altered. Then he went to a spa and dropped a few pounds, went back to pick up the coat, and worried that it needed altering again to take up the slack.

And if some of the humor ebbed with time, it did not all ever completely leave. As the situation in the Middle East deteriorated in late 1991, several Bears were talking about it in the weight room. Among them was guard Mark Bortz, a serious student of warfare and history. Bortz was asked what he thought the percentages were for America going to war in the Gulf against Iraq.

"Probably 70-30," Bortz estimated.

Perry saw things differently. "I think it's more like 75-35," Perry said.

"Fridge," one teammate pointed out, "that's 110 percent."

Fridge reflected, then emphatically declared, "Well, if you go to war, it *should* be 110 percent!"

In 1985 Iraq was still far away for most Americans. Perry was not. Folks wanted to know more about this Perry phenomenon and what Ditka had planned for him.

Ditka fueled local imaginations when he said, "Gives you a little food for thought on the goal line, doesn't he?"

Once again, the Bears had the stage to themselves, and it was again a national stage. This time, it would echo far beyond the United States.

OCTOBER 21, 1985, MONDAY NIGHT FOOTBALL—GREEN BAY PACKERS, SOLDIER FIELD

The Bears trailed Green Bay 7–0 in the second quarter, once again setting themselves up for another comeback. The ball was at the Green Bay 2, first-and-goal. Perry trotted onto the field, and the roar started at Soldier Field. The television cameras locked onto him and millions leaned forward for a clear look at their TVs.

Perry lined up behind Van Horne with the assignment of leading Payton into the end zone. The ball was snapped and Perry fired out of his stance with the power that Hilgenberg and the offensive linemen knew he had and with a forward lean that was frightening from where Packers linebacker George Cumby stood. Perry hit Cumby and simply engulfed him, folding him backward like a reed in a wind. Touchdown, Payton.

One possession later the Bears again were at the Green Bay goal line. Perry lumbered in, this time with McMahon and half the offensive huddle leading the cheers. No decoy this time, no lead blocker. McMahon gave the ball to Perry, who exploded into the right side of the Packers defense behind crushing blocks by Bortz and Covert. The only man in Perry's way: Cumby, again.

At 224 pounds and an 80-pound disadvantage, Cumby was roadkill.

Perry barreled into the end zone, shook himself free of bodies on the ground, and then unleashed a spike that could have sent the ball into Lake Michigan.

Soldier Field was mayhem. Fans were high-fiving in bars all over Chicago. In Los Angeles, Chicagoan and actor Joe Mantegna watched and called to his wife, "Honey, hurry, you have got to see this!"

Perry was not done. Once more in the first half, the Bears drove the ball at the Green Bay 1-yard line. Ditka had the spirit of the moment. He sent in a couple other goal-line substitutions and then hesitated to let the anticipation build. The crowd now was chanting, "PER-RY, PER-RY!" and players could feel the ground shaking. Ditka motioned to Perry. The big fella was in again and hurrying out onto the field like a high school kid.

Another explosion into the line, this time leading for Payton. Perry hit Cumby again, and he and the Packers just disappeared. "It was like stealing," Payton said. "I just walked into the end zone."

Chicago Sun-Times columnist Ray Sons offered that it was "the best use of fat since the invention of bacon."

Reactions were instantaneous and had nothing to do with the 23–7 final score. Some commentators complained that the Bears were piling it on and making a travesty of the game. They were missing the point. Of course Ditka was piling on. This was the Packers. This was Forrest Gregg. Players said Ditka shot Gregg a look after the Perry touchdown and made sure Gregg saw him looking. Piling on? No problem. The Bears' final points came when Wilson blew in on a blitz and sacked Jim Zorn in the end zone.

The NFL knew something was up. Commissioner Pete Rozelle was at Soldier Field for the game and came in to say hello to Bears personnel chief Bill Tobin, who had drafted Perry.

Rozelle was giddy. He spread out his arms and shook his head. "This is really something!" he said. "You guys are a bonanza for football." How much of one he would find out in time, personally.

The next morning, America was in love with the Refrigerator. And the Bears were along for the ride because now this Fridge was national.

Phones at Halas Hall began ringing as early as 7:00, and receptionist Louise Johnson was swamped. Everybody wanted Fridge. "No, Mr. Perry's agent is Jim Steiner and he can be reached at, . . ." she answered over and over and over.

Steiner, who at one point represented Perry, Hampton, McMichael, and others, was not any readier than the Bears or Perry were for what was happening. But he would now move to the center of a national marketing phenomenon.

When Ditka sent Perry in against the 49ers, Steiner was watching the game at home in St. Louis. Never suspecting what the next stage would be, Steiner was on a recruiting trip at Notre Dame in South Bend the next Monday and was again watching the Bears, this time on *Monday Night Football* like the rest of the country. There was no way he could make it back to St. Louis that night, but his office could have used him.

The phones in his offices began ringing early Tuesday morning, with calls eventually numbering in the thousands. It would go on all year and throughout 1986, never stopping. The hard part was knowing when and to whom to say yes.

Steiner had some foresight on his own behalf too. The week before the Green Bay game, Steiner was in Las Vegas and saw the betting spectrum ranging from game winners to who puts their pants on first. There was a line on Fridge scoring a touchdown, 10 to 1. Steiner put $100 down and won $1,000.

Steiner's thinking with Perry, who could become just another fat guy if he was not careful, was near opposite that of Zucker's strategy with McMahon.

Perry was a novelty. He was a hotter marketing commodity than McMahon at that moment. Among the callers that first day was McDonald's. Perfect. Their Chicken McNuggets were Perry favorites, and he laughed at having once had a $55 bill for one trip to the Golden Arches. McDonald's hopped on the fastest of any national advertiser, wanting, like Steiner, to take advantage of the immediate swell of Fridge Mania. McDonald's also was a local Chicago-area company, a big one, and the ideal match for Perry.

> "Our approach ended up being just grab everything we could because it was not something that was going to be a long-term deal. We had some discretion, but he did as much as he could and enjoyed doing it. But he never got wrapped up in the seeming importance of it or how long it would go on. He just wanted to take advantage of it, have some fun, and make some money."
> –Jim Steiner

McDonald's chose not to go for the cheap laugh. Perry was not going to be the buffoon or glutton and devour a dozen Big Macs, although he certainly had done that. The commercial just had Fridge being Fridge. He walked up to the counter with a tray, flashed his gap-toothed grin, delivered his line to the girl behind the counter, and it was done. Not a lot of takes.

Teammates got in on the deal as well. Another spot had Perry sitting at a table and having his meal with McMichael, Duerson, and Hampton, which quietly galled the two linemen, being extras in a cash windfall for a player nowhere near their equal on the field, their standard of measure.

> "His first year, he was a rookie and I treated him like nothing. Then he gets handed a job that costs one of my best friends on the team [Hartenstine] a job. In 1986 we start practicing with Fridge at linebacker. Talk about a silly waste of time. Sure everybody was jealous, including me. Then his wife is dictating shit off the field too, and that stuck in everyone's craw. By '88 and '89 I had really gotten closer to Fridge and now, of all the guys I played with, he was one of my favorites."
> *—Dan Hampton*

The jealousy was understandable, if through no fault of Perry's. He simply was now the leading edge of the change the Bears were effecting in sports marketing. The money generated was "earned" on the field, irrespective of personality.

Perry was reaping millions precisely because he *was* a personality. Perry had a childlike innocence and manner of speaking in his rural black Southern dialect that conveyed a sense of delight and wonderment that was simple Fridge. He was not acting. "Open da do', light goes on," he proclaimed delightedly in an appliance commercial.

The expectation was that endorsements and their accompanying dollars traditionally went to the best athletes. The reason Fridge was doing what he was doing, as some saw it, was because he was some sort of freak.

Steiner was faced with another challenge: figuring out what Perry was worth in this market, because there had never been a "market" like this one. There was no going rate. Most athletes' commercials were little more than a pose with a product; Perry was part of every product's identity and image now. McDonald's was not where great athletes ate; now it was where *fun* athletes ate. Steiner had been in the business for seven or eight years and had done marketing deals, but this was different and new. There was only one Fridge. He was The Guy.

Steiner did exactly what the Bears themselves were doing with their season: he rode it and felt it out as he went, creating a market as he went along. As the demand went higher, so did the price. McDonald's was the first and got the best deal, one that would net Perry millions. The price started in the high five figures and quickly jumped into six figures. Perry's fee for one 30-second TV spot initially was $5,000; a month later it was $25,000 and climbing.

Steiner handled licensing for Fridge Wear and other products by striking a deal with NFL Properties, the league's marketing arm. They handled his licensing opportunities, a one-stop shopping deal where they took his image and put it on cups, caps, shirts, everything they could get their hands on. They paid him an up-front fee and royalty on everything that was sold.

After McDonald's, Coca-Cola was right behind with a deal that brought Perry and McMahon together, Perry hawking Diet Coke. Naturally.

In February 1986 *Advertising Age* evaluated Ditka, McMahon, Perry, and some others and concluded that Perry was the only player who transcended football and declared him the big winner in the endorsement sweepstakes. McDonald's was pushing him, Coke was going hard with him, and he was even appearing in ads for the stock brokerage Drexel Burnham Lambert. They predicted he would double and possibly triple his on-field income with endorsements.

They were low. Way low.

Before he was done, with Steiner handling things for him, his deals included McDonald's; Coca-Cola (Diet Coke); Wilson game jerseys; Royal Textile Mills' "Duke" Brand of thermal underwear; NutraSweet artificial sweetener; Kangaroos USA's apparel, glassware, and other merchandise; Carrier commercial refrigeration for trucks and trailers; Rath Blackhawk bacon; Pontiac Motors; Georgia-Pacific "Mr. Big" paper towels; Alberto

Culver hair care products, with print ads in *Jet*, *Ebony*, and *Essence*; Hasbro toys; White Hen Pantry, a 32-ounce cup promotion that did 1,250,000 cups; and Kraft Foods' macaroni dinners.

It was not all fun for Perry, however. His wife, Sherry, had an inviolable condition written into his endorsement contracts: William was prohibited from having his picture taken alone with women. Usually at the end of a commercial shoot the workers wherever he was shooting were standing and watching. They and the production people liked to have their picture taken with the celebrity. It was standard stuff, and the affable Perry was happy to oblige.

That was not allowed with the "Sherry clause" unless the photographer positioned all the men next to Perry and the women to the outside. And under no circumstances was Perry to be photographed one-on-one with a lady.

Sherry Perry annoyed more than the McDonald's workers. At the Platteville pig roast toward the end of the 1986 training camp, Wilson was surrounded by the ladies. They also wanted Perry's autograph, and Wilson guided the group over to Fridge.

Sherry berated Wilson, who waited until she was done ranting and then went over to Perry. "Fridge," Wilson said, "I think you better get her in check because I will go off on that bitch."

A bunch of plump ladies, all in the range of 200 pounds, started a cheer-leader group calling itself "the Refrigerettes." They were not exactly the Honey Bears, the Bears' sideline eye candy, but perfect for Fridge Mania.

One of Perry's first public appearances after the Green Bay game was at a Montgomery Ward's store outside Chicago. From the helicopter Channel 2's camera operators beheld a line that was out the doors and all the way around the massive department store. The filming of the McDonald's commercial drew thousands of onlookers.

Perry learned more football his rookie year than at any other time, which was only natural because he had Dent, Hampton, Hartenstine, and McMichael teaching him NFL football. But once the circus started, it was difficult for him to be just a football player, and he was never the player he could have been.

Remarkably, or maybe not so remarkably, Perry never seemed to lose his focus amid all the insanity. He liked the money but he really did not care about the marketing deals or all the trappings of success. He was not one of those who, once they had it, could not let it go. Perry was having fun with it, was glad to have the money, and if it lasted three weeks, fine, and if it lasted three years, fine too. He never thrived on it or became intoxicated with what the moment made of him.

It all gradually went away over the years, bearing out Steiner's instinct to take what was there when it was there. Perry would play for the Philadelphia Eagles and eventually would go to London to play for the London Monarchs of the NFL Europe, which was a whole different marketing program once his career was over. He was doing TV shows, making appearances, and doing some endorsements. He capitalized on his European popularity, which was immense after what he had done in the United States and after he had gone to London in 1996. He did not really have to play much football; the public just wanted to see him. His knees were shot, but for his fans in the United Kingdom, it did not matter. Eventually he would return to his Wrestlemania "roots" and sign a wrestling contract.

For the big man from rural South Carolina whose favorite activity was just to relax while fishing, all of the fame and acclaim exacted its price.

In early 1993, the year Perry was cut by Dave Wannstedt, Chicago sports talk-radio host Coppock did a luncheon with Perry. Something was clearly bothering Perry, who uncharacteristically did not want to sign autographs and only grudgingly did the requisite dispensing of signatures.

"William, what's wrong?" Coppock asked.

"You know, I really don't like this," Perry said.

"I know," Coppock said. "But the people really love this. They really love meeting you."

"I know that," Perry said. "But did you ever think how great it would be just once to just play football on Sunday, and there was nobody in the stands, no media? Just to play."

To Coppock, Perry looked as though he was about to cry.

CHAPTER 8

MANURE AND WOOFING

"Talk about the Raider skull and crossbones, the patch over their eye? We're going to put patches over both your eyes."
—*Otis Wilson*

THE BEARS WERE HERE. McMahon had seized the football spotlight in Minnesota. Perry and *Monday Night Football* had taken them far beyond even that with Steiner's marketing plus Letterman, Carson, and others lining up to get him on their shows. The Bears were now moving way beyond just a football story.

The national media descended on Halas Hall and would very soon learn and report that the team had far more characters than just Ditka, McMahon, and Perry. The locker room was an orchard of sound bytes, and reporters rarely needed to ask questions, just wait for ripe ones to fall off. Wilson, Hampton, McKinnon, McMichael, and others could not help themselves.

The Bears' timing could not have been better for a country that could use a diversion or two other than the premiere of Sylvester Stallone's *Rambo* sequel. In October, Rock Hudson died of AIDS, dramatically upping the awareness and concern about that global killer. In November, reports first started mentioning a new drug, something called "crack."

The Bears were 7–0, their best start in decades, which made them a legitimate football story as well as a burgeoning personality feature. They were the NFL's only undefeated team, leading the league in both scoring and fewest points allowed.

The demand on the Bears' time was for more than just Perry or McMahon. The telephone lines and PR offices were swamped with appearance requests as well as endless calls for one-on-one interviews, which were quickly becoming impossible, regardless of price.

The team now had taken Chicago firmly in hand and was offering hope for a city that had gotten its sports heart broken too many times. Something may have been happening with the Bears, but how long would it continue? Chicago fans did not trust easily.

OCTOBER 27, 1985—MINNESOTA VIKINGS, SOLDIER FIELD

The Bears had an answer, again at the Vikings' expense.

The second 1985 game against Minnesota ended 27–9 and may not have drawn the headlines of the Green Bay game, but many players regarded that as a true turning point in the season. The offense was dominating. The defense never gave Minnesota quarterback Tommy Kramer a chance. The day was the start of Singletary, Marshall, and Wilson christening themselves the "Bermuda Triangle" and making a shared mission of being the greatest linebacking group of all time.

The Bears ran over the Vikings for 413 yards, divided almost evenly between rushing and passing. They allowed Minnesota just 30 rushing yards; the defense intercepted five passes, one returned by Wilson for a touchdown; and Minnesota quarterbacks went down over and over. Most notably, Perry had his first sack and saw his highest amount of playing time of the season, a foreshadowing of a change that was coming.

After the Minnesota game, Ditka's pressure on Ryan escalated again. Perry would start the rest of the season; Mike Hartenstine was out of the starting lineup, replaced at left end by Hampton.

It was not a popular move.

Perry was a first-round draft choice, and the organization looked bad if that player was not a starter, no matter how good the team was. But it bothered players that Ditka forced him into the lineup on Ryan, taking Hartenstine's job away from him. Hartenstine had been there for Ditka through the coach's arrival and orientation, had been part of the NFL sack record setters of 1984, and now felt he was being told, "OK, go stand over there and watch."

Hartenstine had been a successful defensive end for almost a decade, picked after Payton in the 1975 draft. His starting job was given to a player that his coach, Ryan, refused to put on the field because Perry was not one of the four best defensive linemen. It was Ditka's decision, but it was Ryan who delivered the news.

By this time, Perry had gotten closer to being in shape, in no small part

> "The media's loving Fridge and I'm outplaying the guy, but they had to play him, almost because of the media. Plus, they didn't want to look bad blowing a number one pick. Ultimately Fridge was a good player and I liked him; it wasn't anything personal. I just hated that I lost my job in a situation where I shouldn't lose it. Ditka made him a media hero letting him run the ball and catch the ball."
> *—Mike Hartenstine*

because Ditka offered the carrot of running with the ball if Perry was up to the workload. With the new defensive line of Dent, Hampton, McMichael, and Perry, Hampton was the senior member now with seven seasons.

Fair or not, the change had a tremendous impact. Opponents averaged a paltry 79 rushing yards per game against the Bears without Perry starting. With him, the average dropped to 74. Dent, already protected with Hampton or McMichael guarding his inside, now stepped up his rushing to new heights because he had no need to worry about anything to his inside.

But the Packers were looming, and there was quite a lot to worry about.

NOVEMBER 3, 1985—GREEN BAY PACKERS, LAMBEAU FIELD

Lambeau Field may have its mystique because of Vince Lombardi, Ice Bowls, and its Titletown, USA, self-proclaimed mailing address. But it has some of the meanest fans in the NFL. Among the first pieces of advice given to Bears rookies is to never remove their helmets entering or leaving Lambeau. Players were pelted with batteries, heated coins, beer, and every form of bratwurst in Wisconsin, which is a lot of flying foodstuff just by itself.

When the buses carrying the 8–0 Bears pulled into the parking lot before the November 3 game, fans were lined up for turns with sledgehammers bashing refrigerators. That was mild compared to what would take place on the floor of the stadium that afternoon. Or on the floor of the locker room, for that matter.

When the Bears got to their locker room there was a five-pound bag of cow manure opened on the floor, with a note from a Green Bay radio station, "Here's what you guys are full of."

Hampton had said he would not give two cents for the whole Green Bay Packers team, to which Packers tackle Greg Koch responded, "He must be giving a penny a sack."

For reasons that are unclear, Ditka had taken to calling them the "Red Bay Packers" and did his bit to inflame tensions. And it was personal.

"Men, I'm not going to scream," he began his pregame talk to the team. Of course, he was. "I'm not going to holler."

He started pacing the floor like a caged big cat knowing feeding time is at hand, which in fact it was. The predator was starting to snarl and turn his usual violent red.

"You know I really don't like these guys! They have been calling us cheap-shot artists, lowlifes! That is what they're saying about you!" He paused, then, in case his team was not clear on one point, "You know I really don't like these guys! I just want to let you know how I feel!"

His mood did not improve with the game, which was a street fight. Green Bay safety Ken Stills smashed McMahon in a pileup after the ball was dead on the second play. Packers corner Mark Lee drove Payton over the Bears' bench and into a wall on the ninth play. The Packers claimed that Payton created the problem by grabbing Lee by the face mask as Lee was making the tackle.

The low point came as the first quarter was over; Stills ran halfway across the field to level Matt Suhey long after the whistle blew. Six personal fouls were called in the first quarter, only because there was not any point in calling five on the same play.

The Stills incident did not end with the game. When Suhey encountered Gregg at a New Orleans restaurant during Super Bowl week, he had to be pulled away and held back from going after the Green Bay coach.

The shots at McMahon served to anger the defense. Wilson ended one play near the Green Bay sideline and turned toward the Packers sideline with a warning. "You got a quarterback too, remember that!" McMahon soothed the situation by running past the Green Bay bench and flipping Gregg the finger.

The Packers had been humiliated by Perry and Ditka in the Monday night game, and they were talking revenge for the Bears hurting quarterback Lynn Dickey, blocking him while well away from the play on an interception. The Bears actually trailed 10–9 in the second half before Payton took over the game in one of the greatest performances of this or any season. The more the Packers talked and punched, the more Payton hammered at them.

Perry had caught a touchdown pass in the first quarter, running right at Cumby on the right side, then cruising around him when Cumby set himself for the hit. The next day he was headed for the David Letterman show and the start of a new level of Fridge Mania.

But this was Payton's game. He put the team on his back and carried it 28 times for 192 yards, his most since 1977. The Bears-Packers rivalry had rarely been so heated as it was in this 16–10 brawl.

"Everybody should've taken their face masks off and put on black high-tops," McMichael said.

The Bears could have suffered a letdown after a game with the venom of the game in Green Bay. They were, in fact, just getting started.

Perry especially. He was off to do the Letterman show, which unfortunately increased some of the jealousy, particularly for Hampton and McMichael, who now were grumbling openly about Perry's success. Perry was now getting about half the requests for personal appearances that were flooding into the Bears offices, and scoring the touchdown, this time catching a pass, at Green Bay just heightened the legend. He was having fun, and America was belly laughing right along with him, even if not all his teammates were.

Bob Hope was calling, and there was talk of a book deal. With Bears staffers Ken Valdiserri and Bryan Harlan handling things with a sense of humor as well, *Omni* magazine's editors were talking about Fridge being on their cover as part of a story about pregnancy in men. By now Perry's price for an hour of signing autographs had gone up more than 10 times what it had been; it was going to cost $5,000 for an hour of his time—if there was an available hour to be had.

Meanwhile, the season was going on and heading toward more historical moments.

NOVEMBER 10, 1985—DETROIT LIONS, SOLDIER FIELD

McMahon was hurt again, bothered by tendinitis in his throwing shoulder, and Fuller was back in the starting lineup against Detroit, the first time since the Thursday night game at Minnesota when he was pulled for McMahon. This time the Bears made a statement that they absolutely could win and win easily without McMahon, unlike that night in the Metrodome, and in the process revealed how much better they had become in a matter of only weeks.

Ditka did not ask much of Fuller at the outset. The Bears ran the ball on their first 21 plays and ran it a total of 55 times for 250 yards that included Payton (107) and Suhey (102), marking the third time in Payton's career that he and a backfield mate had gotten 100 yards together in the same game.

The 24–3 bashing was the fifth-straight game in which the Bears allowed 10 or fewer points. Perry had two of the Bears' four sacks, and the defense forced four turnovers. Detroit gained 106 yards, 1 fewer than Payton alone, and the defense was not happy about even that many.

But the Bears now were 10–0, and the hysteria and fascination showed no signs of abating. The Bears had become a traveling rock show.

NOVEMBER 17, 1985—DALLAS COWBOYS, TEXAS STADIUM

The team arrived at its hotel in Dallas the Saturday before the game against the Cowboys at about 3:00 in the afternoon. The buses pulled up to the hotel and found people 15 deep—not Cowboys fans, but Bears fans and what were becoming Bears groupies and just plain curiosity seekers. This was simply the team that had to be seen.

To many of the Bears, the season to that point had been building toward precisely this game. Ditka spent 13 of his football years in Dallas, winning a Super Bowl ring as a player there and another as an assistant as Tom Landry's tight ends coach. The Bears had not beaten the Cowboys since 1971, a stretch that had included six straight losses.

The worst was a 37–7 devastation in 1977 when the Bears had squeezed into the playoffs only to be crushed in a game that left a bitter taste. Then-coach Jack Pardee was preparing to leave for another job and seemed to the players to be more concerned with staying around Chicago to get his house ready to sell than taking the team down South to prepare in better weather. No member of this Bears team had ever beaten the Cowboys as a Bear.

> "The Dallas game was fun because I saw [Cowboys personnel legend] Gil Brandt on the sidelines in warm-ups and I told him 'You know, I owe you an ass-whuppin',' I told him that and I told Al Davis of the Raiders the same thing, in a nicer tone. I told them I owed them ass-whuppin's and they're going to get it today. I was pissed off at a lot of teams because they'd knock me and didn't draft me. I owed them. And they both got theirs. I saw Al not long ago, and he said, 'I remember that game.' And we just laughed about it then, because we're 20 years older now. 'Course, they weren't laughing much at the time."
> *—Richard Dent*

The Cowboys sold out every game, but Bears fans got their hands on tickets. Tickets that retail priced at $19 were going for $250. Folks were coming down from Chicago looking for the Bears to crush the former "America's Team." They would not be disappointed.

Ditka was concerned that the players were feeling the pressure. Saturday night, for the only time all year, Ditka came in and ordered a change.

"We're not watching game film," he said. "If you guys don't know it by now, you never will." And he put in a film of comedian Rodney Dangerfield, appropriate for his season-long mantra that the Bears got no respect.

"America's Team" was a marketing ploy concocted by the Cowboys in the sixties and seventies and it was good marketing for the star on the helmet, Navy man Roger Staubach as quarterback, and the Dallas Cowboys cheerleaders in hot pants and white boots.

The Bears destroyed all of that in one afternoon.

The score was 44–0. It was the worst defeat in Cowboys history, the first time Dallas was shut out in 218 games and 15 years. Payback.

Fuller was the quarterback. Perry picked up his first offensive penalty with another Fridge moment when he grabbed Payton as Walter was being tackled at the Dallas 2, lifted the 200-pound runner, and tossed him into the end zone. Not that Payton needed a lot of help; he finished with 132 yards, his sixth-straight 100-yard game, which gave him a record nine 1,000-yard seasons.

Once the game started, all the tension was on the Dallas side. There was no score 12 minutes into the first quarter, but the fuse was lit. The Cowboys had run for 22 yards on their first play and -5 on their next five.

The Cowboys were still distinguished by their shifting and their offensive linemen standing straight up before they settled into their stances. The Bears startled the Cowboys by shifting constantly on defense at the same time, based on a complete knowledge of Dallas habits and tendencies. The Cowboys began looking at each other; the Bears sensed growing confusion and, even better, fear. The Bears stopped the run and then went after the quarterbacks and began knocking them out of the game. Dallas' final 16 plays in the first half were all pass plays. The Bears caught almost as many Dallas passes as the Cowboys did, intercepting three while Dallas completed exactly four, one for each sack of a Dallas quarterback.

Hampton started the Dallas collapse after Maury Buford punted and stuck the Cowboys on their 2-yard line. Danny White dropped into the end zone to pass, and Hampton collapsed the right side of the Dallas line and got a hand on the ball. Dent heard the slap when the ball hit Hampton's hand and immediately started looking up for the ball. He found it, went up like a basketball player for a rebound—Hampton claimed that Dent had the vertical leap of the Grapevine, Texas, phonebook—intercepted it at the 1, and scored.

Eleven minutes later Richardson intercepted another pass and ran it back 36 yards to put the Bears up 14–0. It was turning brutal fast. Wilson knocked White out in the first quarter—he would knock White out again in the second half—and Gary Hogeboom came in, which was blood before sharks. Wilson and Dent swarmed in on him, and Hogeboom just got rid of the ball, which fluttered to Richardson. The next Hogeboom pass was picked off by Frazier, who ran it back 33 yards to set up another score that put the Bears ahead 24–0 at halftime.

DESTROYING "AMERICA'S TEAM"

Down inside the lines, where few people watched and fewer still grasped the level of gladiatorial violence, Bortz took on Randy White, the co-MVP of one Dallas Super Bowl win and the so-called Manster. Bortz handed the Dallas terror what teammates simply called "an ass-kickin'."

Bortz kept to himself most of the time but was an executioner, a military historian who had been a defensive tackle in college and converted to guard. And he was more than White's equal in matters of violence. In the 1985 preseason game between the teams, White was being completely dominated and his frustrations spewed out. He punched Bortz through the bars of Bortz's face mask at one point, which only incited Bortz more, and they came to blows. At the other end of the line Van Horne was beating Ed "Too Tall" Jones out at right tackle, and those two were getting into it. Jones had tried professional boxing and considered himself a tough guy. Van Horne actually *was* a tough guy, with a perpetual chill-out look on his face that was somewhere between a sneer and what teammates called a laid-back, "You-got-a-problem?" half grin. Van Horne had taken on half the Green Bay and St. Louis teams on Payton's behalf; Jones was no problem.

White at one point ripped off Van Horne's helmet and hit Bortz over the head with it, which only ratcheted Bortz up another level and brought Hilgenberg, Thayer, and others into the battle royale. White was thrown out of the game and eventually fined $1,000; the total fines against the two teams reached $20,000.

Now, in the game that counted, it was no contest. By the third quarter, White had simply quit. McMichael ran by the Dallas sideline and cursed him right in front of Landry.

But it really did not matter anymore. Dallas was nosing over for its death spiral under Landry that would end with his firing and replacement in 1989 by

Jerry Jones, and then Jimmy Johnson and Dave Wannstedt. The Cowboys made the playoffs in 1985, but they were fading and lost to the Rams. The Bears' arrow was pointing in quite another direction altogether.

Dallas fans were leaving during the third quarter. Singletary started yelling at the leaving Cowboy fans, "Stay here! I want witnesses." By that time the Bears had started the woofing that would become part of America's fan handbook.

Duerson and Wilson started the woofing. The two came off to the sideline after one throttling of the Cowboys offense and Duerson was aflame.

> **"I wish we could've patented that [woofing]."**
> *—Otis Wilson*

"Man, we're like some dogs!" he hollered. "We are like crazed dogs!"

Wilson and Duerson started barking at each other and it spread.

The woofing caught the attention of Irv Cross, a former player who served as CBS' sideline reporter for this game. "Brent," Cross said, back up to the booth and Brent Musburger, another Chicagoan, "I think they're barking like dogs down here."

The game was fast-paced, and it moved the Bears up yet another level. It was in this game that the Bears became the Monsters of the Midway again. They had destroyed, over the previous 12 months, the 49ers, the Raiders, the

> **"We were going to show them, just like the Raiders in '84. Talk about the Raider skull and crossbones, the patch over their eye? We're going to put patches over both your eyes."**
> *—Otis Wilson*

Redskins (twice), and now the mighty Cowboys. There was more than a new sheriff in town. It was more like a task force of Green Berets.

America's Team? Wilson had another take on it.

"Who named y'all?" he yelled at the once-haughty Cowboys. "Just because you got a star on your helmet or whatever don't make you anything."

Hampton was asked if the Bears would now replace the Cowboys as "America's Team." "I don't know if we want to be 'America's Team,'" Hampton said, "but if we keep playing like we are, they might just start calling us 'The Kremlin's Team.'"

The Bears were determined to show that they could play too—and play physical. This was Ditka at his finest, along with Ryan, whipping up the internal passion to epic levels using us-against-them motivation, saying that no one believed in the Bears yet.

> "By the time we got there, we were ready to kick Dallas' ass. We're 10-0 and they're 7-3, and all week, Cowboys defensive back Everson Walls is saying shit like, 'Yeah, the Bears are playing teams like Detroit and all these people. They haven't played anybody.' People pointed out that we're 10-0 and he's still yapping, 'They haven't played anybody.' After we finish up with them and it's 44-0, a bunch of writers are around the locker. 'I have to give Everson Walls credit,' I said. 'He was right. We're 11-0 and we still ain't played nobody.'"
> —*Dan Hampton*

The win at Dallas also gave the Bears the NFL's best record since 1972, the year the Dolphins went undefeated. And they clinched the division in the process, the earliest any team had clinched. Everybody got a game ball after this one.

The Bears did not need any false marketing hype. The hype had to catch up with them.

Driving back to Dallas airport, the team bus was passed by a truck pulling a trailer with a big refrigerator on it with a big red circle with the line through it.

The Bears were drawing red circles and lines through quarterbacks now. It was not to the level of the Packers and their towels with targeted Bears numbers listed, which would happen the next season, but it was enough to create problems. L.A. Mike Richardson declared that he would buy lunch for anyone who knocked a quarterback out of the game the way Wilson had twice to White.

The other players were not amused. McMichael blasted Richardson in the media, and there was some worry that officials and the league would start scrutinizing the Bears unfairly at the suggestion of any sort of bounty on opponents.

They should not have worried. They were about to give opponents a far more inflammatory anti-Bears motivational tool. The following Friday about a dozen players headed down to a Chicago recording studio to cut a record called "The Super Bowl Shuffle."

NOVEMBER 24, 1985—ATLANTA FALCONS, SOLDIER FIELD

The Bears became the third team in league history to open 12–0 when they destroyed Atlanta 36–0 a week after Dallas. With the safety by backup defensive tackle Henry Waechter, the Bears *defense* had scored 27 points on defense over the past six games, the same number it had allowed. In the three games with Fuller filling in for McMahon, the Bears had outscored opponents 104–3.

Suddenly people were wondering if this team was one of the greatest in NFL history.

The number one CBS broadcast team of John Madden and Pat Summerall had called their bosses in New York and ordered themselves switched onto CBS' Bears telecasts for the rest of the season, regardless of what the broadcast staffing schedule said.

Atlanta finished with 10 first downs and 119 total yards, 110 of those by running back Gerald Riggs. Falcons passing totaled -22 yards, and Atlanta never got the ball inside the Chicago 45-yard line in the entire game.

Quarterback David Archer was pulled in the third quarter after throwing 15 passes and completing exactly 2, the same number of Bears interceptions for the game. Waechter had three of the five sacks plus the Bears' third safety in six games.

Payton ran for 102 yards, tying Earl Campbell and O. J. Simpson with seven straight 100-yard games, and Ditka pledged Payton would break that record because Payton deserved to stand above those two, in Ditka's thinking.

Things reached the point where even number three quarterback Mike Tomczak was getting in, and he completed three of five passes for 45 yards.

The Bears were taking another step toward establishing their code. Falcons linemen were cut-blocking Bears defensive linemen until, at one point,

Wilson had had enough. He blitzed, came free, and went right at Archer's left knee as the quarterback delivered the ball.

> "Otis didn't give a shit. He was a badass. Wilber was a badass."
> —*Dan Hampton*

The Falcons were fuming. Wilson could have torn Archer's knee up. As Wilson walked back to the huddle, the Falcons were yelling, "Hey, motherf***er, we'll get you! What's that shit?"

Wilson just turned and answered, "Hey, you pieces of shit, you're chopping our guys. I'm f***ing chopping him."

"Our defense ripped them apart," Ditka said. "They must've felt like it was Sherman's army marching through them."

A week later, however, it was the Bears' turn against Sherman's army.

CHAPTER 9

M̲ONDAY N̲IGHT I̲N M̲IAMI

"We were just stupid."
—Gary Fencik

AS THE CALENDAR SWUNG INTO DECEMBER, the mania was in full throttle. Players were doing commercials and appearances weekly, many of them more than one, some thought at the expense of game preparation. Madonna came out with "Like a Virgin," but it was in danger of getting lost in the shuffle. *The* "Shuffle."

Records and videos were not the only place where Bears confidence was in bloom. Duerson had planned on starting law school at Loyola in January. The Notre Dame safety contacted the school and put his enrollment off because the Super Bowl was in January.

The team was getting dozens of appearance requests each week. Ten players already had their own radio shows, including Fencik, Gault, Hampton, McMahon, Payton, Ditka, and Van Horne. Backup quarterback Tomczak had a show. Backup wide receiver Ken Margerum had one. Backup tight end Tim Wrightman had one. The number would climb well past a dozen in the weeks ahead. The 40-ring circus was always in session, in a renewable cycle that began with the game on Sunday, gathered speed with Ditka's postgame press gathering and team locker-room interviews, shifted up again with Ditka's and the other players' "Sports Extra" shows, and then swung into the week: two days to cover the events of the past weekend and the next four to build toward the next.

The offensive line was lined up for a poster titled "Black 'n' Blues Brothers" for area Chevrolet dealers, in which each of the linemen were in uniform but with Blues Brothers hats, sunglasses, and briefcases as well.

Ditka had ads running on Channels 2, 5, and 7 on the same day, and Payton was in on the Diet Coke parade.

The woofing by the defense brought an instant ad campaign. The "Junkyard Dogs" poster was done, sponsored by Chicago-area Chevrolet dealers, and featured Dent, Duerson, Hampton, Hartenstine, Marshall, Wilson, Rivera, and Richardson.

> "Fridge and Ditka, the media, you couldn't wait until the game was over. The reporters I think waited more for what Ditka was going to say after the game than they were the game. You might win and Ditka would be up there and rip apart everything."
> *—Jay Hilgenberg*

The players wanted to grab what was there while it was there. The front office had told players that personal appearances would be curtailed by mid-December to focus on the playoffs. Contracts are not guaranteed in the NFL, and certainly neither are undefeated seasons. The standard $250 fee for a luncheon speech was now $2,500 for a half hour of signing autographs on up to $5,000 if it was a corporate appearance. And the fee was spiraling higher.

At a charity auction, dinner at Maxim's with Payton and his wife, Connie, went for $3,800. Dinner at the 71 Club with Jim and Nancy McMahon was worth $2,100 to the winning bidder.

The accomplishments of both the offense and defense had become the talk of the NFL and more. In the six-game stretch before Miami, opposing offenses scored a total of 29 points; the Bears' *defense* scored 27 points. In the previous three games, even without McMahon, the Bears outscored opponents 104–3. In the nine games since the Miracle in Minnesota, only one team had scored more than one touchdown in a game against the Bears.

Still, there seemed to be something. . . .

Maybe it was Ditka's intimating that he did not think McMahon was as much a part of the team as he should be. Friction between those two was never far below the surface, and although McMahon wanted to start in Miami, Ditka stuck with Fuller. Maybe it was the first spasm of overconfidence. Maybe there were too many distractions.

Players cut "The Super Bowl Shuffle" record before the Atlanta game. It was a blockbuster around Chicago, receiving airplay on virtually every radio station, AM or FM, and it was spreading outward fast.

Almost half the team was planning on doing the video the day after they got back from Miami.

DECEMBER 2, 1985, *MONDAY NIGHT FOOTBALL*—MIAMI DOLPHINS, ORANGE BOWL

The Dolphins were one of the last two teams, along with the New York Jets, on the Bears' schedule that represented a problem. The Jets were a playoff team. Miami was the other half of Super Bowl XIX, having lost to the 49ers 38–16 two weeks after the Bears' 23–0 embarrassment, and the Bears already had slapped down San Francisco in their swath through Super Bowl teams on the way to one of their own.

The matchup was *the* national sports story because the 12–0 Bears now had to go through Miami, the last NFL team to go undefeated with their 1972 championship team that went 14–0 and ran it to 17–0 with the playoffs and the Super Bowl.

Because the Bears were the Bears that year, they were the story even more than the Dolphins.

Veteran *Miami Herald* columnist Edwin Pope surveyed his town and concluded, "In nearly 20 full Dolphins seasons, including five Super Bowls, none of us has heard this much to-do before a game."

The Dolphins themselves played up the history of the moment. Nick Buoniconti, Larry Csonka, Jim Kiick, Bob Kuechenberg, and other members of the 1972 team were conspicuous in their attendance of Dolphins practice during the week. Some were on the sideline Monday night after finding their way outside the Bears' locker room earlier, just to make conversation.

Miami radio stations played made-up songs about defrosting the Refrigerator. A South Florida newspaper offered reader advice for the Dolphins, things like hijacking the Bears' plane. A Miami TV station went to the zoo to interview a bear and a dolphin. *Miami Vice* star Don Johnson called the Bears, not the Dolphins, to ask for a locker-room pass.

Novelist Carl Hiaasen, with the *Miami Herald*, was not in the thrall of the Fridge: "This is what the Refrigerator did to become famous: he took a football, ran three feet, and fell down. It doesn't sound like much, but when you're 307 pounds, this is all the excitement you can stand."

The result of all of this was the highest-rated *Monday Night Football* game of all time. This Monday night game would attract a 31.7 rating and 48 share, meaning nearly a third of all homes with televisions had them on and tuned to the Bears and 48 percent of all people watching television were watching the Bears.

> "Until I went down to Miami to play my last year, I didn't realize what a big game that was for their franchise. When I went down there and would sit and talk with the players who were there, I learned what a big thing it was for them. Against Miami, at their stadium, where they can interrupt our perfect record on *Monday Night Football* with the whole country watching—that's the biggest regular-season game for that franchise."
> —*Tom Thayer*

Intentional or not, Miami coach Don Shula played to the egos of the Bears. He played them for fools, in fact, including Ditka and Ryan. Shula used the defense's strength against itself, giving the sack-hungry pass rushers enough of an opening to the inside to entice them toward center, then clogging them up while Marino slipped outside the rush and completed long pass after long pass. The irony was that the Miami inside gambit was exactly what Ryan and the defense planned for but just could not contain. Nor could they contain Marino.

The collapse was complete. Miami scored the first five times it had the ball. Besides the players losing any semblance of control and game plan, Ditka lost his compass in his play calling while Ryan mysteriously matched up 240-pound linebacker Marshall on 185-pound receiver Nat Moore, a duel not even Marshall had a chance of winning.

The Bears improvised into their own problems. Dent turned to Frazier in one huddle. "You blitz," the defensive end told the cornerback. "I'm going to drop into coverage [against Marino]."

They got Marino in exactly the long-yardage situations they wanted, then uncharacteristically let him go, literally and figuratively. Marino rolled to his right around the rush and threw for 30 yards on a third-and-18 on the Dolphins' first touchdown drive. He converted a third-and-19 with a 22-yard completion on the second touchdown drive and also netted 17 yards on a third-and-18, then picked up the first down.

The core of the third touchdown drive was a 52-yard pickup on third-and-13, followed shortly by 26 more yards on a third-and-7.

Most inexplicable of all perhaps was that the Dolphins were last against the run, the Bears had the greatest back in the game, and yet Ditka opened by throwing the ball on the first nine plays with not McMahon but Fuller. Payton did not carry the ball until nine minutes into the game. The Bears went three-and-out the first two times they had the ball, the Dolphins scored the first two times they got the ball, and the Bears were never in it. Players suspected that Ditka had become caught up in the magnitude of *Monday Night Football* and a chance to show himself as more of an offensive thinker than simply one who owed everything to McMahon and Payton.

> "We let Marino roll all the way to the sidelines on a bunch of third-down plays, so it wasn't all Buddy's fault by any means."
> *—Richard Dent*

Over on defense, Ryan had an axiom that a game plan was worthless after the opponent had gotten five first downs. If it ain't working, he said, don't stick with that. He did that in every game except that one, making Marshall cover Moore. Ryan had supreme confidence in his players, but it all happened so fast. Players said it felt as if they had gotten into their cars, backed out of the driveway, and been broadsided immediately. A whole bunch of shit in a heartbeat was how more than one player put it.

DITKA VS. RYAN

The mistakes of Ditka and Ryan sparked an incident of their own. During halftime Ditka let Ryan know what he thought of Ryan's defensive matchups.

Ryan offered his opinion on Ditka's mental state with the game plan relying on the passing of Fuller.

The argument during halftime escalated, and suddenly Ditka and Ryan were into a swinging fistfight in the shower. Both were in fact right in their criticisms of the other, Ditka of the Marshall Plan and Ryan of the pass-first game plan that Ditka shoved on Fuller.

Shula and Marino knew what they had in Moore vs. Marshall. A twist was that for all of the fixation on Moore, he caught just four passes for 75 yards, although two catches were for touchdowns. If the Bears thought they had any chance, however, that ended when a Marino pass bounced off Hampton's helmet and to Mark Clayton, who turned the freak play into a 42-yard touchdown.

Early in the fourth quarter, Fuller sprained his ankle and limped off. In came McMahon but with no big finish this time. McMahon did find a way to irritate Ditka instead.

Payton needed a few more yards for a record-setting eighth-straight 100-yard game. Ditka was sending in pass plays, but McMahon had his own game plan.

"Screw Ditka," McMahon told his line. "We're going to get Walter his yards."

They did. Payton finished with 121 yards, getting the last ones in the final minute after Miami was kind enough to fumble the ball back to the Bears.

The Dolphins were not amused. Linebacker Bob Brudzinski angered the Bears and left them hoping Miami would join them in the Super Bowl when he observed, "I never saw anybody give up like that at the end just for a record. They had chances. They had time."

McMahon remembered the slight. After the Indianapolis game the following week, he said that the lowly Colts defense was better than the Dolphins'.

"We don't pay a lot of attention to what Jim McMahon says," Miami coach Don Shula said, immediately separating himself from what was a growing percentage of the American public. "We don't know that he's much of an authority."

The eighties saw two of the best centers in NFL history playing at the same time: the Bears' Hilgenberg and Miami's Dwight Stephenson. That night they were on the same field.

Hilgenberg, a former standout college wrestler, was adept at letting a larger defensive lineman go the way the rusher wanted, getting the defender off balance using the man's own weight and speed, and then dumping him. Hilgenberg was rarely on the ground himself.

Stephenson was the same. He took Perry down effortlessly over and over, letting Perry charge into him and then just throwing him to the ground. Afterward Ryan, not a fan of Perry's to begin with, gave Perry a brief critique.

"Here you are, 400 pounds," Ryan said, "and the guy's throwing you around like a bag of shit."

Not that it was entirely Perry's fault. Stephenson put Pro Bowl players down too. Hampton and McMichael did not want any more to do with Stephenson than they had to, so they took their own liberties with the scheme and called stunts that had Perry occupy Stephenson and a guard while those two looped or did whatever gaming they wanted. Perry was too easily persuaded, too nice a guy, and just plain too rookie to argue.

WHO ELSE?

Some believed Ryan wanted the Bears to lose that game, to take them back down closer to Earth. Ryan was too smart to let a matchup like Marshall on Moore happen by accident. The Bears did not need the game. They had clinched home-field advantage through the playoffs on Sunday by virtue of the Rams losing, so this game did not matter in the standings. Miami, on the other hand, was in a desperate battle with the Jets and playing for something.

One disappointment that would follow later was Miami's loss in the AFC Championship Game to New England. The Bears wanted the Dolphins in the Super Bowl, but the Patriots, with the game plan Ditka forgot, trampled the Miami defense with 59 rushes for a total of 255 yards.

The anxiety bubbling up in Chicago was palpable after the 38–24 loss to Miami, understandable for a city that had so often had its sports dreams turned to nightmares. But there was some perspective to be had.

Hub Arkush did an interview with Hartenstine for WGN right after the Miami game.

"These guys think the world just came to an end, that we're not going to be undefeated," the veteran defensive end said.

"What about that fact, knowing that now you can't be undefeated?" Arkush asked.

Hartenstine ignored the point. It simply did not matter in the overall picture.

"Who else is going to beat us?" Hartenstine said. "They didn't beat us. We show up flat, fall behind, then early in the third quarter, if Marino doesn't bounce that ball off Hamp's helmet, we probably win this game too."

> "Buddy always said that losing to Miami made it a cinch that we'd win the Super Bowl. He's probably right. But that didn't make it any less infuriating when it happened, because we were just stupid."
> *–Gary Fencik*

The plane ride home was quiet. A few hours later, however, the Bears would make some noise of a far different kind.

Chapter 10

"THE SUPER BOWL SHUFFLE"

"Any time you start patting yourself on the back, you've only got one hand to play with. . . . Any time you worry about looking in the rearview mirror more than looking out the windshield, that's when you're going to run off the road."
—Dan Hampton

BROOKLYN NATIVE WILSON WENT HOME to New York not long after the Super Bowl. He and Dent, the MVP of the Super Bowl, met up with Giants star Lawrence Taylor and did the Big Apple, just hanging out. The three were walking down Fifth Avenue one afternoon when a young boy and his mother passed them walking the opposite direction.

The little boy stopped and pointed, his mouth open in disbelief. And why not? L.T. was Mr. Giant and Dent was the Most Valuable Player of one of the most memorable—and watched—Super Bowls in history.

Except that it was Wilson the boy was in awe of as he yelled to his mother.

"Mom, that's the guy, 'Mama's Boy Otis,' from 'The Super Bowl Shuffle'!"

"The Super Bowl Shuffle" was the defining signature of the '85 Bears. It set down many of the nicknames and identities and put faces and voices with the names for all to see and hear. It came to epitomize the '85 Bears— the swagger, the superconfidence, the fun, the bigger-than-life personalities, the rise to rarified heights followed by quibbling over how money and fame would be divided up.

"The Super Bowl Shuffle" happened in stages. First came the song itself, released as a 45 rpm record and a cassette single, with 10 solo rappers: Dent, Fencik, Fuller, Gault, McMahon, Payton, Perry, Richardson,

Singletary, and Wilson. That was recorded the Friday after the destruction of Dallas. Two weeks later came the filming of the video, with additional players becoming involved as backups.

The whole project was very bold, even to some of the participants. By comparison, Joe Namath's "guarantee" of victory in Super Bowl III somehow seemed quaint.

> "This was magical. For me the one thing about it that stands out was the audacity of them, making that 'Super Bowl Shuffle' video. You think about it: who would do that today? Who would be so bold as to say, 'This is how good we are!'? I think that that in a way set the tone for so much, in a good way."
> *—Joe Mantegna*

A BREAKTHROUGH IDEA

"The Shuffle" was the idea of Richard Meyer, president of Red Label Records, and was proposed to the players by Gault, who knew Meyer through working with Jovan cosmetics, Meyer's previous business. Gault was also a good friend of Chicago mayor Harold Washington, and Gault wanted to do something that would draw more attention to Chicago as a favor to the mayor. The project was presented to the players as an endeavor to raise money for charity.

Three Nashville songwriters had written something called "The Kingfish Shuffle," a spoof rap based on the colorful George "Kingfish" Stevens character from the old *Amos 'n Andy* television show. Meyer heard a demo recording of "The Kingfish Shuffle," bought the rights, and changed the lyrics. The project began with Meyer and Rich Tufo penning rap-style lyrics for each of the solo singers. If someone did not like what Meyer had written, Meyer wrote a new version on the spot. The lyrics involved some changes for the players' images. Wilson had been the self-styled "Big O"— "Sit down and tell Big O what's happ'nin"—but Meyer recast him as "Mama's Boy Otis," a sobriquet that would stick as his identity for ever after.

The initial recording was a sensation far greater than anyone expected, with tens of thousands of copies selling daily both in Chicago and else-where in a country that had become enthralled and infatuated with the

Bears. The original "Super Bowl Shuffle" recording sold more than five hundred thousand copies in its first two weeks, during which it was played upwards of four or five times daily on some Chicago stations. It ultimately sold 2 million copies, reaching double-platinum status and receiving a Grammy nomination. That startling

"We were saying those words but I don't think we really truly believed everything we were saying. We were just having fun with it. We knew we were capable of winning, but *damn!*"
—*Otis Wilson*

success fueled the idea of making a video of the song with what amounted to nearly half the team—which would involve paying the players.

THE VIDEO

The team arrived back in Chicago in the early morning hours of Tuesday, December 3, after the Miami loss. Gault and Meyer had scheduled the shoot for 2:00 P.M. downtown, at the Park West Theater on Chicago's north side, located at the trendy south end of Lincoln Park. Gault was late, getting his hair styled, and the production did not get underway until about 5:00 P.M.

In the downtime before Gault arrived, there was some debate over whether the backup singers should be paid shares equivalent to those of the "featured artists." The final plan was to have the solo verses performed by the 10 players who had done the original record. A second set of players served as musicians and backup singers: Buford, Frazier, Gayle, all-purpose back Dennis Gentry, guard Stefan Humphries, defensive lineman Tyrone Keys, linebacker Jim Morrissey, receiver Keith Ortego, linebacker Dan Rains, running back Thomas Sanders, defensive backs Reggie Phillips and Ken Taylor, running back Calvin Thomas, and Tomczak were choreographed as the backup artists, some dressed in a "Blues Brother" get-up of sunglasses and top hats. Humphries performed on the drums, Thomas was on the saxophone, Buford banged away on a cowbell, Tomczak strummed an electric guitar, and Keys played a keyboard.

Some of the Bears were a little embarrassed by the whole idea. Fencik was the embodiment of cool, but sadly *not* the embodiment of dance. Neither was Fuller, a country kid who was hurt and on crutches at the time—and who danced like he was on crutches anyway, injury or not. The group needed two and a half hours just to get the chorus down, with Singletary working at choreography to get the backups in synch. Dent could not keep his voice level constant enough to satisfy the sound technicians; Wilson needed two-dozen takes to get his rap down; and Fencik, Mr. Yale, took constant repeats to get his right. Frazier was acrobatic on defense, but decidedly not so on stage, prompting Wilson to holler, "Leslie, man, I don't know how you could have ever made kids!"

If there was a major surprise it was Perry. Fridge was there with wife Sherry and daughter Latavia, and he looked stiff in the early takes—not the William that was there before the fame and acclaim began to pour down over him. Sherry Perry was becoming a more intrusive figure in her husband's dealings, and she was not sharing any of the fun of the video shoot. At one point, however, Perry appeared to teammates to just ignore all the undercurrents. He cut loose and began a routine that turned on the entire set—except, of course, Sherry.

They were all there to do the "Super Bowl Shuffle." All, that is, except McMahon and Payton. The cover story put out was that McMahon and Payton were too banged up after the Miami game to participate, but McMahon had played only as a fourth-quarter mop-up and Payton was seldom too banged up to do anything. In reality they were having reservations about participating, especially in light of concerns about how much of the money would actually go to charity.

McMahon and Payton were central figures of both the 1985 Super Bowl run and in Bears history, and without them, particularly because they were a part of the original recording, the video might have been seen as lacking some of the star power. They also lent the project an air of credibility that no other players could bring to it. Besides, Payton was a former dancer on *Soul Train*, and the quality of the video's dancing would go up dramatically with him involved. At McMahon's request, Steve Zucker made some inquiries and talked with Payton's agent, Bud Holmes. Finally, McMahon and Payton agreed to participate.

When matters were finally settled, McMahon and Payton filmed their routines separately against a blue background and were dropped into the video electronically. McMahon, true to form, "audibled" away from the prepared script and did his own rap.

The video took off immediately on its way to half a million dollars in sales and became an instant cult classic, that cult by then being a Bears Nation that was growing weekly as radio stations continued playing the record repeatedly. Estimates of sales from the record and video run beyond $10 million.

The explosion of success for the record stunned the players and started them wondering about the money. They were specifically concerned about how much money really was coming in, whether or not they should be getting something more, and if there was as much money going to charity as they'd been led to believe. For the video, the 10 soloists were paid $5,000 each, with the promise of more from the sales as they rolled in. The backups for the video were given checks for $400 each and also expected to share in some of the post-charity proceeds. The office of Illinois attorney general Neil Hartigan initiated a series of discussions regarding the actual level of charitable contributions, and, through subsequent negotiations, a distribution plan was worked out whereby more than $300,000 was eventually given to the Chicago Community Trust, which used the money to help the city's needy and abused.

> "It was like, 'Uh-oh, I didn't know I said that.' I didn't know we said we're going to win the Super Bowl. That was pretty bold, but it was where we were. I liked the hook, the idea, but when I started seeing the lyrics, I thought, oh God, no. Then to play three games and give up 10 points. . . ."
> *–Richard Dent*

THE AFTERMATH

Though the project was criticized by some outsiders and players early on, significantly, it did not divert any of the players' eyes from the real

> "The biggest problem I had with "The Super Bowl Shuffle" was that they did it the day after the loss to the Dolphins. We're on the plane coming home from Miami and everybody's talking about going down to do 'The Super Bowl Shuffle.' I was like, 'We just lost a goddamn game and we're going to do a video about the Super Bowl after we got our asses handed to us?' I probably would have done it if it were a different set of circumstances, because it was a team kind of thing and I'm about the team."
> *—Mike Hartenstine*

prize, the Super Bowl. If anything, it made them even more dedicated because they now had a lot of promises to keep.

But the idea of the video did divide the team. Those doing it were having fun, not necessarily even believing the goofy lines they were putting out. Other players expressed opposition that "The Super Bowl Shuffle" was being filmed the day after the team's first loss, and a bad loss at that. When they were finished, some felt an immediate flash of "what have we done."

Ditka had told the players they should not do it—all the more reason why McMahon would. McMichael was particularly angry. Hampton was against it. So were Hilgenberg, Hartenstine, and others. The reasons varied. Some thought the timing was just bad. Others reasoned that now opponents would not need any special motivation to go out on Sundays and blow up this mouthy bunch of Bears.

Hampton, McMichael, and the other high-profile players who passed on the project missed out on the $5,000 each soloist was supposed to get up front. They also would have to hear about it in the years afterward from fans who wanted to tell them how much they loved "The Super Bowl Shuffle."

So successful and popular was "The Super Bowl Shuffle" that it inspired immediate copycats. In a very short time, teams and athletes were heading into recording studios to do songs of their own. The staid Dallas Cowboys recorded "Living the American Dream." The Cleveland Browns

produced "Masters of the Gridiron." The
Raiders came out with "Silver and Black
Attack," and the Rams foisted "Let's Ram
It" on an unsuspecting public. The follow-
ing year, New York Mets Rick Aguilera,
Len Dykstra, George Foster, Dwight
Gooden, Howard Johnson, Kevin Mitchell,
Rafael Santana, Darryl Strawberry, and
Tim Tuefel took the Bears' idea into base-
ball with "Get Metsmerized." Not to be outdone, Ditka came out with
"The Grabowski Shuffle" in 1987, also produced by Meyer, who had not
paid all the bills from "The Super Bowl Shuffle" and had to settle his
debts before the editing studio would let him record again.

> "I have a gold record and a platinum video. A bunch of guys doing something they don't normally do, wearing tight pants. I was thinking, 'Heck, we're going to win it anyway, so why not?'"
> *–Richard Dent*

Michael Jackson's "Thriller" (released in 1983) and "The Super Bowl
Shuffle" stand as two of the early big successes that helped propel videos,
then still just an emerging idea, into American entertainment. For many
years, "Thriller" would be the only video to outsell "The Shuffle."

The Bears indeed were going to win it anyway. And it was going to be a
win for the ages.

CHAPTER 11
ON FINAL APPROACH

"All of a sudden they know it's time to turn it up a notch.
No one has to say anything. It's just a look."
—Mike Singletary

AMIDST THE SOUR MOOD AFTER the Miami loss, those members of the McCaskey family in charge of the team decided that the Honey Bears cheerleaders, 38 beauties who had provided eye candy for fans for eight seasons, most of them dismal, were passé. Michael McCaskey announced that "the concept of cheerleaders has outlived its time."

Players were less irritated by the removal of the cheerleaders than they were by Michael McCaskey's decision that there was insufficient justification for an indoor practice facility. They were apparently fine with the greatest team in franchise history making two-hour round trips by bus to Morton High School in the city's western suburbs.

The city may have been troubled by the Miami game, but that didn't stop the fun. The following Friday the Chicago Art Institute installed massive football helmets on the two bronze lions in front of its building on Michigan Avenue. Enterprising fans stole them—of course. Kids were wearing Bears headbands to school and businessmen were donning Bears T-shirts under their pinstriped suits. Talk of the games and the latest comments (usually from Ditka) put commuters in a good mood and provided a universal conversation-starter for folks on their way to work. Perry was sworn in as a voluntary Lake County deputy sheriff working with kids programs. As to whether he would carry a gun, officer Mickey Babcox explained, "Anybody who weighs 304 pounds doesn't need to."

The end of the undefeated season temporarily staunched the torrent of national media streaming into Chicago, if only for a few weeks. But it did nothing to damn up the local flood of Bears mania. The offensive line's poster for Chevy featured the "Black and Blues Brothers": linemen attired in their uniforms along with Blues Brothers–style hats, sunglasses, and briefcases. Hampton, Dent, Marshall, Wilson, Ron Rivera, Hartenstine, Frazier, Richardson, and Duerson had a "Junkyard Dogs" poster picturing them sitting around a junkyard looking hostile. Fencik was modeling hair mousse; he was also a spokesman for a bank, had his own TV show, three radio shows, and a newspaper column; and held a big stake in the Hunt Club bar and restaurant, a location from which radio shows were paying to broadcast. Sir Georg Solti, conductor of the Chicago Symphony Orchestra, directed a CSO performance wearing a Bears hat. The enormous metal Picasso sculpture in the Chicago Loop turned up one morning sporting a headband. The advertising machine was gathering speed as well. From November 1985 through January 1986, sports-talker Chet Coppock made $100,000 with Bears doings alone, from commercials to emceeing events.

MEDIA MAGNATES

The change in the faces and voices representing sports in America was continuing and the pace was accelerating. The ascendancy of the Bears was producing an insatiable media appetite for not only what the Bears said and did, but also for the Bears themselves. This was the true advent of athletes being enlisted as members of the media—and getting paid for it. Sterling Sharpe, "Neon" Deion Sanders, Tom Jackson, Boomer Esiason, Sean Salisbury, Ron Jaworski, Howie Long, Terry Bradshaw, Cris Collinsworth—all the players who have gone from gridiron performers to gridiron commentators owe a tremendous debt to the 1985 Bears. The thing that made this team new and different was that it featured personalities who could all speak and think for themselves.

Chicago was becoming all Bears all the time. Fencik did the *Johnny B in the Morning* radio show with Jonathan Brandmeier. Thayer was a regular with Steve Dahl. Kevin Butler began joining Kevin Matthews on the air, an association that lasted many years. Bears flagship station WGN-AM had the *Three*

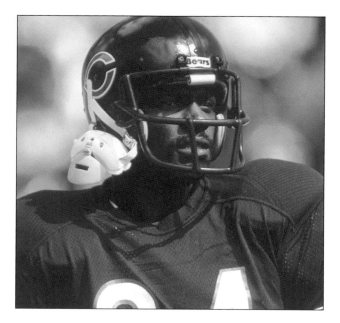

In 1985, the next-to-last season of his storied career, Walter Payton accounted for more than two thousand total yards rushing and receiving.

Dan Hampton (No. 99) let some words by defensive coordinator
Buddy Ryan motivate him in his earliest NFL days, and then went on
to change the face of the vaunted Chicago Bears defense.

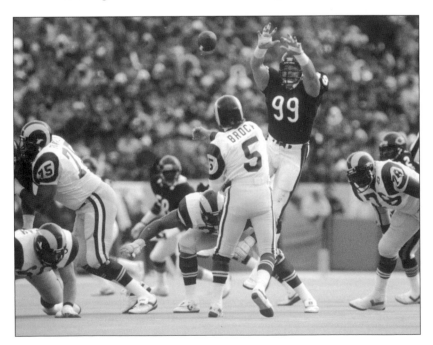

Steve McMichael (No. 76) didn't have a lot when he arrived in Chicago, but he left an imprint on the city and the opposition.

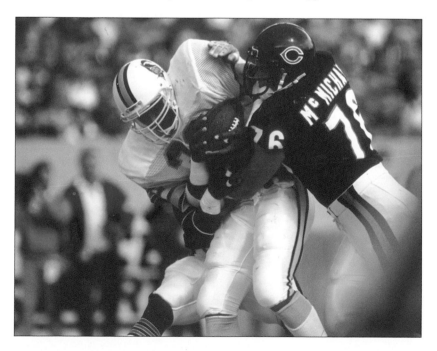

Otis Wilson (No. 55), a second-round draft pick in 1981, and
Wilber Marshall (No. 58), a first-round draft pick in the early eighties,
made huge contributions during the championship push.

Buddy Ryan's "46" defense worked largely because he knew how to get the most out of his players, and because he had the players, including (below, from left): Hampton (No. 99), William "Refrigerator" Perry (No. 72), Richard Dent (No. 95), Marshall (No. 58), and McMichael (No. 76).

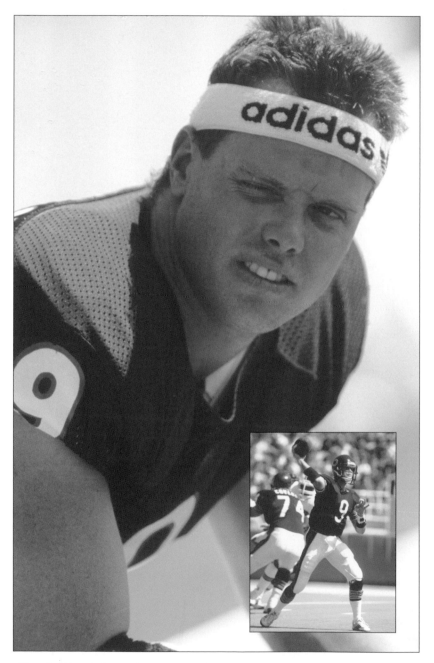

Despite his plethora of NCAA passing records, Jim McMahon was considered too small, too fragile, and generally unpredictable by many NFL scouts.

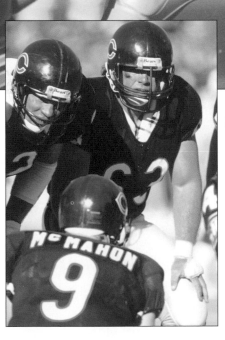

While future Hall of Famer Mike Singletary (above) directed the defense, McMahon always had support from the likes of offensive lineman Jay Hilgenberg (No. 63).

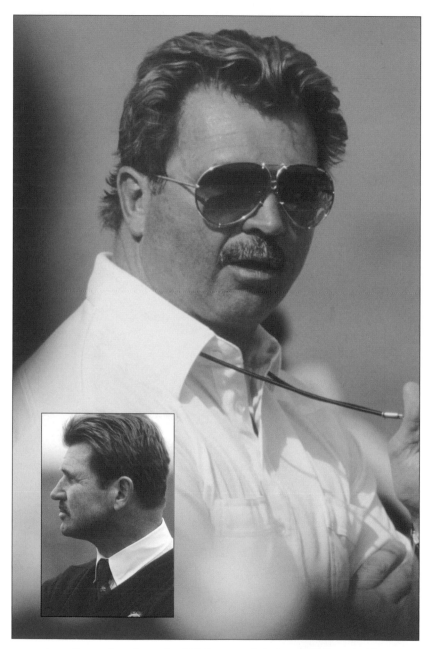

Any discussion about the '85 Bears and their subsequent demise begins and ends with Mike Ditka, who, in the words of Dent, was "the reason we won that Super Bowl and the reason why we didn't win three."

Bears with Duerson, Hilgenberg, and Hampton. Hub Arkush hosted the weekly show, meeting with the three players in a tiny room at Halas Hall every Friday. The questions were really just points to get the trio talking. It did not take much for them to fill air time. McMichael was added to the local NBC affiliate's sports telecast, and his show was more highly rated than Ditka's at times, which irritated Ditka.

But Ditka was Ditka, which made his show "must-view," even for reporters. If Ditka had had too much to drink before the show, it only added to the image and built viewership. The front pages of the papers occasionally carried pictures of him from his TV show. Ditka made $250,000 for the television shows with Johnny Morris and another $100,000 for his radio show with Mike Pyle, both teammates of Ditka's on the 1963 championship teams. Ditka came into the local CBS studio on Thursday and taped the show in front of a live audience; it was then televised on Sunday before the game. After the game he went into the studio, typically after he had had some drinks with dinner while he killed time. Eventually the show was shot immediately after the game; it was safer. While he and Ditka had been friends since their playing days, Morris was intensely competitive about getting stories. So if Ditka gave a vapid answer to something, Morris was comfortable enough and motivated enough to push: "C'mon, Mike. What about this?"

Fencik did his show from the Hunt Club, with host John Landecker and reporter Les Grobstein at times, and always, 80 percent of the audience was female. They all wanted Fencik; when they realized there was no chance, they went after Landecker. After a while some were even coming on to Grobstein. When

> "You know, I suspect it was Thayer and 'Horne who started all that. They were on a show and somebody asked them who the 'biggest' guy on the team was and I heard they said me. Hey, I didn't need no advertising at that point. I guess I got more than my share. Single, great body, age 25. . . . [Laughs.] Wednesday, Thursday, Friday, and Saturday, before the games, I didn't do anything; just took care of my business. I did all my 'damage' Sunday night, Monday, and Tuesday."
> —*Otis Wilson*

Wilson visited the show a woman named Debbie called in. "Otis," Debbie began, "I gotta ask you a question: how big is it really?" Wilson started laughing and never did answer the question. Debbie was not a teenager, either. It was just one more example of Wilson's "growing" reputation.

Payton's commentaries during the 1985 season for the local ABC affiliate, which earned him a tidy $100,000, were done in-studio in downtown Chicago from 10:30 to 11:00 on Sunday nights. Payton usually went home after the games to the far northwest suburbs, then turned around and drove like a madman to make it back in time for the show. The race was part of the fun.

If some distractions were threatening to divide the team and create grumbling, there were still strong forces keeping them together. The offensive line had started the "Friday Pump Club," a group consisting of all the offensive linemen, who hung out and lifted after Friday's light morning practice. The same went for the group dinner every Thursday, a tradition that would still live on two decades later. McMahon, by now head-butting his offensive teammates after touchdowns, was invited with his linemen and took his turn picking up the check, which ran into four figures, when the rotation got around to him. His place of choice was the Prime Minister out on Milwaukee Avenue in the suburb of Northbrook. McMahon was pals with owner Gus Pappas and the players were well taken care of. Later, McMahon and Pappas would have an acrimonious falling out in their own restaurant venture, but till then it was good times.

McMahon was not the only one who took care of his protectors. Payton bought shotguns for each member of the offensive line, at a cost of about $5,000 apiece. Hilgenberg thought the gun would look good above his fireplace mantle; he hoped Payton would provide that next.

The media crush occasioned some jealousy and required some delicate

> "Walter was so great. Was he spectacular like Barry Sanders? Probably not. But he was just incredible. And those offensive linemen had a lot to do with Walter's success. He slowed down a lot at the end but he was still effective because of the offensive line. There were times when he did it without a lot of help, but that offensive line of the eighties was great. Those guys helped make Walter great."
> —*Dan Hampton*

handling inside the Bears. While McMahon, Perry, and Ditka were still the targets of choice for national advertisers, the staggering demand for their time left plenty of spillover for teammates. Seven Bears stepped in and did a McDonald's commercial worth $4,000 each just to sing "It's a good time for the great taste of *victory!*" After the circus of "The Super Bowl Shuffle," that one was easy.

And somewhere in all of that, they still had to play some football. With everything that was going on, it looked at times as if football was an afterthought.

> "We didn't create it. We were just trying to maintain and manage it and it was very, very difficult. There was some resentment from the players thinking that we pushed this guy or that guy forward, always giving so-and-so the *NFL Today* show interviews. They'd ask for a lineup of people and a lot of times we were caught in the middle. Some guys got left out just because they weren't as charismatic and that was what they [the TV shows] were after. If you had to build a scale from charismatic to dull, it would be almost completely opposite the scale for pure football player from excellent to poor. Walter would be a 10 on the football scale, but maybe in the low range to middle for charismatic where something like national TV was concerned. He was aloof but had a great way about him that he just didn't show to outsiders."
> —*Ken Valdiserri, Bears marketing and communications director*

DECEMBER 8, 1985—INDIANAPOLIS COLTS, SOLDIER FIELD

Whatever the distractions, the Bears did not help themselves by looking at film of the underdog Colts and underestimating them. Somewhere along the line they decided that the Colts were bad to the point of not requiring total attention and preparation. A combination of factors was at work. It was the short week after a *Monday Night Football* appearance, and teams typically were not as sharp the following Sunday. The Bears had already clinched all they could: the division title and home field through the playoffs. And to top it all off, the Colts were indeed not very good.

With the score 3–3 at halftime, the anxiety left over from the Miami debacle six days earlier bubbled up and the team heard boos cascading down.

"I'd have booed us too," Hilgenberg said. Ditka was incensed. "I told you this was a good football team," he said, having already cautioned the Bears that the Colts were a lot like the Bears were three years ago: hungry. He wondered if perhaps the team was playing with pillows, since he had heard none of the noise from tough hitting that he was accustomed to. He told the Bears that unless there was a change, they were about to be embarrassed. Really embarrassed.

While the Bears managed to eke out a victory, the rest of the game was just as lackluster as the first half. The score was still 3–3 midway through the third quarter and Payton had only 18 rushing yards. The Bears offensive line then controlled the ball almost 19 of the final 23 minutes, letting Payton hammer away behind his line and finish with 111 yards in the 17–10 win.

In total the defense managed only one sack and did not take the ball away from the Colts once. The Bears had 22 first downs to Indianapolis' 10, but no Bear was pleased to see quarterback Mike Pagel slipping outside the pass rush containment the way Marino had, even if Pagel did complete only 10 of his 24 passes. McMahon was pedestrian in his first start in a month. Bothered by continuing shoulder soreness, he completed only 11 of 23 passes for 145 yards and ran the ball five times—not what the offense needed him to do but what the aggressive young Colts forced him into.

Overlooked in the win was punter Maury Buford, who pinned the Colts deep in their end of the field a couple of times—and no team without a Dan Marino was going to drive 90 yards on the Bears defense even on its off days.

"Sweetness" showed some of what made him great off the field that day. Backup safety Shaun Gayle had mentioned to Payton during the week that Gayle's parents were coming up from Virginia and would be at the game. Gayle also said that his father was in a wheelchair, and really wanted to meet Payton. After the game there was a sea of fans and well-wishers hanging around Bear Alley under the stands. Payton came out and immediately made his way through the tide of fans, found Gayle's father, and visited with him.

Payton was not respected by teammates—he was *revered*. Prior to the December 22 game in Detroit, Gayle went into the trainers' room for taping and Payton was on the table next to him being treated for "turf toe." Payton abruptly grabbed Gayle's hand and squeezed it as doctors slid a huge needle underneath the nail of his big toe to deaden it so he could play. Payton rushed for 81 yards in that game. The next morning the headlines read, "Payton may be losing a step." And Payton said not one word to anyone to explain his performance. Not to the press, not to teammates—no one.

DECEMBER 14, 1985—NEW YORK JETS, MEADOWLANDS

In the next-to-last game of the season, the New York Jets were a far bigger problem than the Colts had been the week before. The Jets were finishing an 11–5 season that would make them one of three teams from the AFC East to make the playoffs. Their defense, with Pro Bowl end Mark Gastineau and tackle Joe Klecko on the defensive line, ranked third in points and rushing yards allowed. Not surprisingly, Payton's string of consecutive games with 100 yards ended at nine; he finished with 53 yards on 28 carries, 9 of which lost yardage.

The defense came in feeling anything but special. The Indianapolis and Miami games had not been close by their standards, and Ryan gave them three written tests on the game plan in the week leading up to the game.

The work and preparation paid off. Dent punched the ball away from Jets quarterback Ken O'Brien to force turnovers with sacks on consecutive possessions in the third quarter. The Jets managed just 70 rushing yards and lost three fumbles.

The player of the game this time was kicker Kevin Butler, the rookie from Georgia with one of the strongest sets of legs in the NFL; he would set a franchise and league record that season with 144 points. The Bears had thought so much of him that they cut kicker Bob Thomas during the 1985 preseason even though Thomas, who would go on to become a judge, scored a career-best 101 points in 1984. Butler kicked four field goals in the 19–6 vanquishing of the Jets to give him 28 for the year. With a short-sleeved uniform like those of the offensive linemen, even in frigid conditions, he was fast becoming part of what made the team special.

Former President Richard Nixon's football interest was piqued. Living in New Jersey, the country's ex–No. 1 fan let it be known that his heart was with the Giants and Jets, living as he did in New Jersey, but that his head said this year was all Bears.

DECEMBER 22, 1985—DETROIT LIONS, PONTIAC SILVERDOME

Marshall established that the finale with Detroit was not going to be simply a walk-through. On the third play of the game, quarterback Joe Ferguson made the mistake of starting to roll to his left without looking, and as he did, Marshall hit him and knocked him out. That hit, which film showed to be violent but hardly cheap or dirty, would cost him a $2,000 fine. Ditka suggested that everyone chip in to pay it.

The rest of the defense did some hitting of its own, although they squandered the NFL pass-defense lead.

Ditka went off on the team after the game, 15–1 record or not. They had thrashed the overmatched Lions 37–17, yet Ditka started ranting in the locker room, "You guys aren't worth a damn. I ought to fire all of you! You guys better go home and find yourselves before the holidays!" The players were surprised at the eruption even though they were used to it from Ditka. He even threw in that maybe they were doing too many "Super Bowl Shuffles." Gault muttered that the "Shuffle" was five weeks ago and that maybe they were doing too many McDonald's commercials or car commercials, a dig at Ditka.

But it was true that since the Miami game, they clearly had not been up to the standards they had set for themselves. The Jets game had been merely a workmanlike affair, and signs of bad attitude were turning up in practice arguments, often between members of the same unit.

"It's a different kind of feeling. When I'm out there, even in training camp, you get in a situation that might be a little tight, and you start looking at the guys all around you. It's game time. All of a sudden they know it's time to turn it up a notch. No one has to say anything. It's just a look."
—*Mike Singletary*

What appeared to set Ditka off was that they were up only 6–3 at halftime and 16–10 at the end of the third quarter. The Bears also lost four turnovers.

After Ditka told the players that they needed to go home and find themselves, McMahon felt compelled to offer directions. On the flight home, he got on the PA system. "When you find yourselves, come find me," he said. "I'll be in the gutter somewhere."

The Bears frankly had gotten bored in the closing weeks of the season against the likes of Detroit and Indianapolis. Now the games were going to matter again.

The frenzy was building. Seven thousand playoff tickets sold in only 30 minutes. Northwest National Bank in Chicago sued former employee Robert Hahn, charging that Hahn had changed the mailing address for the bank's Bears tickets from the bank to his home. The bank thus lost its chance to buy Bears playoff and Super Bowl tickets.

It was time.

Chapter 12

The Playoffs—Now Everybody Believed

"I didn't do nothin' to y'all. Why'd you treat me like that?"
—*Eric Dickerson*

THE REGULAR SEASON WAS OVER. Actually, it had been over for quite some time; the schedule just had to be played out. Now that was done and the time was coming to prove that the Bears' magic was all real.

The beauty of a 15–1 record was the extra week off while the wild-card games were played. Ditka let the Bears off early from practice to do their Christmas shopping, and Marshall Field's made arrangements for the team to come in through a private entrance so they would not be mobbed. It did not work; the sidewalks were solidly filled with people after they learned that the Bears were in town.

Perry, however, had an idea. He decided not to put in his false tooth in, figuring that with the tooth missing, people would not recognize him as quickly.

With two weeks' run-up to the divisional playoff game, the Bears had time to mix their unique blend of civic angst and puffy-chestedness. Another round of craziness was coming. As usual, McMahon was in the middle of it.

Many of the players wore manufacturers' logos for the equipment deals they had. The league did not like it because of its desire to centralize and control—and take in all the money—from endorsements arising out of NFL play. McMahon wore an Adidas headband in the Giants game, as he had done during the season, but this time it was a finable offense. Payton wore a Roos headband, and about 15 players had something going with equipment deals, and the NFL was not going to allow that.

The league fined the Bears $5,000, more than twice what they took from Marshall for the hit of Joe Ferguson in the Detroit game that they considered heinous—evidently less than half as heinous as circumventing or diverting NFL revenue streams.

The responses of McMahon and the Bears would lead to millions raised to fight diabetes, remembrance for U.S. POWs and MIAs, support for children's hospitals, and a gesture to remember a friend. And a little fun at the expense of the NFL commissioner.

JANUARY 5, 1986—NEW YORK GIANTS, SOLDIER FIELD

The Giants were first in the playoff run, and there was some concern, certainly among the oft-jilted fans of Chicago. The New York defense was supposed to be a problem for the Bears, who had not managed a 400-yard game since midseason. The Giants were the NFL's number two defense, behind the Bears. In the wild-card game against the 49ers they had sacked Montana four times and hit him over and over again on his 47 pass attempts. Giants linebacker Lawrence Taylor was third in balloting for the NFL's defensive player of the year, behind only Singletary and Dent.

The Giants led the NFL with 68 sacks, topping even the Bears by 4. Just as the

> **"We could have played those guys 15 times and wouldn't have beaten them once."**
> *—Giants linebacker Harry Carson*

Bears had done, however, the Giants simply beat up the 49ers 17–3. San Francisco dropped 10 passes; running back Roger Craig and receiver Dwight Clark both were knocked out with injuries. The 49ers did not cross the New York 20-yard line until three minutes remained in the game and did not sack Giants quarterback Phil Simms even once. The San Francisco "dynasty" would have to wait another year.

So would the Giants. Bill Parcells or not, they were not ready for what they were about to encounter in Chicago.

Before the game, the Bears had traveled down to Suwanee, Georgia, for some practice away from the madding crowds. But they brought some controversy with them.

Dent had been brought to his knees during training camp in contract negotiations, and there were hard feelings still lingering, for more than Dent. The ill will was becoming public with Dent's agent threatening that the defensive great might not play in the Super Bowl if—when—the Bears got there.

No one liked the idea, least of all Dent. His teammates, however, were going to do something to help him out. Their idea was to concoct a defensive maneuver that would loose Dent on the Giants as never before, a gambit that would likely turn him into the defensive MVP of the game at the very least and net him some serious negotiating leverage at the very best. His teammates knew what the Colonel meant to them, even if McCaskey and the Bears refused to acknowledge it sufficiently.

> "[Dent is] one of those guys you like to play football with. I wish we had more of that type of guy. Unfortunately you don't get that type of guy all that often. He's a tough individual. Anything he takes on in life I know is going to turn out to be successful because he knows dedication and hard work."
> *—Mike Singletary*

The plan was to use a line stunt they called "echo." In the echo alignment, used in passing situations, Hampton and McMichael lined up at the tackle spots, slanted to their right, and tied up all three of the interior offensive linemen while Hartenstine went to work on the right tackle one on one. Dent lined up at right end, then at the snap he looped around both Hampton and McMichael and ran in through the vacated spot in the pass-protection pocket. Dent was fast enough to cover the distance in an instant, and the Giants were not good enough to stop him, not with Hampton and McMichael creating havoc inside.

Echo created a monster. Dent sacked Simms three times and shared in a fourth sack as the Bears took the Giants' linchpin down six times in the slaughter. Dent's sacks accounted for 33 yards of losses for the Giants; the New York offense had only 32 yards rushing for the game, one of the rare times that a defensive end has truly "out rushed" an opponent's featured running back by himself.

Joe Morris had rushed for 142 yards against the San Francisco defense and had piled up 1,336 yards and 21 touchdowns for the regular season. The Bears were certain Morris could not run against their front seven and the variations of the 46, but that did not stop Ryan from concocting more than a dozen different fronts and nearly 20 different coverages to throw at the New York offense.

Besides the echo plan of Hampton and McMichael, Ryan sent Shaun Gayle in as a replacement for Perry as the Giants tried to thwart the Bears' power by throwing more and using a third wide receiver. Ryan then moved Dent inside over the right guard and left Marshall and Wilson at either end of the line.

"They didn't know who to block," Marshall said.

Morris was being systematically crushed. Wilson afterward remarked, "One time I looked down and thought it was a poster of him."

Simms really got nothing going the whole game. The Giants could not run, but unlike a lot of teams, tried to stay with it.

> "A lot of things I did weren't all planned, just things happening and you react. I'd tell guys, 'You see ball, you get ball.' If I'm going a little outside the rules or the scheme at the moment, it's because I'm going to make plays. And when I do it, 95 percent of the time, I'm making something happen; I'm not hurting anybody or the scheme. And if you have to be somewhere, yes, you have to be there."
> *—Richard Dent*

"THE WHIFF"

The Giants game would be by turns enigmatic, then laughable. The Bears did virtually nothing against the New York defense, although Covert, Van Horne, and the offensive line were dominating the rush demons of Taylor and Leonard Marshall. And it might have been a closer game if not for the Landeta Whiff.

Indeed, the only score of the first half came when New York punter Sean Landeta, who would go on to a long and distinguished NFL career, if always remembered for this instant, moved to punt from near his own goal line only to have the gusty, swirling winds of the lakefront blow the ball sideways. He barely ticked the ball in his motion.

Landeta's style was exactly the wrong method for Soldier Field in January. While some punters hold either the side or the tip of the ball, Landeta's way was to cradle it, meaning it was at the mercy of the winds. Landeta dropped the ball as the wind kicked up. His foot missed the ball, which fell to the ground next to Gayle, who picked it up at the 5-yard line and stepped into the end zone for the Bears' first touchdown.

"I don't know what you call it," Gayle said. "A foul tip?"

Landeta always maintained that the wind blew the ball, and it probably did.

> "They had this look that they were someplace they had never been before and they had no idea what was happening to them, what this was about. They had a look like 'This is a foreign land and we don't know anything that goes on here.'"
> –*Shaun Gayle*

The Bears sensed something else they had seen all year: fear. Gayle was lined up alongside Dennis Gentry on the left side, and the two just began yelling, screaming at Landeta.

Gayle saw him miss the ball, grabbed it, and spiked the ball in the end zone.

When Gayle came to the sideline, offensive coordinator Ed Hughes gave him a "lecture." Before you can spike a ball, you have to really score a touchdown, Hughes explained.

"You just picked it up and stepped into the end zone!" Hughes said.

That was more than any Giant was able to do.

The Bears were talking and baiting the Giants. Simms jogged over to the sideline at one point to confer with Parcells on the merits of going for it on a fourth-and-inches. Dent started yelling, waving his arms.

"C'mon, go for it," the Colonel dared them. "Go for it."

Wilson and the rest of the pack were right behind: "C'mon try it. Just try it once."

It was not a good day for the great Lawrence Taylor. Covert, whom Dent considered the greatest offensive tackle he ever faced, battered L.T. and at one point drove him backward onto his shoulder pads.

Adding insult to insult, Taylor and the Giants thought they were the Bears' equals and ran their mouths right back at the Bears. The Bears responded by running behind Covert right at Taylor, and by days' end, Bears backs had rushed for 138 yards, plus 18 more by McMahon, who at one point went right at Taylor to throw a block. Eventually the future Hall of Famer was screaming at Suhey, McMahon, and McKinnon because of their blocks.

> "After Jimbo Covert? C'mon. Whoever I was playing against after him was a joke."
> *−Richard Dent*

McKinnon's blocking was not the problem for the Giants: it was his receiving. McKinnon caught seven touchdown passes in the first eight games of the 1985 season. Over the last eight, he caught seven passes, period. He had injured his knee back in July and had been limited in practice ever since.

For this game McMahon and Ditka turned to Gault as the bar for prying open the New York defense. Gault caught three passes in the first half, and his world-class speed was forcing the Giants to tilt their defense in his direction as the second half opened. Time for McKinnon.

With the Giants worrying about Gault, McMahon, wearing sticky batting gloves because of the cold, broke the game open with touchdown passes of 23 and 20 yards to McKinnon, both against the wind in the third quarter. The Giants, for their part, ran 11 plays in the third quarter and lost 11 yards.

"This is the time to show what you're made of," McKinnon said.

It was that for the Giants too. Parcells was fuming. If Ditka resented the adulation given to Bill Walsh for his genius, Parcells had no use for the elevation of Ditka and his team to such exalted "tough-guy" legend status. He gave the Bears no credit for their 21–0 win.

"I'm unhappy," he said tersely. "I want to go to the Super Bowl. This team got in our way."

The Bears did a little more than that.

JANUARY 12, 1986—LOS ANGELES RAMS, SOLDIER FIELD

The Bears were back where they had been a year earlier in San Francisco. But very little was exactly the same.

Their fan base certainly was not. For this NFC championship they had followers that included Keith Richards, John McEnroe, Bill Murray, the Jackson Five, Dennis Franz, Tom Dreesen, Greg Norman, and others, many of whom would find their ways to the sideline to see up close what everybody wanted to know: what are these guys going to do *next*?

The Bears themselves were not the same team that had been told as they left San Francisco in defeat to bring its offense next time. They had McMahon at quarterback now instead of Fuller, which was a huge difference, if only for purposes of confidence. McMahon had quietly taken over the New York game in the second half after the Bears managed little in the first. When the Bears got close to the red zone in the third quarter, McMahon changed almost every play that Ditka and Hughes sent in. The results were the McKinnon touchdowns.

The Bears had laid waste to the 49ers and everyone else in their path except Miami. At this point, with Miami going against New England in the AFC Championship Game, the Bears were starting to salivate at the chance to complete the circle with a revenge demolition of the Dolphins in the Super Bowl.

But first there were other matters requiring attention.

Their wardrobe had indeed caught the attention of commissioner Pete Rozelle and the NFL, which was handing out fines for the headbands and other sartorial mischief. By now McMahon's headband was drawing as much attention as his play, and he had an eloquent answer planned for Rozelle.

In the locker room minutes before the Rams game, McMahon secured some plain white headbands and a marker and proceeded to write "Rozelle" on a couple of them. Payton saw him and got one for himself, and the two of them took their helmets off time after time during the game so the league and everybody else could see them. Rozelle was laughing.

"Guys were in the locker room, puking, taping up, getting ready for the game," broadcaster John Madden said, "and there's this guy McMahon just writing a name on his headband. It was hysterical."

Afterward, McMahon got a note from Rozelle, which Zucker had framed and put in McMahon's restaurant, thanking McMahon for making Rozelle famous. Rozelle had taken it well.

Dear Jim,

I was really upset yesterday with your headband because:

1—I didn't have my shoe model ready to sell so the promotion was useless.

2—I lost a little of what's left of my personal privacy.

It was funny as hell!!

You and your friends have done a tremendous job on the field and captivating the entire country. Looking forward to seeing you in New Orleans.

Regards,

Pete

The Bears already had taken care of the team from New York, a small measure of revenge for what the Mets had done to the Cubs in 1969, perhaps the greatest sports scar on any city outside of Boston at the time.

Now came Los Angeles, the city that was supplanting Chicago as the Second City, at least in population. And the Left Coast's cultural arrogance grated on Chicago, not to mention sizable chunks of the rest of the nation, so there was business to be done.

The first thing was to establish the appropriate sense of Armageddon. Ditka had the perfect idea.

"There are teams that are fair-haired, and there are teams that aren't," Ditka explained. "There are teams named Smith and teams named Grabowski. The Rams are Smiths. We're just Grabowskis."

The line was drawn. Ryan drew it even sharper and made it personal. "We're going to make Eric Dickerson fumble three times," the defensive coordinator declared. "He'll lay it on the ground for us."

This was a serious challenge. Dickerson, on his way to a Hall of Fame career, had devastated the Cowboys with 248 rushing yards, one of the great playoff performances of all time, while the Bears were disposing of the Giants. He had run for 1,808 and 2,105 yards in his first two NFL seasons, and even though he had slipped a little in 1985, he was still projected to break Payton's rushing records.

Dickerson was 6'3", 218 pounds, and partnered at SMU with Craig James (later with the Patriots) in the "Pony Express" backfield. Against Dallas he had run for 78 yards in a 3–0 first half, then erupted to easily shatter the previous postseason mark of 206 yards set in 1963 by Keith Lincoln of the San Diego Chargers.

Rams quarterback Dieter Brock, in his first NFL season, completed only 6 of 22 passes in the 20–0 mugging of the Cowboys. It did not matter. Dickerson scored from 55 yards out on the first play of the second half, then added a touchdown run of 40 yards in the fourth quarter, slicing through Dallas defenders Randy White and Ed "Too Tall" Jones as if they were tissue paper.

Added to that was a Rams defense that intercepted three passes, recovered three fumbles, and collected five sacks against Dallas. Three of the sacks were by rush specialist Gary Jeter, who then started the war of words with the Bears.

"We don't want those guys up there [at the Super Bowl]," Jeter said. "They talk too much."

The Bears had their own issues to settle with Dickerson. In the turnaround year of 1984, the week after the Bears made their violent statement in the landmark Raiders game, the Rams knocked the Bears around 29–13 in Los Angeles. Just as he had with Dallas, Dickerson had a respectable 50 yards in the first half, then turned a 13–6 Bears lead into shambles, finishing with 149 yards and two touchdowns while the Bears did nothing on offense. It was a game, however, in which neither Hampton nor McMichael had played, if the Rams cared to look a little closer.

Ryan's prediction on Dickerson was bold to the point of being insulting. The Rams responded to questions about their toughness by showing up for practice in freezing Chicago wearing shorts and T-shirts.

The night before the game, Rams coach John Robinson had dinner with Madden. Robinson asked Madden how good he thought the Bears were.

"They're the best I've ever seen," Madden told him.

"Well," Robinson said, "they haven't seen us yet."

CBS and Vegas legendary oddsmaker Jimmy the Greek picked the Rams.

Word got back to the Bears that the Rams were declaring that they were going to stomp the Bears and that Dickerson was strutting around saying that he could not wait to run against the Bears.

He should have waited.

Before the game, McMichael looked across the field and saw Rams defensive coordinator Fritz Shurmur, who had been with the Patriots a few years back when McMichael was drafted by New England.

"He's the f***er that cut me in New England," McMichael told Hampton.

> "Even 20 years later, I'll see Eric at charity events or wherever and he still remembers and brings up that game. 'I didn't do nothin' to y'all,' he'll say. 'Why'd you treat me like that?'"
>
> *—Otis Wilson*

In the fourth quarter, with the mighty Rams in shambles, Shurmur was on the sideline, waving to catch McMichael's attention and calling, "Steve, Steve."

McMichael gave him the finger.

That was more than the Bears gave Dickerson. The Los Angeles strongman ran 17 times and took home all of 46 yards against a new version of the 46 that Ryan concocted and which confounded the Rams, who were looking at Gary Fencik jumping up on the line across from the center and slashing in to drop Dickerson. The Rams finished with 130 yards—total—although Dickerson made a liar out of Ryan.

He lost only two fumbles, not three.

Hampton was asked when the Bears took control of the line of scrimmage. "Kickoff," he said.

When the Rams won the toss and chose to receive, Fencik applauded.

The Bears systematically took the Rams' hearts. McMahon ran in from 16 yards for the Bears' first score. Butler added a field goal, and it was 10–0 late in the first quarter when Dickerson took the handoff on third-and-one and headed over left guard. Singletary, who had felt Dickerson's power when the two faced off in college, was there.

"Mike hit him so hard, I don't think he knew where he was," Marshall said.

Neither did Brock. The Bears sacked the Rams quarterback three times, and he completed only 10 of 31 passes.

McMahon threw to Gault for a 22-yard touchdown in the third quarter, and the score stood 17–0 when Hollywood—the real one—wrote the final act to a game and a season.

Dent slashed in on Brock in the fourth quarter and knocked the ball loose. It bounded free on the ground for a moment. Wilson tried to pick it up first but was too eager to get running and dropped it. Marshall then grabbed the ball and a trip into Bears history.

Marshall gathered the ball in just on the Bears' side of midfield and headed for the Los Angeles end zone with Perry, Wilson, and others on escort duty. Suddenly, the snow started—snow that all were sure was George Halas' way of saying he was watching.

For the numerologists there was some symmetry too. The Rams had smashed the Cowboys 20–0 in the first round. The Bears beat the Rams 24–0. So the math says they should have been 44 points better than the Cowboys, which they were, 44–0 when they destroyed Dallas. Dickerson ran for 248 yards against the Cowboys. He had 46 against the "46."

There was some celebrating afterward, but it was mild. After all, this was not the game the Bears really wanted. That game was still two weeks away. Singletary was interviewed afterward on field by WLS' Les Grobstein.

"Champagne in the locker room now?" Grobstein asked.

"We got work to do," Singletary said simply. "We've got a ton of work to do. We're going to celebrate a little, and then we gotta get to work."

In the locker room there was emotion. Ditka had tears in his eyes as he drew on his cigar, collecting himself.

"I want to say, you guys accomplished something special today," Ditka began, then halted. "There's a poem. We've gone many miles but there's more to go before we can sleep. We've got a job to do. We're on a mission, but that mission won't be accomplished until we take care of business in New Orleans. Now take a few days off, but don't get too relaxed. Remember, we've got the big one coming up."

CHAPTER 13

THE CRAZIEST WEEK OF THEM ALL

"I thought I was in some Twilight Zone."

—Les Grobstein

FINALLY, THE BEARS WERE INDEED ON a stage with the whole world watching.

By this time national and international interest was reaching its zenith. The Super Bowl would draw the largest viewing audience of any television show in history—127 million. Not the biggest audience for a Super Bowl, the biggest ever for a TV show. *Any* show.

The November summit meeting between President Ronald Reagan and Soviet Premier Mikhail Gorbachev drew one thousand accredited media to cover the event. The Bears being in New Orleans attracted a press corps of twenty-five hundred, from all over the world. The *Chicago Tribune* sent 27 reporters, editors, and photographers. The *Boston Globe* was number two with 23, just edging out the *Chicago Sun-Times'* 22.

And the world was listening. The Bears were a living, breathing, nonstop sound byte.

The zaniness of that Super Bowl was apparent almost immediately. Wilson explained to reporters that the barking the guys on the defense were doing was "Woof," not "Arf." What did they think they were, anyway, Wilson mused, a bunch of Chihuahuas?

Wilson also let it out that he thought the Rams were better than the Patriots. As the week went on, he elaborated; he said he saw a goose egg, that the Bears would shut out the Patriots. That might have upset New England, but it was the truth. And the Patriots knew it.

"If we play our defense right, no one can run on us," Wilson said. "No bragging intended. I'm telling it like it is."

Wednesday Hampton was watching the major press conferences on television. Tony Eason, the New England starting quarterback, was on the screen, and Hampton could see fear in his eyes. He knew. They all knew.

"I know that some of the Patriots took offense at what we were saying," Fencik said. "They thought we felt superior to them. I guess now they know why we had reason to believe that."

The Patriots tried whistling past the graveyard. Cornerback Ronnie Lippett made a prediction. "I am quite sure our linebackers are going to get to [McMahon] and take him out," he said. "They won't go for his arm. They'll go for the head."

If they wanted to do some real damage, they needed to go for more of his anatomy than that.

ACUPUNCTURE

Much of Super Bowl week revolved around McMahon. Many people inside and outside the team thought he made it that way intentionally. Those close to him say otherwise. Besides, neither he nor anyone else could have scripted all that was about to happen.

Pat McCaskey, another one of the grandsons of George Halas and in charge of Bears PR before being relieved in 1984 and replaced by Ken Valdiserri, was in New Orleans and met McMahon's father before the Super Bowl.

"You should have given Jim more spankings," McCaskey said.

"I know," McMahon's father said.

The week began with McMahon in serious pain where he had been hit in the hip region while sliding during the Rams game. While the team practiced in Champaign, Illinois, Gault told McMahon that he was bringing over noted acupuncturist Hiroshi Shiriashi from Japan to help Gault deal with the nicks from a season in the NFL. Gault had developed a relationship with Hiroshi while running track around the world.

McMahon was in such pain on Monday that he needed help putting on socks. He went to Halas Hall in Lake Forest and got a treatment from Hiroshi that gave him some immediate relief, and he was looking forward to continuing that in New Orleans.

Michael McCaskey had other ideas. Ditka, Vainisi, and virtually everyone associated with the team wanted Hiroshi as part of the program in New Orleans. But when the team, Hiroshi included, got together Monday at O'Hare Airport for the trip to the Super Bowl, McCaskey said the acupuncturist was not coming along.

McMahon and others were livid. Gault had lobbied for Hiroshi and was told in no uncertain terms that he—McCaskey—was running the Chicago Bears. Nobody else.

The problem for McCaskey, however, was that an incensed McMahon was about to be given an international pulpit. And he was going to use it.

The first thing up for the Bears upon landing was a round of mass press gatherings at the Hilton. Ditka, Hampton, Singletary, and McMahon did the first round of interviews. Reporters asked, and McMahon vented. He told the entire story about how McCaskey had killed the treatment. Instantly McMahon's became the most scrutinized butt since George Brett's 1980 World Series hemorrhoids.

On Tuesday, matters came to a boil. McCaskey arrived in town, and McMahon left him in no doubt what he thought. In the meantime, the Illinois Acupuncture Association noted the furor and arranged to fly Hiroshi to New Orleans, whether or not the Bears paid for or wanted it.

At practice that afternoon a helicopter carrying a local news camera crew flew over. McMahon saw it, turned around, dropped his pants, and mooned the crew.

"Just showing them where it hurt," McMahon explained.

RESOLVING ISSUES

The question of whether or not Dent would play because of the contract concerns was being put to rest by the Colonel himself. He was not going to sit out the Super Bowl.

"I remember walking in the locker room and somebody gave me a newspaper and said, 'What's up with that?' 'With what?' I said. 'Says here you're not going to play.' But pretty soon guys are looking at you, thinking you're doing something selfish. I didn't want to hear that. I just wanted to do my job. So I felt like I had to go out at practice and kick ass because I could just see it in the headlines or guys' faces: 'Bears lose, Richard's fault.' So I went out and was all over the place in the Super Bowl."
–*Richard Dent*

The Patriots had health problems of their own but hardly with the panache of the Bears. Some of them came down with cases of the flu, with Eason catching it the worst and being unable to practice late in the week.

And they were not pleased at the national love affair with their opponents. "I don't understand it," guard Ron Wooten said. "We're America's team. The Patriots: red, white, and blue. They are the Russian mascot, the Bear. Who do you think President Reagan will be rooting for?"

His point was well taken. Hampton himself had volunteered after the destruction of Dallas that maybe the Bears were the Kremlin's team.

One annual Super Bowl rite is to chronicle the worst, most outrageous, or most whatever questions of the media. Now, however, the answers were far beyond anything the media could have come up with.

Ditka was asked to describe his relationship with McMahon.

"Strange and wonderful," Ditka said. "He's strange and I'm wonderful."

New Orleans is America's Paris, an endless spectrum of exquisite dining establishments. Perry, clearly the gourmand if not the gourmet, couldn't cite any one spot as his favorite.

"I don't notice names," Fridge said. "I just browse."

Naturally there was interest in what individual members of this character cluster planned to do after the season. "Cheese sculpting," Hampton said.

Headbands were taking on a life of their own, fueled by McMahon's scribbling "Acupuncture" on one for practice.

The Bears were doing their part to keep the French Quarter in business. "I know I was getting back at 2:00 and 3:00 in the morning," Thayer said.

> "We came in most nights about 1:00, 2:00, some guys at 4:00, 5:00. And I had a personal driver that I could get at any time. That was a good thing. In the Super Bowl I got a chance to play against my old buddy Steve Moore from Tennessee State. The Patriots had curfews, 12:00 or 1:00, and they couldn't do certain things. I told him, 'You guys are all uptight. We're going to enjoy ourselves.'"
> *—Richard Dent*

In the course of wanderings, a few met up with some Patriots and the talk got around to tickets and all the requests the players were getting.

"Well," said one Patriot, "at least we've got 30 so it'll work out."

"What?!" the Bears said at once. "Thirty?!"

The Bears organization had kept 10 of each player's tickets and given them only 20, not 30.

Worse from an internal PR standpoint, there were plans to bar former players from the post–Super Bowl party. That was finally resolved. What was ultimately done, however, was to shorten the party.

Tickets, of course, weren't the only things on people's minds at night.

HEADBANDING

Headbands were never far from the headlines and were now, in the wake of the "Rozelle" version, about to take on another life of their own.

The league had passed the "McMahon Rule" decreeing players were not allowed to wear unauthorized apparel. The mystery, however, was not whether McMahon would comply but rather how the NFL's ranking rebel would tweak the league.

By the time he got to New Orleans, McMahon was getting headbands from all over the country and beyond. He already had *Rolling Stone* magazine trailing him around, working on a cover story. This was just adding to the ambient hysteria.

Stores and souvenir stands were already selling all kinds of headbands before the team even got to town. Some were "Rozelle" headbands. Some were mailed to the Superdome. Some went to the hotel. Some had blinking lights. Some were fur. Many had names of one sort or another.

Zucker had another idea.

Zucker's son Herbie had diabetes; McMahon was close to the family and knew Herbie.

"You know Herbie and you could really do a lot for diabetes if you'd wear a 'Diabetes' headband," Zucker said. "You almost have to do a 'charity' headband because otherwise they're going to crucify you. This way, nobody can say anything."

McMahon, who privately raised thousands for charity, liked the idea and agreed. Zucker called the Juvenile Diabetes Foundation, which made a headband saying "JDF-Cure" and overnighted it to New Orleans. They managed to get it to somebody on a plane to New Orleans and also did a one-page statement as to what it meant. Zucker took the statement up to NBC's booth for the Super Bowl broadcast and made sure Dick Enberg and Merlin Olsen had the explanation so they would know what McMahon was doing.

Mary Tyler Moore, a diabetic and national spokesperson for JDF, was ecstatic because McMahon raised the awareness to a tremendous level and raised a lot of money for research in the

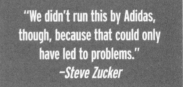

"We didn't run this by Adidas, though, because that could only have led to problems."
—Steve Zucker

process. McMahon and Zucker had turned a problem into a good—for McMahon, the NFL, and the fight against diabetes.

Adidas had given McMahon a lot of money to wear its headbands, plus a trip to Germany and France via the Concorde and a future contract. McMahon did not ask for anything from JDF.

McMahon had enough problems already.

"SLUTS"

Things went from wacky to truly bizarre on Thursday. Again McMahon was right where he liked to be—in the center of a media firestorm. But this one was different.

All the Chicago TV and radio stations were doing their shows or some parts of them from Bourbon Street that week. Les Grobstein was down doing

WLS-AM's 5:30–10:00 A.M. show with Fred Winston from Tony's House of Spaghetti, which served breakfast—which is great for those who like noodles for breakfast.

Everything was going fine, and Grobstein was doing his sportscast at 8:25 A.M. on Thursday. Then during a commercial break he got a call from one of the newscasters back in Chicago, Katherine Johns.

"What's with this McMahon story?" Johns asked.

"What McMahon story?" Grobstein asked.

The night before, a New Orleans DJ going by the name of "Boomer" was on for the 6:00–10:00 P.M. shift and got a call on the request line from some local claiming that McMahon had been on WLS's morning show from "some spaghetti place," broadcasting back in Chicago, slurring New Orleans women and men, calling the women sluts or whores and the men idiots. The caller even mentioned Grobstein as the one McMahon did this morning interview with.

Boomer hung up and didn't do anything at first. Then he got a second call, then more. At about 9:45, a newsman for one of the New Orleans stations, a man named Buddy Diliberto, called Boomer and said he was going to check it all out. Then, without checking anything out, Diliberto went on his 10:00 sports broadcast announcing that McMahon had said these things and suggesting that all the women of New Orleans should show up at Bears headquarters the next day with rolls of toilet paper to throw at McMahon. Sure enough, there were women outside the Hilton the next day with tons of toilet paper.

When Grobstein got the call from Johns, he had no idea what she was talking about; he had done no such McMahon interview. But New Orleans was inflamed. When he got the full story, the Grobber was flabbergasted. He was well connected, rarely slept for all of the circulating he was doing that week, and likely would have heard something about it if indeed it had ever happened. He also knew McMahon. He told Johns and the station it did not happen. It occurred to him to ask what time McMahon supposedly said this.

Johns told him it was 6:30 in the morning.

"No *way!*" Grobstein yelled. "There is no way on God's green Earth that McMahon got up that early and sure as hell not to talk to the media!"

But this was not long after McMahon mooned the helicopter, so the public was on the lookout for possible McMahon actions. Boomer had warned Diliberto to check the story out, and Diliberto did not, which confirmed that at least one man in New Orleans indeed was an idiot after all.

All the media outlets were carrying events like Ditka's news conferences live, interrupting regular programming during the day. Grobstein began setting up in the interview ballroom for his station's broadcast. Sports anchor Mark Giangreco from Channel 5 in Chicago came in and asked Grobstein to come on the air. Giangreco brought his crew over and asked Grobstein about the story.

"Nothing happened," Grobstein told Giangreco. But with this team, anytime nothing happened, even that was news. Grobstein kept saying it was a nonstory. Except that all of a sudden, the Grobber was a story himself.

The Giangreco crew shut its lights off and Grobstein saw dozens of writers standing by, taking notes and quotes, wanting to be sure who Grobstein was. Anchorman Jim Rose from Chicago's Channel 7 came over.

> "I thought I was in some Twilight Zone."
> *—Les Grobstein*

"I gotta get you next," Rose said, waving his crew into position. Then Johnny Morris from Channel 2 came in, doing the on-location work for his then-wife Jeannie; then came WGN, a New Orleans station, CNN, ESPN, and a Rockford, Illinois, station.

By this time Ditka had come in. He had perhaps a dozen reporters around him. Singletary had some. Hampton had some. Grobstein had probably 300 around him. So there it was, the Thursday Bears news conference, days before the Super Bowl, and Les Grobstein was the man of the hour.

Joe Mooshil, the legendary Associated Press writer, ambled over to Grobstein, his usual huge cigar in his mouth, and said he had to ask Grobstein some questions. The Grobber just started to laugh.

"What's so funny, ya' silly cocksucker?" Mooshil growled in one of the great gravel voices of all time. "Moosh" was one of Grobstein's idols, and from Mooshil, "silly cocksucker" was a term of endearment.

"This has to be killing you," Grobstein said, "getting quotes from me."

The Bears' team office was set up there and got a call from some disgruntled native.

"Y'all bettuh git outta thayuh 'cuz I'm gunna blow that place skah-hah and get that Mack-Ma'n guy, blow his ass clear intuh Lake Pontchatrain," the caller snarled, in one of the more notable and articulate bomb and death threats of the week.

Zucker was walking with the Adidas folks, discussing headband strategies. Someone ran up to him and told him about the incident—that McMahon was in his room and people were picketing the hotel, phones were ringing, and everything was out of control.

Zucker ran back to the hotel and into the lobby, where he saw Vainisi, who was fuming. The only ones besides Grobstein and Zucker who believed McMahon did not make the offending comments appeared to be Ditka. Zucker went up to McMahon's room and told him he should get downstairs and deal with everything.

"F*** 'em," McMahon steamed. "I'm not talking to anybody. I've been accused of all kinds of bad stuff that I didn't do and now this. I do enough bad things; now I don't do something, and they're crucifying me."

Zucker persisted. "You have got to talk to the press. Come with me."

McMahon wasn't convinced, but he trusted Zucker and went down on the elevator with him. Zucker arranged for McMahon to be at the big podium in the ballroom instead of at a table, which was where most of the players sat. This was too big for one table. The press was interviewing Bears all over the hotel, but when Zucker announced that McMahon would be available in five minutes, the stampede was on and the room filled up. McMahon went to the podium.

"I didn't do it," he said, confronting the whole situation. "Anybody who knows me knows I'm not up at 6:30 in the morning."

Well, that was true. But ironically, McMahon *had* said it, just not publicly. So had other Bears. Women in fact were trolling for Bears all week, some ticking off the ones they'd "done."

Grobstein then was summoned to a private meeting at the hotel and saw Bill McGrane, one of the top Bears officials, with a very serious look on his face. McGrane motioned Grobstein over to a secluded area that is posted as off-limits to everyone not authorized.

Inside sat some NFL heavies: information directors Pete Abitante and Dick Maxwell; Paul Tagliabue, then Rozelle's right-hand man; security people; Ed and Michael McCaskey; and Kenny Valdiserri. They started grilling Grobstein.

> "No 'accused' about it. He did. He just said it somewhere else. Lotta guys did. Women were throwing themselves at us. Then the death threats started and nobody would stand next to Jim at practice."
> *–Otis Wilson*

"Are you *sure* he didn't say it?" they asked Grobstein.

"Not only am I sure he didn't say it," Grobstein answered, "but the interview didn't even happen! As far as I know, McMahon has never been in that spaghetti house the whole time we were there."

Finally they let Grobstein go and he went back to his room where there were 20 more messages. Then the *Boston Globe* ran a column about the whole crazy business, asking, "Who's this 'Les'?"

Diliberto went on to do Saints pre- and postgame shows. He was suspended for two weeks after apologizing to everybody, and then he came back a celebrity. More than

> "I'm convinced that McCaskey privately wanted McMahon to screw up and be guilty, because those two didn't like each other."
> *–Les Grobstein*

just the players were the centers of attention at this Super Bowl.

Grobstein never spoke to McMahon again until the next training camp. Then McMahon came up to Grobstein and thanked him for what he had done and how he had handled it.

"You're OK," McMahon said, one of the only nice things anyone can remember McMahon ever saying to anybody in the media.

GOOD-BYE, BUDDY

All four Bears defensive linemen made the 1985 All-Madden team, a tongue-in-cheek all-star team picked by the NFL's foremost color commentator. Perry of course made it as a running back. Perry also made it as a wide receiver. McMahon made it, too, and shared the quarterback "honor" with Joe Montana. Covert and Hilgenberg made the offensive-line group. All three linebackers were All-Madden. Fencik and Frazier were All-Madden defensive backs. Butler, whom McMahon had tried unsuccessfully to con into wearing a "McMahon" jersey at practice with the death threats flying, was the All-Madden kicker.

As the week wound on, an advanced headband strategy was forming beyond even the diabetes issue. McMahon ultimately prepared headbands honoring and remembering American prisoners of war and missing in action with "POW-MIA." He made one up with "Pluto" in honor of close friend Danny Plater, with whom McMahon had played at BYU and who had been diagnosed with a brain tumor that ended his college football career.

Children's hospitals and the United Way also were designated 'band honorees. McMahon enlisted Gary Haeger, one of the Bears' equipment assistants, to keep the headbands during the game, and McMahon switched them off and on, with suitable TV exposure for each.

On Friday it was time to do the *Mike Ditka Show*. Two cars left from the Bears' hotel, which was the Hilton on Poydras Avenue. One car contained Ditka and Johnny and Jeannie Morris; the other carried Payton, who was Ditka's guest that night on the show, and Bob Vasilopolous, with Vasilopolous driving. The show was going to run live.

Payton and Vasilopolous were in the first car, driving down Poydras. They were making some of the lights and suddenly Payton, from the passenger's seat, reached his left leg over and stomped on Vasilopolous' foot, ramming the gas pedal to the floor. They began hurtling down Poydras approaching 100 miles per hour, blowing red lights until a crowded intersection loomed not far ahead.

Vasilopolous, determined not to show fear in front of Payton, let it go and just tried to control the car. But the intersection was seriously dangerous. He started punching Payton in the thigh, and Payton started laughing like a madman as he took his foot back.

"You were scared, weren't you?" Payton said, howling.

"Walter," Vasilopolous said, trying not to hyperventilate, "can you imagine what would have happened to me or my family if something happened to you just before the Super Bowl?"

They drove at a respectable speed the rest of the way to the Superdome and got out of the car. Ditka and the Morrises had caught up by then. Ditka burst out of his car.

"What the f*** were you doing?!" he raged at the pair.

"Just ask your running back," Vasilopolous said.

"I don't know," Payton said, innocently. "I didn't do nothin'. He just started drivin' like a crazy man!"

Amid all of this, the Bears were preparing for the Super Bowl. They may have been living the "Shuffle," but they knew exactly why they were in New Orleans, and the occasional circus was hardly going to divert them from a course that had been set a year earlier on a plane ride home from San Francisco.

As he had in Dallas, Ditka chose to go light in his last meeting with the team. He came in with a salute to the madness, particularly McMahon, wearing sunglasses and a headband, and talked about the insanity of the previous week, the acupuncture. Then he abruptly turned, dropped his pants, and mooned the team. The players roared.

The closest thing to a true distraction for the team was a cloud that was forming but which not all of the Bears knew was there. Whispers were everywhere that

> "Buddy didn't tell us, any of us, before the end that he was leaving. He didn't even tell Samurai. And for a long time that hurt some of us. I know it had to hurt Samurai. But now I know why. I wasn't mature enough, a lot of us weren't, and he was thinking, 'C'mon, man, I need you at your best.'"
> —*Dan Hampton*

Ryan was going to leave to coach the Philadelphia Eagles after the Super Bowl.

Ryan all but told them he was leaving in their last meeting the night before the game. In fact, however, he had confided his plans only to Fencik, no one else.

At the meeting, they went over the game plan for the final time. Then Ryan stopped. There were tears in his eyes and running down his cheeks when he told his defensive players, "Whatever happens, I want you to know you're my heroes."

Hampton said they'd seen enough damn film, and he knocked a reel off the projector and sent the projector flying off the table. McMichael went one better, picking up a chair and throwing it so its legs stuck through the blackboard.

It was time.

CHAPTER 14

A GAME LIKE NO OTHER

"The only real chance the Patriots had was if we got so wrapped
up in the nonsense and forgot to show up."

—*Dan Hampton*

WHILE THE BEARS WERE "SHUFFLING" to their January 26 ren-
dezvous with destiny, America was flexing its muscles as well. Reagan was
standing up to Libyan dictator and terrorism-backer Murammar Khadafy—
freezing Libya's assets, ordering Americans out of that country, locking
down economic sanctions, and sending a naval task force to do maneuvers
in the Mediterranean.

Reagan did not bother with diplomatic niceties. He simply said that the
fleet was there to "demonstrate U.S. resolve." America was mad as hell and
wasn't going to take it anymore. America was woofing.

Down at Cape Canaveral, Florida, Christa McAuliffe, a high school teacher
from Concord, New Hampshire, who had been chosen to take a ride in space,
was busy making final preparations with the crew that would fly Tuesday on
the *Challenger* space shuttle.

But there was time amid those preparations for a Super Bowl. The Super
Bowl is America's sports Mardi Gras, and Super Bowl Sunday is the biggest
national party day of the year outside of New Year's Eve. Nobody was going
to miss this one.

Not the glitterati that had become fixtures in the Bears' entourage: Michael
and the Jacksons, Don Johnson, the movie stars, the TV stars. Shaun Gayle
ended up in a limousine with Vanna White and some other people after the
team's Super Bowl party, having no idea who or how.

> "The audience just seemed to keep calling for more. We gave it to them. After the shutouts against the Giants and Rams, the Super Bowl was just about settling on a score. The result wasn't a question. We knew it. They knew it. The only things that could screw it up were us. By that time the hoopla was getting so insane, between the endorsements and everything else, that the only real chance the Patriots had was if we got so wrapped up in the nonsense and forgot to show up."
> *—Dan Hampton*

Not the stars of the first 19 Super Bowls. The league brought the MVPs of the previous games to New Orleans and introduced them at a pregame ceremony.

There was already some particularly nice Super Bowl karma for the Bears. Pat had met his wife Gretchen on Super Bowl Sunday 1983. Exactly nine months after Super Bowl XX, they were blessed with a son, who "reported" two days early. Said McCaskey: "I thought it showed good initiative."

The affair turned out to be everything most thought it would be and more.

"We just kicked the door in and said, 'We're here! Let's rumble!'" Wilson said.

JANUARY 26, 1986, SUPER BOWL XX—NEW ENGLAND PATRIOTS, NEW ORLEANS SUPERDOME

Rumble indeed. What transpired was a blizzard of "never-befores"—the culmination of everything that had led to this moment.

The Patriots gained only seven yards rushing—a record. The Bears sacked New England quarterbacks seven times. The Bears set records (since broken) for point total (46) and winning margin (36).

Dent was voted the game's Most Valuable Player, although there were opinions that the vote was a case of the media taking its chance to show McMahon some of the contempt that he had shown them. The Colonel forced two fumbles, collected 1½ sacks, and was in so many tackles that it was difficult to keep an accurate count. McMahon scored two touchdowns and completed 12 of 20 passes for 256 yards. For the third straight playoff game, he was not intercepted.

Wilson had two sacks. New England finished with 123 net yards. The Patriots' starting quarterback, Tony Eason, ran 15 plays before he was taken out. Only one of those gained yardage. "The look in his eyes said, 'I hope we're not in for another one of these,'" Singletary said.

There was a brief spasm of unpleasantness. On the second play of the game, Payton took a handoff from McMahon and was hit immediately. The ball came loose, and the Patriots recovered at the Chicago 19.

An instantaneous, anguished gasp took the breath away from Bears faithful no matter where they were. After three incompletions, the Patriots kicked a field goal and became the first opponent to beat the Bears to the scoreboard since Miami.

> "When the Patriots scored first on Walter's fumble, I know everybody got that little pang, like, 'Uh-oh, here we go again!' And what primed us for that was the Miami game on *Monday Night Football*. It proved they weren't indestructible, so you knew it could happen. And after all, this was Chicago."
> *–Joe Mantegna*

But this was not the typical Chicago team. Kevin Butler squared matters with a field goal after McMahon unsheathed the Gault sword and struck for a 43-yard gain down the right sideline. That the drive didn't produce a touchdown did not matter. Events had been set in motion, and the timer on the bomb was ticking for the Patriots.

New England called three more pass plays; two throws went incomplete, and then Marshall and Wilson blitzed to sack Eason, who was clearly beginning to show signs of panic.

With good reason.

Patriots coach Ray Berry had seen how New York and Los Angeles fared on the ground, and he wanted to use passes to get the Bears' attention right away. Instead, they got his.

Two plays into New England's second possession, Dent blew past left tackle Brian Holloway and stripped the ball, which Hampton recovered at the New

England 13. Ditka had decided he did not much like the Patriots, so on second-and-goal from the New England 5, he sent in the play: halfback option pass by Perry. Fridge brought thousands out of their seats in the Superdome and millions out of their chairs at home as he took the pitchout from McMahon and looked for tight end Emery Moorehead.

There was no Moorehead, but Patriots nose tackle Dennis Owens was there, bringing down Perry to become the first player to sack a defensive tackle in a Super Bowl.

Another Butler field goal, 6–3.

Over on the Bears' sideline, offensive line coach Dick Stanfel, the Most Valuable Player on the 1953 Detroit Lions' NFL championship team, knew it was over. Indoors or not, no-smoking ordinance or not, Stanfel lit up a victory cigarette.

Finally a Patriot run. Craig James right at Dent. Bad idea. James found out exactly what his former SMU "Pony Express" backfield mate Dickerson did two weeks earlier. Dent knocked the ball loose, and Singletary recovered again at the 13. This time, the Bears finished. Suhey for 2 yards, then for 11 behind Van Horne for the touchdown, 13–3.

There was blood in the water now. Hampton ended the next New England possession with another tackle in the Patriots' backfield. McMahon then scored, 20–3.

"NOW WHAT?"

Three more Patriots pass plays: no gain, 2 yards lost, 11-yard sack of Eason by Wilson and McMichael. In the New England huddle, one lineman turned to All-Pro guard John Hannah and said, "OK, we can't run. We can't pass. Now what?"

Then: disaster. Bears cornerback Leslie Frazier, who had never returned an NFL punt, went into the game as part of the punt-return team. He took a handoff on a reverse and suffered a knee injury that ended the career of the 46 defense's best pass defender.

Ditka was criticized for putting Frazier in for the punt. But Frazier was not someplace he did not want to be. The idea was to give Frazier the reverse so he would have a chance to score. He was not inserted against his wishes. He wanted to be out there.

Finally, with four minutes left in the half, it happened: New England made a first down. One. For the half. Then another Butler field goal, 23–3 at halftime.

It was a half of running uphill into cliffs for New England. The Bears had sacked Eason three times, and the Patriots quarterback missed on all six of the passes he did manage to get off before he was pulled with 5:08 to play and replaced by Steve Grogan. On their first nine plays, covering four possessions, the Patriots lost 22 yards and the ball twice on fumbles.

The play that gained the New England first down was the Patriots' 18ᵗʰ and only the 3ʳᵈ to gain any yards. The Patriots had -19 yards of offense, -5 rushing, -14 passing. All were Super Bowl records for a half.

Worse perhaps, at halftime, huge portions of the crowd of 73,818 stood up and belted out "The Super Bowl Shuffle." If there was ever a home-field advantage for a Super Bowl, the Bears had it now.

The Bears allowed 132 yards for the game and would easily have broken the Pittsburgh Steelers' record of 119, but Ryan trotted out the second teamers—"F Troop," as he called them—for most of the fourth quarter when New England gained 37 yards.

The only points scored by the New England offense in the first half came on a zero-yardage drive. The Patriots' only touchdown drive did not come until early in the fourth quarter, against Bears backups, and it accounted for 7 of their 12 first downs for the game.

"I'm not embarrassed," said Patriots guard Ron Wooten afterward. "I'm humiliated."

The day was not all Bears defense. The offense was about to set a Super Bowl record with 21 points in the third quarter, beginning with another McMahon-to-Gault long lance. Starting from their 4 after a New England punt, McMahon heaved the ball to Gault, who would have turned in a 96-yard

> "This was the early days of VCRs, so I started mine going at something like 10:00 that morning, and I really didn't want to watch. I would pop in and out of the room, watch a little bit, but knowing it was being taped, I ducked back out. Same thing during the game; I could not watch the whole game. I just wanted it to be over and say YES! WE DID IT! I could not bring myself to join the ranks of those in bars and at parties, living and dying on every play. I was like a little kid with horror movies. There was a little boy who would hide in his parents' bedroom and stick his head out from this place of safety and peek at the TV. Or he would hold a mirror up and watch in the mirror. That's the way I felt about the Bears in that game. When they won and it was all done, I started screaming and then, only then, did I start calling everybody. And Bears fans like me understand that. You want to enjoy it but you want to be safe too and not ruin it."
> *–Joe Mantegna*

touchdown but for having to slow down to catch the ball out near midfield. McMahon's second touchdown of the game started the bloodletting again.

Enberg and Olsen, NBC's game announcers, were pouting, ex-Ram Olsen perhaps because of the dismemberment the Bears had performed on his old team two weeks earlier. NBC also was the AFC's network, so Enberg and Olsen were hoping the Patriots would do more than just show up, if only to keep viewers interested. Instead, the Patriots were sparring partners. But the Bears were the heavyweight champions, and few TV sets were clicking off, regardless of the score.

At one point the Patriots snapped the ball and all Enberg said was, "Here they come again." In the third quarter the broadcasting great mumbled, "If it was a prizefight, they'd have to stop it."

If it was a prizefight, they never would have scheduled it in the first place.

Not every fan was riveted to a TV to hear Enberg's lament, though.

NO WALTER TD

By the fourth quarter, even Perry had scored to bring the score to 44–3. Perry's touchdown, like the Frazier knee injury, would be the subject of controversy and second-guessing long after the game was history.

By that time in the game, McMahon and Ditka knew the starters' time in the game was virtually at an end, and they knew that Payton, the franchise's greatest player, deserved his moment. Yet neither made the call, even though Payton was on the field when Perry burst into the end zone for the Bears' final touchdown. Ditka sent the call in for the ball to go to Perry; McMahon, however uncharacteristically this one time, did not change the play.

Fittingly, perhaps, as Perry was tumbling to the ground after his run, Payton was one of those with his arms raised, celebrating even this meaningless score by his team.

> "I couldn't enjoy the Super Bowl because they let Fridge score and not Walter. After all that buildup, the game was such an anticlimax. And then Walter looked so glum after the game. It was a first for Chicago, a foregone conclusion, and everything was sitting there for Walter to be honored."
> —*Mike Hartenstine*

AFTERMATH

As the seconds ticked away, members of the defense sought out McCaskey on the sideline to plead with him to keep Ryan as the head of the defense, to make it worth his while to stay. McCaskey had no interest in anything but being seen at this climactic moment as the head of the Bears. He brushed off the players with platitudes that left them irritated. They knew he would do nothing to keep Ryan.

Accordingly, they then got to Ryan and, while Ditka was being hoisted onto the shoulders of players that included McMichael and Perry, Hampton and Wilson gave Ryan a matching ride of coronation. They would have been pleased to know that a number of Bears front-office executives were appalled to see Ryan so celebrated.

In the locker room afterward, McCaskey was hugging the trophy as if it were one of his children and nobody could get it away from him. Fortunately, with all the drinking and celebrating, eventually he had to use the bathroom.

He put the trophy down in the men's room and instantly it was grabbed. Disappeared. McCaskey was frantic.

One of the other McCaskeys—not all of the numerous brothers got along and there was real acrimony among some—had plucked it and headed off behind some curtains so he could have some pictures taken with his own family and the trophy. Meanwhile, Michael went on searching desperately.

Secure behind the curtain, the brief private photo shoot went off without interruption. The other McCaskey finally poked his head out from behind the curtain. One of the young backup players was walking by.

"Hey," the pilfering McCaskey whispered, gesturing the player over and looking around to see if Michael was anywhere close. "Do you know me?"

"No," the player said.

"Good!" McCaskey said as he thrust the trophy through the curtain, handed it to the player, and ducked back behind the curtain.

Other of the postgame activities were not so amusing. Players began arguing over the "Super Bowl Champion" hats in the locker room, which were free but were also a prized souvenir of the moment. Some thought the supply got curiously short quickly and said McCaskey had had a couple boxes taken away for his private stock. In any case, with the millions of dollars being made every day by and surrounding this team, a battle was joined over free hats.

To Hilgenberg and many others, that was the first clue that the Bears would never be back.

Hats were not the only thing missing.

Payton had locked himself in a storage closet under the Superdome, alone. He was fuming. After the most dominant game in Super Bowl history, one of history's greatest players was so upset that he would have nothing to do with the celebration, revelry, media, well-wishers, and hysteria of the locker room.

The reason: nearing the end of his storied career, which finished two seasons later, Payton had been one of the few Bears not given a chance at a touchdown in this, the climactic hour of his Hall of Fame career. The Fridge had scored, McMahon had run for two touchdowns, but not Payton, the one

> "I'm not sure that it was a selfish anger or depression as much as he was just mad at his own performance. On the biggest stage of all, he had 61 yards. They had keyed on him. Walter didn't score a single touchdown in any of the three playoff games. His rushing totals of 93 yards against New York, 32 against Los Angeles, and 61 in the Super Bowl against New England. It was probably the worst three-game run of his career."
> —*Ken Valdiserri*

player who had kept the franchise interesting for a decade. Equally disappointing was that the three epic playoff games were three of the worse all season for Payton. The Giants, Rams, and Patriots had built their game plans around stopping Payton.

But he never was entirely stopped, certainly not then. Payton was refusing to come out for the interviews and the rest of the Mardi Gras of sport. Finally Bill McGrane, Ken Valdiserri, and a few others talked him into coming out, and the secret of his anger was kept hidden.

It truly was about more than just the no-touchdown slight. Payton's anger was born of frustration. The night before the Super Bowl, he had told the team that this was the game he had been trying to reach his entire life. Then to have it turn out like this. . . .

Payton did not make much of it in the years that followed. He said all the right things, that his career was about more than scoring a touchdown in a Super Bowl. So he said he was past it.

The culmination of a historic career that was now on its downside, the highest-profile game of his career, had been a disappointment. He wanted to win a Super Bowl. Then in the first series, through no direct fault of his own, he fumbled the ball and the opponent scored first. Then to be passed over and to have the playoff games be three of his worst all season in terms of yards gained . . .

The darkest suspicions in sections of the team were that both Ditka and McMahon were determined not to be upstaged by Payton at this, their own personal climactic moments. Ditka called Payton the greatest Bear. McMahon, who always had complete mastery and grasp of game situations, had defied Ditka to get Payton his needed 100-rushing yards even in the loss at Miami. For both to have overlooked Payton at that moment in history seemed more than chance to some. Had Payton scored a couple of touchdowns, he was a virtual sentimental lock to be the Super Bowl MVP and the game would have been remembered as Payton's, not Ditka's, McMahon's, or anyone else's.

Payton was not alone in feeling some personal pain at the moment that should have been one of life's greatest. For Van Horne it was the highest point of his professional career and the lowest in his personal life. His father had died the week before the Rams game. "That's why I wish we would have gone back and won another, because I would have been able to enjoy it," he said. "I was just kind of in a trance."

The Friday back before the Bears opened the season against Tampa Bay, Ryan had gone on Coppock's radio show. Coppock asked him whether, because he never got Todd Bell and Al Harris, the defense was still a work in progress.

Ryan instead gave Duerson a nasty review.

"You want to know how bad Duerson is?" Ryan said. "If Todd Bell shows up tomorrow, I'm going to start him on Sunday."

Ryan spent a lot of that season making life miserable for Duerson, even though Duerson had been voted to the Pro Bowl as a rookie and would go on to win a second Super Bowl ring with the New York Giants. On the night of the Super Bowl party, when all should have been rejoicing and enjoying, Ryan walked over and found Duerson and his wife, Alicia.

"I want you to know," Ryan said, "that if Todd Bell had been here, I still would have played him instead of you."

Alicia Duerson had had enough: "Why don't you just shut up!"

Chicago wasn't shutting up. Expressways into downtown were clogged as people headed for Rush Street and every other street. The city seemed to be hosting one giant party. The next day, more than a half-million celebrators lined LaSalle Street in subzero weather for the parade. Mayor Harold Washington renamed the Daley Civic Center "Bears Plaza" for the day and said he had a city street all picked out to be renamed "George S. Halas Drive."

The party went on most of the night, at locations untold. The next morning, Coppock did his last *Ditka Show*. Coppock opened up the show with a trademark long soliloquy about how this moment belonged to Nagurski, Luckman, Halas all the greats. And he finally asked Ditka, "Coach, this was so decisive, so overwhelming. At what point did you feel you had to call off the dogs?"

Ditka had had several hours to become thoroughly overserved: "I don't think much of those guys to begin with. When they started comparing themselves to us, they're lucky I didn't run the score up to 60!"

CHAPTER 15

LIVING THE BIG CRAZY

"I felt like I was at a Tom Jones concert. Any minute
I expected to see panties flying up on stage."

—Chet Coppock

THE SUPER BOWL WAS HISTORY. So were the Bears. They would go
14–2 in 1986, set an NFL record (since broken) for fewest points allowed
even without Ryan, and still, it was over. Bit by bit, one management decision, one game, one injury, one blowup at a time, it had begun its inexorable
slide toward the end.

The fall was gradual at first, almost imperceptible, like a single brick falling
out of a wall, then a while later, another. But it had begun. Whether in a
squabble over free hats, a contract dispute, jealousy over an endorsement, the
bricks had begun loosening.

And yet only the Bears could make their demise nearly as memorable as
their ascent. In the afterglow of the Super Bowl, they were at their apogee.
Nine of them went off to the Pro Bowl in Hawaii. Between television's
demands and an endless stream of advertising spots, their national presence
was never higher. Their international profile would reach staggering levels as
the NFL staged its first-ever game overseas, sending the Bears to London in
August to play the Dallas Cowboys.

Soon after the Super Bowl, history suddenly supplied a tragic metaphor for
what was to happen to the Bears.

Tuesday morning, as the horrified world watched and sat in spirit alongside
Christa McAuliffe, the *Challenger* space shuttle exploded 74 seconds after
leaving the launchpad at Cape Canaveral. America's best and brightest went
down in flames.

The Bears shared in the emotional and spiritual devastation that swept the country.

But before the downfall, the Bears had their victory parade down LaSalle Street, eventually coming to a complete stop as fans mobbed the bus, the team inside behind closed doors and windows. McMichael decided the fans deserved better. He opened the hatch in the roof of the bus, and he and a few of the Bears popped out as the crowd roared.

In the frigid weather, bottles of liquor were enjoyed in the crowd, and some were tossed up to McMichael, who took drinks and then threw them back to the people. Not surprisingly, when his turn to speak came, Mongo gave the people a show: "That's right, Chicago," he bellowed, "we got f***in' bragging rights over the whole goddamn country now!"

> "I remember going up to Halas Hall and sitting in my locker, the TV on, and watching that shuttle blow up. That just ended it, the end of the celebration, and I had a feeling that maybe more than that was ending. We weren't invited to the White House. I just saw Bill Belichick going for the second time with George Bush; I didn't get there with Reagan the first."
> —*Gary Fencik*

REAPING REWARDS

The Bears had more than just bragging rights. Right after the Super Bowl, *Advertising Age*, the bible of the ad business, assessed the commercial outlook for the Super Bowl Bears. They went through McMahon, Payton, Ditka, Gault, Ryan, and of course Fridge. McMahon, they thought, was too much of a smart-ass to do much nationally. Taco Bell, Coke, Honda scooters, Revo sunglasses, and others thought otherwise.

In the McMahon section of the story, *Ad Age* quoted none other than Doug Flutie, Heisman Trophy winner, quarterback of the USFL's New Jersey Generals, and everybody's pet. Eventually, as fate would have it, Ditka's.

"I admire [McMahon] for standing up and saying what he feels," Flutie told *Ad Age*. "This is something I would like to do every now and then, but

I guess I'm a little afraid of the ramifications. In Jim's case, I don't think he cares."

To the Bears, that was the Flutie they would come to know: the politician. When Flutie got to Chicago, he found out how much McMahon really did not care, especially about him.

Ditka did an American Express commercial in front of the polar bears at Brookfield Zoo not long after the Super Bowl. A Chicago clothier provided a wardrobe that was a long way from his customary sweaters and sideline wear, and he launched his restaurant operations with Ditka's and City Lights in the city's chic Near North area.

> "To me, football was something that allowed me to do a lot of things for myself, for my family, let me put my mother on her first flight to Hawaii. She never flew before in her life. That was 1986, right after the Super Bowl. She wouldn't go to the Super Bowl because the seats were so high. She didn't like being so high up, going up escalators for seats. If anything I could do over, I wish I could've made it to the parade. I went to bed at 4:00 after the Super Bowl and had to do *Good Morning, America* at 6:00, then had a flight at 8:30–9:00 to Hawaii, and was nervous about my mom."
> *–Richard Dent*

Amid the dizzying spiral, however, some of the Bears were seeing some of their most personal dreams realized as well.

Backup quarterback Tomczak opened T 'n T's pub out on the South Side with Thayer. Fencik was part of the attraction at the aptly named Hunt Club. As Ryan prepared to leave for Philadelphia, he wrote a letter to each member of the team. Fencik framed his and hung it above the urinal in the Hunt Club.

Butler had an interest in a restaurant. Payton's 34 restaurant out in Schaumburg had spectacular ribs and frequently Walter himself on the dance floor.

But resentment over the dollars and exposure was simmering. Ditka, McMahon, and Perry were turning requests away while others felt they were being overlooked, especially for television. Ditka, McMahon, and Singletary all had book deals in the works. McMahon's all but assured his eventual departure from Chicago several years later. His attack on McCaskey, with McCaskey still draping himself with Super Bowl adulation, was scathing and not something McCaskey forgot or forgave.

Dealing with McCaskey was not helping the players' dispositions either.

Super Bowl rings typically cost somewhere between $5,000 and $10,000, depending on each team's own unique design. The NFL paid half, the team paid half, and the team's board decided, in a judicious manner, how much the rings would cost. The Bears' committee consisted of Michael McCaskey, Ditka, Ed McCaskey, and Payton.

The Bears went with the bare minimum. McCaskey explained it with accountantlike precision: "Oh, we plan on going and getting a lot more of them, so we want to have money to buy more."

Oil was selling for $15 a barrel at that point. McCaskey was not the only thing that was relatively cheap.

Not only the Bears were prospering from the popularity wave that was sweeping over the country. In the year from the time the Bears started exploding on America, Coppock picked up thousands of dollars just doing the voice-overs for commercials like Perry's for McDonald's or Kevin Butler's for Merlin Mufflers.

In February, Coppock was enlisted to emcee the Bears' portion of a Caribbean cruise that would include Emery and Leslie Moorehead, Shaun Gayle, and Stefan Humphries—Bears, but not the megastars.

On the boat they found that word had spread:

"There are Bears on board!"

"Bears?"

"Yes, *Chicago* Bears!"

Throngs lined up along the pier to say good-byes to their friends and families, then scanned the ship with binoculars searching for Bears.

The trip called for several sessions of football talk that all assumed would provide a small diversion for those on the tour. Instead, the turnout was so huge the event had to be moved from the small salon expected to be sufficient to the grand ballroom. People from New Orleans, Edmonton, Paris, and all over the world were lined up hoping to get in to see real *Chicago* Bears.

> "I felt like I was at a Tom Jones concert. Any minute I expected to see panties flying up on stage."
> *–Chet Coppock*

Coppock brought out Gayle first— handsome, young, bright—and the women started swooning. And, of course, woofing.

Moorehead came up, sheepish, and opened with a preemptive public-service announcement.

"I'd like to remind everyone that my wife Leslie is here in the front row," Moorehead said.

When they reached Cabo San Lucas, the group tried parasailing. Moorehead was 150 feet up when the rope broke and he came crashing down into the water. He immediately waved that he was OK and was brought over to the beach.

"Everything's fine, everything seems to be where it belongs," he said, checking his arms and legs. Then he stopped. "But I lost my watch."

His $18,000 Rolex watch, as a matter of fact. Instantly there were 50 young Mexican boys flying into the water and out to hunt for the missing timepiece.

McMahon was continuing his help for research on juvenile diabetes, now with far more than just a headband. He appeared at a special benefit wearing a tuxedo and sneakers. Jim Belushi was there; comedian Tom Dreesen was there. With McMahon, the JDF could not have done better if it had gotten Ronald Reagan.

WRESTLEMANIA II

In April, while Clint Eastwood was being elected mayor of Carmel, California, and Reagan was bombing Libya, wrestling's legendary Vince McMahon turned to the Bears in what would be the true launching of the wrestling craze of the eighties.

The event was Wrestlemania II, a three-site extravaganza that would play out in New York, Chicago, and Los Angeles—appropriate, considering the Bears' path of destruction in the playoffs.

The centerpiece was a "Battle Royale," a match with a dozen wrestlers, including world heavyweight champion Andre the Giant and other wrestling characters, in the ring for an over-the-top-rope donnybrook: last man in the ring wins.

Covert picked up $35,000 for the extravaganza. Perry was paid $150,000. Ironically, the event did not sell out; later research revealed that thousands thought there was simply no chance whatsoever of getting tickets to a function with Perry, so they did not bother trying.

The night before there was a rehearsal at the Rosemont Horizon. At the rehearsal, Perry was the show. Vince McMahon was giving his spiel at the press conference. Coppock asked McMahon, "Vince, regarding the pay Fridge, if—"

Perry jumped in, completely in wrestling character.

"It's not about money!" Perry declared. "I want my piece of John Studd! They say he's never been pinned before? I'm going to pin him! I'm going to pin Andre the Giant! I'm going to throw them over the top rope! This isn't about money! It's about *wrestling!*"

Covert would joke that he got $35,000 for 30 seconds. He was tossed over the top rope by a journeyman named King Tonga. The gimmick with Perry was to have him get tossed out of the ring and then extend his hand to whomever tossed him. Fridge eventually got tossed after putting on a good show and delivering some hits on Big John Studd. He did the obligatory mope and stomp, then in good sportsmanship went over to the ring and extended his hand to Big John.

Big John took the sportsmanship gesture, and Fridge responded by immediately jerking the wrestling star over the top rope! The crowd roared as Studd stomped and blustered.

So did professional wrestling. The impact on the sport was stunning and immediate. Suddenly wrestling as entertainment became trendy. Frank Sinatra, the Beach Boys, Andy Warhol, Elizabeth Taylor—all of a sudden, they were ringside.

Rock legend Ozzy Osbourne was in attendance, acting as a "manager" for one of the wrestlers on the Chicago card. He sought out Coppock: "Do you think you could arrange for me to meet Mr. Perry?" Osbourne asked. "He is such a legend in my country."

Vince McMahon had spent massive energy and funds promoting Hulk Hogan, Macho Man Randy Savage, the Iron Sheik, Rowdy Roddy Piper. He had a stable of the best in wrestling personalities, grasping completely that it was indeed about personality, not wrestling.

For McMahon to reach out and decide he needed the Chicago Bears to put his growing dream over the top was one of the greatest tributes paid to the '85 Bears. They had sold products. Now they were selling a sport.

Sometimes too well. In July the wrestling tour swung back to the Rosemont Horizon with Hogan and King Kong Bundy as the main event. Wilson secured tickets and was down near ringside. Coppock, announcer for the evening, spotted Wilson and prior to the Hogan-Bundy match gave him a long buildup and introduction that culminated with a sustained, roaring standing ovation from the crowd.

The introductions then turned to Bundy, then to Hogan, who glared at Coppock, enraged at being upstaged.

Shortly afterward, a nuclear disaster in a place called Chernobyl in the Soviet Union drew attention to another spot on the globe in late April and early May. The sports pages were dominated by news that Len Bias, a Maryland basketball All-American who was the first selection of the Boston Celtics in the 1986 draft, had died from cocaine use.

Meanwhile Jim McMahon's stature was rising. Caesar's Palace held a roast for him June 1 that drew Bruce Willis, boxer Boom Boom Mancini, and Raider Lyle Alzado. Madden came all the way up from Southern California in his Madden Cruiser.

Meanwhile, as July drifted on and Coca-Cola announced it was bringing back Classic Coke, the Bears headed for England.

TALLY-HO

The NFL, perhaps recalling the barnstorming tour of Red Grange after he signed with Halas in 1925 and truly launched the NFL, wanted to reach markets outside the United States, so they occasionally scheduled one preseason game outside the United States. In 1986, wanting to capitalize on the international fascination with the Bears, the NFL went one step further: it created the "American Bowl," and made the game an annual event, kicking it off with a matchup between the Bears and "America's Team," the Dallas Cowboys.

England was waiting for them when the Bears arrived.

"Kids used to walk around wanting to look like [race driver] Jackie Stewart or John McEnroe," wrote Barry Flaxman in the British paper the *Daily Express*. "After the Super Bowl they were walking around in their Jim McMahon headbands."

The Bears spent no time on the sports pages of the English press. They were front section, usually front page: daily Fridge stories, paparazzi snapping frenzies, and an insatiable curiosity among the British over the size of these Yanks: one photo featured Perry hoisting 6'8", 290-pound Van Horne up as the flashbulbs popped.

Van Horne drew his own cluster of the curious. A *Sunday Times* columnist puzzled over the infatuation of his countrymen and women with Perry's bulk. "Keith Van Horne, the stupendous offensive tackle, is bigger by six inches [than Perry] with the sort of physique which encourages its possessor to kick sand in the face of Charles Atlas."

McMahon came off the plane wearing fatigues and sunglasses, christened "Your Outrageousness" by Payton, who was content to enjoy a lower profile than McMahon, Perry, and the rest.

> "Van Horne, Margerum, myself, and some others were invited by the Bee Gees up to their personal estate near Oxford. We're going up there to meet Eric Clapton. Clapton doesn't show up but Ringo Starr is there with his wife, Barbara Bach, and our photographer, Bill Smith is there so we have him get ready to get pictures with Ringo and each of us. But Ringo is so shitfaced that when we ask him, he just kind of slobbers, 'I m- muss-t regr'fully decline your offer.'"
> *—Gary Fencik*

Size was viewed as a main reason why American football could be successful in fan following but would never be a game in which the English could field competitive teams of its own because of "a general paucity of behemoths," *The Observer* said. Columnist Hugh McIlvanney suggested to readers that "the best way to deal with someone like Singletary is by telephone, starting with an offer to pay the ransom money."

The Bee Gees hosted a party for the Bears in their 800-year-old mansion, attended after a $171 cab ride by Fencik, Margerum, Van Horne, Suhey, and Valdiserri along with George Harrison, Phil Collins, Rod Stewart, and Ringo Starr, who was quite drunk but whom the Bears found amusing.

Collins went out with his son to watch practice on Wednesday. Collins went to Perry and asked for an autograph. Fridge obliged and went away with no fanfare.

"Fridge, do you know who that is?!" he was asked.

"Sure," Perry said. "That's Su-Su-Ssudio," the monster hit from Collins' *No Jacket Required* album. Perry was not swept away with his own celebrity status, and he certainly was not by others' either.

Players went to a club and found Chaka Khan performing. Before leaving, they were up on stage dancing and singing. The crowd's demand: "Sing 'Supuh Bowl Shuffle'!"

But Perry was the biggest single attraction, if not always in the best taste. The BBC's version of Johnny Carson's show, called *Wogan*, and the editorial cartoons fixated on his size and presumed appetite. Some editorial interests ran to other appetites.

"FRIDGE IS RED HOT IN BED, SAYS WIFE!" screamed a headline in the Saturday *Sun*, accompanied by a photo spread of Sherry Perry sprawled on a bed, starlet style. She played to the media and the moment, explaining how she ran instantly when Perry called and how she just hung on. Perry was not as taken with the hype: "Get real, man," he told reporters.

Sherry Perry contributed to the allure of the Bears. Just the name—"Sherry Perry"—had a ring that struck the Brits as funny and added to the novelty.

The British tabloid media, given to excesses whenever possible, devoured every utterance and nugget from the Bears. But they were completely baffled by the notion of a preseason game, a "Match on the Pitch," as their soccer games were called, that didn't count. What exactly did this mean? they kept asking. What are they playing for? What do they win if they win? Did the players have some sort of wager going on the side?

Exasperated, Bears PR man Bryan Harlan finally reached the end of his tether with all the questions but decided to have some fun with the moment.

A reporter from one of the tabloids asked what would happen based on the result of the preseason game.

"Well, if the Bears lose, Mr. William Perry must go over to the other side and kiss the feet of Mr. Ed 'Too Tall'

> "They loved Fridge over there. He was like the Beatles. If he was big in America, he was beyond huge over there."
> *—Otis Wilson*

Jones," Harlan deadpanned earnestly. "If the Cowboys lose, Mr. Jones must kiss the feet of Mr. Perry."

Then he added with some solemnity. "It's a ritual."

One day later, the headline screamed, "LICK MY BOOTS!" with pictures of Jones and Perry.

Soccer attendance in the United Kingdom was down because of hooliganism and a fire in the stands of one stadium. Hooliganism was at its peak, with more than 39 spectators dying in a fan riot at one European finals match. Efforts to transfer sports across the Atlantic, whether soccer to America or baseball or football to England, "have been about as rewarding as booking a passage in the *Titanic*," wrote Dr. Desmond Morris, author of *The Naked Ape*. Morris noted the down status of soccer coinciding with increased popularity of football, a sport that was built for an entire new group of (larger) athletes and that had a fresh enthusiasm. It was as though soccer was the much-loved but drab, nagging wife, while American football was the "colourful, classy, wide-eyed young mistress."

British and European fans in general were open to something new. Into that void came not only American football but the '85 Bears. They came along with almost tabloid-type characters like McMahon and Perry, with nicknames and personalities. They filled a niche.

Super Bowl XX was the first time that British tabloids like the *Sun* sent reporters to the American championship football game, doing double-page spreads on players and the game and vaulting the Bears and the game into mainstream British news coverage for the first time.

What started off as almost a cult sport had become mainstream. Brits arrived at work on Mondays during the football season talking about what they had seen on the NFL highlights the night before. Usually that meant the Bears.

FRIDGE INTERNATIONALE

By the end of the 1985 season, in addition to his staggering commercial load in the United States, Perry was appearing in TV ads in England for British products: chocolate bars, cereal packets—the kinds of things that English soccer players no longer could get because of the stigma their sport had acquired. No English soccer star in the mideighties earned as many advertising dollars in England as Perry did.

"If you found 10 people on the streets of London even today and asked them to name an American football player, more than half of them would name the Fridge. Even now, 20 years later," says David Tossell, now the PR director for NFL Europe and a member of the British press corps in 1985. Before the 2005 Super Bowl, Perry was a prominent figure on British TV and in print coverage.

Even "The Super Bowl Shuffle" made a connection with English fans. While the Bears' chest beating irritated numbers of players and fans in the United States, British soccer's top teams regularly did some sort of cheesy song or entertainment routine each year. The Bears were their kind of team.

A significant novelty for English fans also was the concept that a star player could be 300 pounds, or 22 stone. Soccer and even rugby are not sports played by the giants that are standard in American football. And then to have a 300-pounder like Fridge. . . .

Perry's popularity indeed had staying power. He returned in 1996 to play for the London Monarchs, one of NFL Europe's developmental teams, in what was as much a victory tour. The team had been folded for a couple years, and the operators looked around for a device to help relaunch the team and sport in England's capital city. They hit upon Perry, who was finishing his career with the Philadelphia Eagles.

In England, Perry was still the biggest name in American football a decade after his Super Bowl season. The result from his several-day 1996 visit to London was the

> "Fans stood in the rain the entire time for this game. It was like a Papal visit. You could be in the back of a crowd of a million people, not hear a word he said, but just to be able to say you were there, that was what counted really."
> *—David Tossell,*
> *former London journalist,*
> *now public relations director for NFL Europe*

most coverage the Monarchs ever had. The team hired a London cab, painted it with the colors and design of a Monarch helmet, and chauffeured Perry everywhere in it.

Perry was on breakfast and daytime television shows, including *They Think It's All Over*, the number one game show in England. One of the games was to blindfold a contestant, bring a mystery guest out, and let the contestant, by touching the guest, try to determine the identity of the mystery figure. A tennis player might hold a racket to help.

Perry was brought out, in shoulder pads and uniform. As soon as the blindfolded contestant felt the size of the guest and the shoulder pads, "The Fridge!" he blurted instantly.

The 1985 season was the peak of interest in American football in the United Kingdom. The weekly highlight show, running late on Sunday nights, drew four to five million viewers, comparable to *Match of the Day*, the main soccer show in England. Rozelle, in his letter to all U.K. fans in the program for the Bears-Cowboys game, set U.K. viewership of Super Bowl XX at 12 million.

The press and public indeed struggled to truly understand American football. London's *Sunday Express* TV critic suggested "a cross between chess and grievous bodily harm."

The Bears did their part to "help."

"It's men trying to knock the crap out of each other," McMahon explained on one talk show. "That's really all there is to it."

When Fencik was the featured speaker at the American Chamber of Commerce lunch in London, introduced by McCaskey, his advice to British fans was, "Get a set of rules."

Moments later he was asked his thoughts on soccer and admitted that he found it boring. "Get a set of rules," suggested one Brit in the crowd.

Or get "Dave the Brain." Linebackers coach Dave McGinnis spent an hour each day meeting with fans and explaining the game at either the team hotel or the Crystal Palace Sports Centre, earning the title "Dave the Brain" among the British press and fans.

The Cowboys fared considerably worse in England than they did in the States, although it did not cost them any foot-kissing. The 17–6 score was an improvement over the 44–0 humiliation of the 1985 season, but the crowd of 82,699 booed their entrance onto the field and roared louder with each appearing Bear, including Brit Russell Willsmer, who was signed by Bill Tobin to kick off if the Bears won the toss. Payton was held back until near the end, and Perry made his dramatic entry a scripted five yards behind him to a crowd on its feet and singing the soccer song "Here We Go, Here We Go."

Perry scored a touchdown, as the fans wanted. "I tell you one thing for sure," said broadcast color commentator Paul Maguire. "If the Bears get inside the 5-yard line and don't put Perry in, the fans'll rip the stands down."

The highlight of the fourth quarter, definitely as far as Fencik and the Bears were concerned, was the sprint by a streaker wearing nothing but a moustache. Diana Ditka was watching the game from the Royal Box and was asked by a *Chicago Tribune* reporter if she had seen the streaker.

"Sure I saw him," she said. "If I had binoculars I would've seen him a lot better. But Michael McCaskey and Jerry Vainisi wouldn't give me theirs."

The Bears began what they intended to be a successful defense of their title with the romp over the Texans, confirming once again, this time for the continent, who was "America's Team."

Chapter 16
STARTING TO UNRAVEL

"They aren't going to win it this year."
-Wayne Larrivee

THE BEARS CAME BACK FROM ENGLAND on a flight into Dubuque, Iowa. Their European vacation was over. But in fact, only the accents had changed.

After 1984, it became nearly impossible for fans to find a hotel room between Platteville, Wisconsin, the site of training camp, and Dubuque, 25 miles to the west over on the Mississippi River. After 1985 it was difficult to find lodging even that close to training camp. Channel 7, the ABC affiliate in Chicago, could do no better than rooms in Lancaster, Wisconsin, 20 miles away.

CAMP CRAZY

If 1985 was a rock show, 1986 was about to become the Bears' North American tour, starting in Platteville. It was Bears Theme Park, Bears Great America. It was the must-have stop on every national reporter's itinerary, sports and otherwise. They were the Beatles of professional football, and they did not disappoint.

Besides the thousands of fans who came on weekdays to the restful campus in wooded southwest Wisconsin, Bears wives and girlfriends all came up to Platteville. Debra McMichael drove up in her gold Mercedes convertible. Sherry Perry made her entrance. Payton arrived in a helicopter, right onto the practice field, while Suhey drove up in Payton's mobile home.

Brad Palmer, longtime color commentator for Bears broadcasts before the contract went to WGN from WBBM in 1985, coined the phrase "From Platteville to Palo Alto" before training camp in 1984, the Bears' first in

Platteville. They missed by a game. Palmer came up with "From Second Street to Bourbon Street" for 1985, referring to the action strip of Platteville, Second Street, and the New Orleans landmark.

It is difficult to say what "street" Palmer would have chosen for 1986. Up in Platteville, between the buildings in town and inside the Patio, the Hoist House, and other institutions, anyone with a Minicam could have made a great porn flick.

In the last half hour before weeknight curfew, it struck no one as out of the ordinary for one distinguished member of the defense to have two women on the pool table, another to be outside getting a little oral sex, and still another Bear to be behind the bar, holding court and making drinks. One starter walked in wearing spandex "slacks," a form-fitting T-shirt, and a knockout on each arm. They disappeared for about 10 minutes and returned shortly, both women adjusting their tops, hair, and lipstick. It was a party, and it seemed everybody was invited.

Well, maybe not everyone was invited. Platteville had a dark underbelly that concerned the Bears, an upstairs area at one of the taverns at the east end of town. Rumor had it that runaways—girls—were finding their way there as a stop on their way to somewhere else, but the "proprietor" was exacting sexual services in exchange for providing a roof and dry room. Special "guests" were invited up to the space to partake in what was rumored to be bordering on sex slavery, and those encounters were secretly filmed. The fear was that a Bear, feeling bulletproof, would be among the performers on film, with the prospects for blackmail or scandal just behind the two-way mirror.

None did. None had to. Those interested hardly needed a procurer. Certainly not with "Mazola Bowling."

The east side bowling alley was closed for a night toward the end of camp for a private Bears party. The lanes were oiled up and players "bowled" using female participants only too willing to be slid down the lanes. Over on the pool tables, one offensive lineman proudly used his male appendage as his cue stick.

In more team fun, posing for the team photo, one of the defensive stalwarts covertly took his spot but without pants or jock, unbeknownst to photographer

Mitch Friedman. The defender worked up a massive hard-on; the instant before Friedman shot the photo, two players in front of him leaned aside, providing a clear shot of the enlarged member.

STARTING OVER

The season started in a manner vaguely reminiscent of 1985. Cleveland came into Soldier Field September 7 and was sent home with a 41–31 loss.

That set up week two and a visit from the Philadelphia Eagles, coached by Buddy Ryan. The Bears

> "Vince turned attack dogs into sentries."
> —Dan Hampton

defense had been taken over by new coordinator Vince Tobin, and he and Ditka did away with the 46 defense, at least in name. The immortal defensive scheme that had brought a reign of terror to the NFL was now simply the "Bear defense."

More than just the name had changed, however. Tobin was in step with Ditka's idea of defense, which was to avoid wanton blitzing and react rather than attack, or so it seemed to the players.

Style notwithstanding, it was still a frightening defense. Unfortunately, so was Ryan's.

The teams played to a 10–10 standoff in regulation, then came out for the coin toss going into overtime. The Bears won the toss and elected to *kick off* rather than receive and go for a field goal. The confidence was well founded. The defense held for three plays, the Bears got the ball on a Philadelphia punt, and Butler won the game with a field goal.

For the next five games (including Philadelphia), the Bears allowed a total of 36 points combined, including a 23–0 shutout of Minnesota on October 5.

But the fabric of the team was fraying. And it had little to do with anything that was happening on the field.

EXPLOSIONS INSIDE

Ditka came in one day and railed at the whole team in the team meeting about how they had forgotten what it took to win and where they came from, about personal appearances and such. That night several went home and saw three different commercials on three different channels, all Ditka.

Ditka accused the players of becoming preoccupied; they saw him as the ad-man incarnate.

The players saw it as hypocrisy. Only McMahon and Perry were even close to his level of commercialization, but those two had credibility among their peers, Perry because he was clearly being swept along, like it or not, and McMahon because his interest in the fruits of the frenzy was only slightly above Perry's; he was saying no more than he was saying yes.

In early 1986 McMahon and wife Nancy had been having dinner at the Prime Minister, a steakhouse not far from their home in the north suburbs, when Zucker called. Perry had canceled out of an appearance at a corporate cocktail party. The deal was for $10,000 to shake some hands and just be a Bear.

McMahon passed, a measure of the kind of money that was flowing. Zucker called again; the offer was now $15,000. McMahon still wanted to just have his evening with Nancy. Then a third call came; the price was now $20,000. McMahon relented, did his appearance, and was back at the restaurant for dinner, 20 grand richer. Doing appearances and commercials in the first months after the Super Bowl, McMahon made more than $1 million and had not done even half of what he'd been offered.

Secretaries in St. Louis sent Zucker a letter offering $15,000 to have lunch with him. McMahon passed when it was apparent the deal was for more than lunch. The producers of *Miami Vice* wanted him to play a drug dealer; McMahon turned that down when the show would not take Becker and Van Horne as well. He said no to a movie deal worth possibly half a million dollars because it would have taken more than a month of his off-season or, rather, his golf season.

Compounding the problem was the perception of the McCaskeys. The team felt that Michael did not take care of players. Michael came in at one point and said they were going to take care of the veterans "because they've been here." But he would not give them the promised incentives. They felt increasingly betrayed by the man and family for whom they'd earned millions and who turned around and did nothing for them.

Lunch with Bears on Tuesdays was fast becoming a Chicago event, something that the public overflowed and the media raced to cover as hard as any news of the week. There were multiple locales and organizations hosting regular luncheons. And players made thousands apiece at special Tuesday events, whether corporate speaking gigs, onetime meeting appearances, store openings, or other functions.

Coppock hosted the first *Sun-Times* luncheon in September. Coppock's legendary extended build-up drove the crowd to crescendo with his Fencik intro that finished with "195 pounds of twisted steel and sex appeal" as the women shrieked and woofed.

The scene was slightly different with McMichael. Coppock went through his elaborate buildup of the mighty Texan, "the longhorn steer come to Chicago," and so on. When he was finished, McMichael just looked at him, then turned to the crowd, nicely dressed professionals, women as well as men.

> "Mike [Ditka] was just starting to rev up. I tried to pick my spots. He was getting into that media swirl, becoming bigger than life and a guy you couldn't talk to. 'Head coach' changes people. I've known guys who were great guys as coordinators who changed completely once they became head coaches. And the wives got into it quite a bit. They're counting commercials and dollars and with a lot of teams are at the root of a lot of problems."
> —*Hub Arkush*

"Do you believe what this f***in' cocksucker just said about me?" Mongo snarled, shaking his head. The fans went berserk. The crazier, the more vulgar, the better.

The flood of money was overrunning some players, and it became more serious when wives got involved in conspicuous consumption. Sherry Perry had gone in for matching Mercedes with engraved door handles.

Channel 2 got a call one day from Loeber Motors, a north suburban European auto dealership, suggesting the station might want to get a crew up there: Sherry Perry had bought 10 "Baby Benzes," the new 190 model.

"It got scary sometimes. Before the playoffs and that season, I would always take my son with me and there would be a lot of people, but it wouldn't be crazy. Then you started seeing the crowds swelling as the season went on and really after the Super Bowl. Eating at a restaurant, it was like you were a rock star, people pushing and shoving trying to get next to you. It really did get to a point where you didn't want to go out anymore because you had no privacy and you were going to get mobbed. People were going to pinch you, take pictures, demand autographs—it was fun at first, but then, 'To heck with this.'"
—Otis Wilson

When Wilson first arrived as the number one draft pick in 1980, appearances typically earned $500 to $800. After the Super Bowl they started at $1,500 on up to $15,000. And more. Wilson got $20,000 for a couple hours of signing things, mingling, and being in some pictures.

At one point, Hampton, McMichael, and Perry all were represented by Jim Steiner out of St. Louis at the same time. Then "the Tire Deal" happened.

Sherry Perry and Debra McMichael were kindred fiscal spirits, with the Rolexes and the Mercedes, and they started hanging out together. There was some shared resentment toward Hampton, who was garnering far more football attention than either of their husbands, if not the advertising dollars of Perry.

A commercial offer came in on a Monday from the Kelly-Springfield tire company, which wanted Fridge because he was the star and Hampton as the "other Bear." It was still going to pay $8,000 to the supporting "actor."

It was supposed to be something they would shoot Friday afternoon after practice. By Wednesday Hampton heard that he was not in fact doing it after all, that Fridge wanted to do it with McMichael because he and Perry were close. Hampton did not think Fridge on his worst day would do something like that. The wives, though, would.

And did. What was worse for the fraternity along the defensive line, McMichael and Perry were seen as letting their wives order their lives around and not standing up for what was right. Hampton was angry and out of the

picture for the $8,000. It deeply
eroded his respect for
McMichael and Perry as well.

With McMahon and Steve
Fuller hurting, and Tomczak on
his way to being driven to seek
psychological counseling

> "The little jealousy in the thing always seemed to be McMichael, who sometimes felt like the lesser wheel among Hampton, Fridge, and Dent, that he didn't get the recognition."
> *–Jim Steiner*

because of his dealings with Ditka, the Bears created a major stir on October
14. Ditka and Jerry Vainisi overrode the objections of personnel chief Bill
Tobin and brought in Doug Flutie. It was a move that would further tear the
fabric as the year wore on.

Because of McMahon's injury woes, Ditka said he was not going to be
caught in that trap again and went out and got Flutie so he would not be at the
mercy of McMahon. The next year the Bears drafted Jim Harbaugh trying to
cure the problem.

FATAL SPLIT

Many felt the greatness really ended after the Minnesota loss on October
19. No one said it at the time, maybe because it was just sad. They had
nothing short of the greatest team in the history of the National Football
League, and it was slipping away.

The Bears were 6–0 when they went up to Minnesota and were beaten by
the Vikings. That put an end to a run of 24 wins in 25 games, including the
1985 season and playoffs, which is a stretch that nobody in the NFL ever
approached.

But there were undercurrents of problems, and everybody knew it.
Something was going to blow.

Ditka came into the meeting room the Monday after the Vikings game and
laid it out.

"There's something wrong with this team. What is it?" Ditka said, standing
in the front of the room, looking at everybody.

Nobody said anything.

"You guys haven't had your attitudes right all year. Now what is it?" he demanded again.

Hampton could not stand it anymore. He stood up.

"I'll tell you what it is," he said.

McMahon had come to camp out of shape that year, no different than he did every year. He was hurting, although how much of that was due to lack of off-season conditioning was questionable. During that Vikings week, he could not practice. Then he went to Ditka during the game and said he could play. That struck some as weird, being in the same place as the Minnesota game in 1985 when McMahon had rescued the Bears and the season with his heroics coming off the bench.

Ditka would not play him this time because he had not practiced. Then after the game McMahon was in front of the media, as some felt he always was when he wanted to help his image, and said he could have played. That made Ditka the scapegoat for making the no-play decision as far as Hampton was concerned.

That angered Hampton. In the meeting room, Hampton pointed right at McMahon. "Everybody's out there, we're all beat to shit, trying to do it.

"McMahon, what the f*** is your deal? Here you say you can play but you won't come out and practice or do any of the things you're supposed to do. Then you throw everybody under the bus and say you can play."

"Well," McMahon said, "my doctor says my shoulder's bad."

Hampton saw red. "What the f*** are you trying to do then, saying you can play?" Hampton yelled. "Trying to make us all look bad and you're the golden boy?"

Van Horne, Hilgenberg, and others of the offense defended McMahon. "If he says he can't play, he can't play."

"My shoulder's injured," McMahon said again.

Horseshit, Hampton thought.

"Oh fine, it's injured but you can go out there and throw the ball around at practice on the sidelines?"

"No," McMahon said. "I can't play because I've got to think about my family and my future."

"Oh," Hampton said, "Hilgy's out there when he can't straighten either arm. Covert's out there with a back so bad he's got to sit in ice for two hours after practice. And we don't have families or futures?"

"Yeah, well, that's your decision," he said.

"Fine," Hampton said, "then we'll do it without you. Just stay the f*** out of our way and quit causing problems and f***ing up everybody."

Hampton sat down. Ditka said a couple things, and the players went off to their individual offense and defense meetings, nobody saying much of anything to anybody. Hampton did not think he created a rift. To him the rift was already there, always had been. It was not really a rift between offense and defense the way people thought. It was between McMahon and a team, in Hampton's thinking.

> "I think it all kind of started in Houston. McMahon was hurt and wasn't practicing; Ditka was frustrated with him not practicing. Guys were talking, and Hampton kind of jumped in all over McMahon."
> —Jay Hilgenberg

After practice that day Ditka came by.

"You're the only f***er who had the balls to say something about that prick," Ditka muttered to Hampton. That's all he said, and walked away.

At that point, big factions did exist. Members of the defense had to support Hampton even if they did not completely agree with him because they had to have a strong group line. But McMichael pulled Hampton aside privately and asked exactly what Hampton thought he was doing. No one was happy.

The real problem was that McMahon was indeed hurt. Seriously hurt. Hampton was accusing McMahon of not playing hurt, a harsh charge under the players' code, but McMahon in fact had, more than once.

CHARLES MARTIN AND LOSING McMAHON

November was full of unpleasant shocks, beginning with Wall Streeter Ivan Boesky rocking the financial world to its foundation with his confession to stocks and bonds trading based on secret and illegal information. Boesky agreed to pay a $100 million fine—Bears players would have preferred the money go to buying out Michael McCaskey—and helped start to unravel the "junk bonds" abuses that were ravaging sectors of the economy.

> "I thought it was jealousy from Hampton. Jim was such a great leader. One thing Hampton said was that Jim didn't play hurt, but my God, he played so hurt in so many instances."
> —*Steve Zucker*

And word was starting to leak out about convoluted arms deals that involved hated Iran and Nicaraguan contra rebels. One name in particular kept cropping up: Oliver North. What Americans were learning was that things are not always what they seem.

Bears fans were beginning to get that same feeling.

On November 23 Green Bay came to Soldier Field for a game and a play that effectively ended the Bears' chances for a return to the Super Bowl. A few Packers were wearing small towels in the waistbands of their uniforms with numbers on them: "hit lists." The Bears were 9–2 but were in a string of seven straight games in which the defense allowed no more than 14 points in any contest, 10 or fewer in five of those seven. The offense was wobbling and was about to take its worst hit of all.

McMahon came into the game with an injured right shoulder, his throwing arm. Midway through the second quarter, Mark Lee intercepted one of his passes. Defensive lineman Charles Martin, whose towel had McMahon's No. 9 on the list, sighted McMahon, ran up behind him, picked him up, and body-slammed him into the artificial turf, injured shoulder first.

Martin was ejected and subsequently suspended two games and fined $15,000. Years later a guy came forward claiming to have been a bag man, delivering money to Martin in return for taking McMahon out, no matter what.

McMahon was done for the year. So were the Bears, who were about to turn to Flutie.

But McMahon's exit from the season was bitter.

The organization turned up the pressure on McMahon, maintaining that McMahon could play, that he just needed to rest the shoulder, that it really was not all that bad, just slight separation.

Zucker took McMahon out to see Dr. Frank Jobe in Los Angeles, which was a huge step at the time, in effect questioning team medical services. The Chicago media followed him. Jobe examined McMahon, then his partner examined McMahon, and they both concluded that McMahon needed total reconstructive surgery on his shoulder. Zucker had a favor to ask of Jobe.

"Will you just announce that right here and now, because we're getting such pressure," Zucker said. "When we come back to Chicago, the Bears are going to pressure him to play."

Jobe had a press conference, and then McMahon had one at which he announced, "I'm not coming back to Chicago. I'm having shoulder surgery in the morning."

> "I could tell by midseason '86 that they were not going to win it. The Packers were not very good and the Bears struggled to put them away. I went home after the Green Bay game that year, the Charles Martin game, and told my wife Julie, 'They aren't going to win it this year.'"
> —Wayne Larrivee

McMahon had taken a position. He had a local doctor in Chicago, Michael Schafer, because Zucker did not think team doctors necessarily put the players' best interests first. The Bears fought Zucker on that, but in fact he did the Bears a big favor. They eventually hired Schafer as their team doctor.

So McMahon was out for the season. But more than just McMahon was lost in the Green Bay game.

They also were losing the cachet of tough-but-fair guys. One week after the Martin outrage, the Bears hosted Pittsburgh. Steelers wide receiver Louis Lipps came hard at Wilson to block the All-Pro linebacker. Wilson reacted instinctively with his forearm, caught Lipps under the chin, and Lipps was out cold on the turf.

Suddenly Wilson was no longer "Mama's Boy Otis" from "The Super Bowl Shuffle," but rather a thug and villain. Announcers Charlie Jones and

Jimmy Cefalo, broadcasting for NBC, denounced Wilson and wrung their hands even though the official right next to the play threw no penalty flag.

Wilson drew a fine, and then the Bears made the matter worse internally. They told Wilson they would handle it, which they did—by deducting $5,000 from his check.

FLUTIE

Prior to the Pittsburgh game, November 30, Ditka had Flutie over for Thanksgiving dinner. It was a nice gesture for a new Bear and now the starting quarterback, but one that blew up inside the team. "He never had me over for Thanksgiving dinner," Hampton groused to McMichael. "How 'bout you?"

"Nope."

> "I don't know why we needed Flutie. We could've won with Fuller the way our defense was playing."
> —*Richard Dent*

Flutie replacing McMahon stirred instant resentment from McMahon, who dubbed him "Bambi," not an endearing moniker. More important, it fanned resentment of Ditka, whose celebrity status appeared to the players to be fueling a raging case of egomania that was growing weekly with every win.

Signs were there that Flutie was not going to work out. As simple as the Ditka's Bears offense was—give it to Payton or let McMahon audible to something else if the defense stacked against Payton—Flutie had not mastered the offense and could not audible, the very thing that made McMahon great.

A bigger—or rather, smaller—problem was Flutie's height. At 5'9", he simply could not see well over an offensive line that included Bortz, Covert, and Thayer at 6'4" and Van Horne at 6'8". The solution was to create rollouts so Flutie could get away from the clogged pocket. But that meant the offensive line, still one of the best in the entire NFL, had to master different, seldom-used techniques and do it in a hurry. It proved difficult, more perhaps for Flutie than for the linemen.

> "Flutie had his nose right up Ditka's ass, and Ditka loved that."
> —*Keith Van Horne*

In the Monday night game in Detroit on December 15, Flutie did call a bootleg, then proceeded to go the wrong way. Instead of rolling left, he rolled right and into a sack. But *MNF* announcer Frank Gifford

> "We should have killed Washington and would have if they hadn't revamped our offense just for that game just for Ditka's pet."
> —Mike Hartenstine

declared, "Well, Van Horne sure screwed that one up." The reason: Ditka had built Flutie up in the pregame meetings with the broadcasters. Flutie was a media darling from his days at Boston College, and somebody else was going to take the fall for Flutie's mistake.

The Rams had gotten their revenge on the Bears in November, handing Chicago one of their only two losses of the season. Now it was January—the playoffs—and Washington was in Soldier Field to face the 14–2 Bears. But the Bears knew something was woefully wrong.

In the locker room before the game, offensive coordinator Ed Hughes was sitting with Flutie, going over the signals to be used for signaling in the plays. The offense already had been simplified for Flutie. Hughes test signaled twenty plays; Flutie got two right.

Flutie completed only 11 of 31 passes, gaining only 134 yards. Worse, he threw two interceptions, one to set up the touchdown that put Washington ahead for good.

The season was over.

After the loss to the Redskins, there was a spectrum of reactions. McMichael, Hampton, Covert, Duerson, and many others wore long faces. But there also were many faces not so down, and even some of the "downs" were not quite as devastated as they might have been a year earlier. There was an air almost of—relief.

Some years later, Coppock had occasion to meet up with Moorehead and his wife.

"Why were there so many guys who seemed, I don't know, casual?" Coppock wondered. "Was it maybe that the weight of the world was off your shoulders?"

Moorehead hesitated, then, "Yeah. We'd won 32 ballgames over a two-year window. The pressure of carrying that load was so, so much. It was on you seven days and nights a week."

For a lot of the guys, the ride was so fast and so steep, it had buried them. It was the old Fireball rollercoaster at Riverview Amusement Park—incredible speed, sharp turns, not a moment of easy.

It was a rock band on a tour that lasted a whole year, even longer. Every day, everywhere, the press, the public, all coming at them. For dozens of them, it was a relief it was over, even if it meant losing.

Chapter 17

FINAL GROWLS

"People say, 'The old gray mare ain't what she used to be.'
Well, all of a sudden I was the old gray mare."
—Dan Hampton

AMERICA LOVES ITS WINNERS. So as 1985 slipped away, replaced by enormous disappointments each of the next three seasons, America gradually moved on from the Bears.

At one point in the 1987 season, McMahon had won 27 straight games as a starter, a record. That string was broken in Denver, a Monday night game. Pete Axthelm of *Newsweek* was doing a cover story on McMahon; Zucker sat with him for several hours and at one point asked a question.

"What happens if they lose?" Zucker wondered. "Is Jim still on the cover?"

"Of course," Axthelm said.

They lost. First thing Tuesday morning, Zucker's phone rang. It was a *Newsweek* staffer.

"Something came up," the employee said. "We decided to go with a different cover."

Despite a 14–2 record in 1986, they were done. There were other cover stories all of a sudden. Along with the nation they so captivated, the Bears were headed for epic falls.

The stock market, which climbed to a record level in 1985 as the Bears were reaching their new heights, kept going up with them into mid-1987, going above 2,500 for the first time in July 1987 as the Bears started training camp.

The Dow Jones Industrial Average then took the greatest one-day plunge in its history on October 19, 1987—the day after the Bears lost to the New Orleans Saints in the last of games played by replacement players, the issue that would irrevocably tear apart the already fraying relationship between Ditka and his players.

Pop-art icon Andy Warhol, among the many glitterati seen around the Bears of '85, died in February. In May, Colorado Senator Gary Hart, riding a wave of arrogance and seeming invincibility toward the presidency, brought down his White House aspirations by his own hand, and other body parts, in his affair with Donna Rice.

The Bears were still *the* show in Chicago and much of the nation, with the Washington defeat viewed as a fluke. Appearances were still drawing capacity crowds, and tickets to *The Mike Ditka Show* were still the hottest in town, an adult *Bozo Show* where tickets were ordered months or a year ahead and schedules were arranged around it if the tickets were secured. People waited in lines that stretched twice around the Channel 2 building hoping for tickets.

One CBS producer carried two *Ditka Show* tickets with him at all times. If he was pulled over by one of Chicago's finest, the tickets worked flawlessly to undo what he had done.

LOSING HURTS

The full 1986 season contained special miseries beyond simply not winning again. The Bears were still dominating sports marketing and advertising, but their year ended with the ignominy of watching the New York Giants utterly dominate a Super Bowl that the Bears knew should have been theirs—the same Giants they had laid to waste on the way to Super Bowl XX.

They had been eliminated from the playoffs by the Redskins, over whom they'd stepped on their way almost to the top in 1984, then again in 1985 on their way to dominance. Their losses in the 1986 regular season had been to the Rams, their punching bag in the 1985 NFC Championship Game, and to the Vikings, in the same Metrodome where all the magic had begun a year earlier with the coming of McMahon.

The 1987 season saw the greatness of 1985 fade even more. Flutie had been traded to New England. The Bears finished 11–4 but lost again to

Washington in the playoffs, this time 21–17 and with McMahon. But McMahon threw three interceptions in what was Payton's last game ever.

Perry's weight, which may have had comedic value in England, was no longer an amusing subject and was becoming a flash point. Ditka angered Sherry Perry when he was asked about Perry's weight. "He's not eating here [Halas Hall], so he must be eating there [home] or between here and there." It threw blame on Sherry and Fridge's home life.

Sherry called Channel 2's assignment desk. "I've got a story to tell," she said. The station sent out a crew and did the interview, in which she claimed that there were wild sex parties going on in Platteville with the knowledge and blessing of Ditka.

The Bears were in Los Angeles on Friday to play a preseason game with the Raiders. Word of Sherry Perry's tell-all meant a need for Ditka's reaction. An hour later, the station called again. She had admitted she was just angry and had made the whole thing up.

Payton brought his own mobile home to Platteville. Perry had his room in the dorm with the players. But Sherry came to Platteville and stayed at a local hotel the entire time the team was in camp. Fridge would join her but not always for the clichéd conjugal visits. The reporter staying in the room next to Sherry's could hear, "Wh-wh-wh-where da fries, Sherry?"

The 1987 regular season started in magnificent enough fashion. In a *Monday Night Football* game that drew even more viewers than the 1985 meeting with Miami, the Bears opened the season against the defending Super Bowl champion Giants, a matchup that brought together the two teams the country really wanted to see face off.

The Bears knocked around the Giants of Bill Parcells again, 34–19. Quarterback Phil Simms began trash-talking the Bears early in what was his chance to atone for the humiliation of the 1985 playoffs, when they had sacked him six times and harassed him into 21 incompletions in 35 passes. He was in their faces with language quarterbacks probably should not use while addressing Hall of Fame defensive players.

The Bears blitzed and down went Simms, looking out the ear hole of his helmet. He had to be helped off the field, dazed and wobbling rather than walking, as Dent and the Bears taunted him to return. "C'mon, Phil, c'mon back," Dent called out. "Aww, Phil, c'mon back."

The players heard that same plea from the fans just a couple weeks later.

"SCABS"

The Bears and the rest of the NFL were beset by the players strike that year about the time the stock market was disintegrating, which seemed prophetic. Two weeks into the season the Players Association voted to cease playing; team owners elected to continue the season with replacement players. Games in week three were canceled, rosters of former and aspiring players were assembled, and the season resumed with replacement players suiting up for three games before the strike ended.

> "It's like in a marriage, if you find your wife is cheating on you, you can stay together, but it'll never be the same again."
> —Dan Hampton

The Bears were doing informational picketing outside Soldier Field, fans told them how much they were missed, then went inside to watch the replacement "Spare Bears." The deepest cut, however, came from Ditka, who declared, "The real Bears are the ones wearing uniforms on Sunday."

Maybe not surprisingly, Ryan over in Philadelphia was contemptuous of the Eagles replacement players and did not care if he angered management by saying so. It was nothing less than his former players expected from Ryan, or hoped for from their own coach.

Before the strike game at Philadelphia, there was concern about union violence, so the team was brought into the building and slept in cots on the floor of Veterans Stadium. Teamsters and others stood outside screaming at the Bears, bringing trucks up to the locked gates and blowing truck horns all through the night. Fueling that was Ryan's declaration that these players were not the real ones.

But when the strike was over, everything was changed. Ditka had lost the players, and the split was far deeper than that from the Flutie courtship.

Ditka's relationship with his team was never the same again, even though he had been trapped on the horns of an impossible dilemma. He worked for the organization, the organization had decreed a course, and Ditka was not going to go against it, particularly with a boss like McCaskey who was looking for reasons to be rid of him—and Ditka knew it.

> "Mike insisted that all coaches put in normal preparation time, do up game plans and play books, and insisted that those kids' names be placed in the media guide. Mike had no choice; the league said you'll play. And I give a lot of credit to our players, who did nothing to harass or do anything irregular to those kids."
> *—Kenny Geiger, longtime Bears pro scout*

And there was more to Ditka's actions than simple self-interest. He felt for the replacement players, guys who were willing to risk being branded and hated for just wanting a chance to play the game of their dreams. In the years that followed, Ditka quietly campaigned to have the replacement players included in the media guide just like every other man who'd worn the Bears uniform. No asterisks.

The irritations were causing raw spots elsewhere as well. What once had passed for fiery motivation was now tearing apart rather than fusing together. Ditka referring to Dent as "Robert" in press conferences was taken as an insult that did not sit well with or motivate the franchise's best pass rusher.

Dent was angry. Ditka was making it personal. Players could not understand the thinking, other than perhaps frustration that Ditka had not been able to get to Dent, who adhered to his own code and program. Dent, for all of his laid-back, Southern veneer, was an intense, serious student of his craft and the game. Ditka did not like that Dent went less than full-out at times during games, certainly during practice. Dent appeared to Ditka to be lazy, something that none of his demanding teammates ever saw or would have tolerated. Dent, like Van Horne, did not have a demeanor Ditka liked, and the coach could not easily accept what he mistook for lack of fire or effort.

"Robert" did not make Dent play any harder, because he was already playing his game as he saw fit. No matter what, Dent was going to go right

"Regardless, I was going to do my job. I didn't give a shit what he said or what anybody said. I was going to do my job. Wasn't but one name on the check that pays me and that's 'McCaskey.' Everybody else I could give less than a shit about because that guy writes my check, and if he can see well enough to write his name on my check, he can see well enough to see that I'm doing my job. They would bring guys in to take my job, but I felt that if a guy ain't willing to die, he won't take my job."
—*Richard Dent*

down the line with Ditka. He did not waver, did not change. The problem was respect; because Dent felt Ditka was not respecting him, his respect for Ditka ebbed.

At this point too, players were irritated at the constant use of the media as a conduit for communications. Ditka felt that he had to do something to motivate Dent to play hard, but his choice of tactic turned off Dent and others.

By the end of 1987, Perry was benched. Fridge had ballooned up over 400 pounds and was even getting knocked off the ball on running plays. Vince Tobin came into the defensive meeting before the Raiders game and said simply, "Hampton, you're starting at right tackle."

GREATNESS SQUANDERED

So many bricks fell out of the wall after the 1987 season that it all started to teeter dangerously. Payton retired after that season, taking with him a huge part of the soul of the Bears. Before the 1988 season, McCaskey traded Gault away to the Raiders for a first-round pick in 1989 and a third-round pick in 1990.

Marshall, by then the single most feared member of the defense, became eligible for free agency and received a big contract offer from the hated Redskins. McCaskey chose not to match the price, which was his option, and let Marshall walk in exchange for first-round picks in 1988 and 1989.

The reality as far as the players were concerned was that management had become insufferably arrogant, figured they did not need anybody, that suitable replacements could simply be inserted into the machine with no loss of power, and that executives like McCaskey truly believed they had won that Super Bowl trophy or had been in some major way responsible. McCaskey to them was the kid who started life on third base and acted as if he had hit a triple.

> "We squandered it. In 1988 we were so beat up by the championship game. We had Ron Rivera and Jim Morrissey as the outside linebackers, good guys, but they weren't Wilber and Otis. There's a saying that caution is a disease that flourishes in opulent environments, and that's almost how that team became. You look at a team like New England since 2000. They identified players who were important to them, cultured them, and took care of them. But with the Bears, the attitude was always, 'Well, they've got those Bears helmets on, of course they're going to win. So we don't need Otis. We don't need Wilber. We don't need this guy, that guy.' Well, we did."
> —Dan Hampton

The problem was not only what was being lost. It was what was being done to replace the losses. Neal Anderson, taken in the first round of the 1986 draft to be Payton's successor, was a quality back and a quality human being. But he would never be Payton.

The Bears used one of the number one picks they had gotten for Marshall on wide receiver Wendell Davis in the 1988 draft—again, a completely class individual and solid player. But he was never to the offense what Gault had been, even though he caught more passes. They used the 1989 number one pick on Clemson cornerback Donnell Woolford, who became a Pro

> "After three years, when everybody started leaving by '87, you tell me what player came in there and made a big damn difference."
> —Richard Dent

Bowl player, but not without serious struggles in his early years.

From the McMahon trade, they netted a second-round pick that was used in 1990 for linebacker Ron Cox, another average player. The 1990 third-round pick from the Gault deal went for Florida State quarterback Peter Tom Willis, who never won a starting job.

In 1988 the Bears opened 7–1, then lost to New England and quarterback Doug Flutie, who threw for four touchdowns.

"Don't anybody ever question my judgment again," a vindicated Ditka bristled.

McMahon pulled a hamstring to go with a knee that was already unstable. Trade talk started. McMahon wanted to play against Detroit in the next-to-last game but could not, and once again some of the animosity simmered.

> "Did Jim take enough care of himself? I'm sure he did; he just put his body in harm's way a lot and he would get abused because he's not a real big guy. If it was third-and-one, he would do what he had to do to get something done."
>
> *–Tom Thayer*

The Bears' 12–4 was the best record in the conference in 1988, but even beating Ryan and the Eagles in the "Fog Bowl" at Soldier Field, when much of the field was invisible to even the players on it, could not save them.

Dent, whose "Flying Sack" of Joe Montana in the 10–9 win over San Francisco October 24 made its way onto posters, broke his leg late in the season and was gone when the Bears met San Francisco again in the NFC Championship Game. Without Dent the pass rush was impotent. Montana threw for 288 yards and three touchdowns, two to Jerry Rice, and the 49ers walked into another Super Bowl with a 28–3 win.

> "I think the hardest thing was losing that championship game to the 49ers in Soldier Field, because we beat them earlier that year 10-9 on *Monday Night Football*. It was everything. We just didn't do it. That last San Francisco game, because we still had a core group of guys from the '85 team, and we had beaten them. The weather and conditions and everything were in our favor, and we were still 12-4 that year. The next year, we started 4-0, then just caved in. I try to repress those memories."
>
> *–Tom Thayer*

END OF McMAHON

McMahon's magic, absent in the 1987 loss to Washington, was now in large measure gone. Soon, so too was McMahon.

Hampton came in one morning during training camp in 1989 badly hung-over. Don Pierson from the *Chicago Tribune* came over.

"Did you hear what McMahon had to say about you in the paper?" Pierson asked.

"What'd he say?"

"Something along the lines of, 'Oh, Hampton thinks everybody can do this or that,'" Pierson said. He did not remember the exact comment, but it was something flip about Hampton.

"He said that about me?" Hampton said, and started over to McMahon's space.

McMahon was by his locker when Hampton came up, and he turned around. Hampton grabbed McMahon by the throat and put him up against the locker.

"Motherf***er," Hampton hissed, "if you ever say one more thing about me, I will kill you. Do you understand? I will kill you."

"Yeah, yeah," McMahon said. Hampton let him go and went back around to his own locker.

The players went out to practice. McMahon was not out there. Twenty minutes later they learned he had been traded to San Diego.

Fittingly the Bears faced San Diego in the second preseason game. Harbaugh caught Tomczak signaling plays over to McMahon, but the real signal was from McMahon to a couple of his buddies. Several Bears had shaved their pubic hair region into the shape of a triangle. McMahon went out into the San Diego game with a wristband that had a triangle on it.

The trade was another crisis crossroads for Ditka. He was in a difficult spot because McMahon had the image, which some felt he fostered but regardless was universally believed, that the team could not win without him. Ironically, the playoff loss to Washington in 1987 showed that the Bears might not be able to win *with* him either. Ditka did not want to see the whole team blow up because of one player, but dealing with that conflict was perhaps his most difficult dilemma.

McMahon would not talk to Ditka. Zucker was the go-between in what was a true love-hate situation. At the bottom of it all, Ditka really did care a lot about McMahon. Zucker went to Ditka after the trade to San Diego—which was the worst thing for the Bears, for McMahon, for Ditka, for everybody— and found that Ditka wanted McMahon back for the 1990 season.

McCaskey said no. He had gotten his chance and rid himself of a player that was the essential anti-Michael. Ditka wanted him back, knew he should have fought more to keep him, but thought they could win without him. Ditka realized he was wrong.

The truth was, however, that there was little Ditka could do to influence McCaskey, as he would increasingly find out.

The losses were costing the Bears meat now, not fat.

Losing Gault to the Raiders hurt in a different way. He was a part of their cachet, the unequaled speed receiver, the best at what he was in his unique niche. And it was taken as a further indication that the organization was willing to lose yet another piece of what they once had.

And yet Gault also had become almost a distraction. His lack of production for his level of talent became a conundrum, and his toughness was always suspect among a group that prized that quality. When he and Ditka clashed over outside distractions, the feeling in parts of the locker room was, fine, let him go. He personally was the antithesis of what the Bears were. He'd catch the ball and, if he was not running free somewhere, he would go into the fetal position.

But oh, that speed. . . .

GUTTED

Wilson hurt his knee in the August 22, 1988, preseason game against Dallas. It was determined that he should take the entire year off, rehab his knee, and come back to finish the last two years of his contract.

Ryan and the Eagles came to town for the Fog Bowl, the divisional playoff round. Twenty-two Bears trekked down to the Eagles' hotel to see Ryan, and some photos were taken.

Unfortunately for Wilson, on crutches and wearing a leg brace, the *Sun-Times* chose to run a photo of Wilson with Ryan on its sports front page for that Sunday, December 31, paper. Just Wilson. Goddamn, thought Wilson, I'm going to hear about that.

Sure enough, just before the 1989 draft, the Bears sent Wilson a letter. No call, just a letter. Some people's loyalty, the letter read, is not to the team. Due to that loyalty factor, it said, Wilson was being given the opportunity to negotiate with any team he chose because the Bears probably would not retain his contract.

Then the team said publicly that the decision was based strictly on the injury factor, which did Wilson no favors in his efforts to catch on with another team. Wilson had gone to Dr. Lanny Johnson in East Lansing, Michigan, who had done successful surgeries on Walter Payton and Magic Johnson and would handle Hampton a year later.

Wilson surfaced in training camp with the Raiders, starting, and there was nothing wrong with his knee. The Bears simply did not want him around. They just used his knee as an excuse.

A greater collapse was coming in 1989.

The Bears started 4–0 but lost Hampton for the year with a knee injury. They then lost their next two games, the second to Houston at Soldier Field. Ditka said after they lost to the Oilers that they'd be lucky to win another game. And he made it personal again, declaring that rookie cornerback Donnell Woolford, one of two number one draft choices that year, could not cover anybody. Then they went to Cleveland and were destroyed, then five weeks later to Washington, where journeyman quarterback Mark Rypien made his first start and dominated them.

"We stink," Ditka told the press and the country. "We're just not a good football team."

They in fact won two more games. But after a 20–0 victory in Pittsburgh, the locker room was like a morgue. They acted as if they had just lost.

They were losing more than they realized. Hampton, whose knee injury had started the slide into the abyss, had been to Lanny Johnson for knee surgery and was starting to jog around the practice field in mid-October, with the team standing at 4–3 and holding on. Ditka came over to him.

"Are you going to take the whole f***ing year off or are you going to play?" Ditka said.

"Well, the doctor said I was done, but I'll play," Hampton said. "But I've got no contract for next year. I'll sign the same contract for next year that I had for this year, so if I destroy myself, at least I'll get half of it and it'll be worth my while. I'm not asking for anything, just a little security before I get into this."

"Fine," Ditka said, "let's go talk to McCaskey."

They walked into McCaskey's office. Hampton sat on the couch, Ditka in one of the chairs.

"So," McCaskey said, "what's going on?"

Ditka explained that the team was down and everybody was saying that without Hampton it was not the same. "Dan's saying he might be able to come back, and even if he plays 10 plays a game, at least he'll be back and be a factor," Ditka said. "He doesn't have a contract for next year and you know the importance of having that before putting him back out there."

McCaskey knew. But he had let Gault, Marshall, McMahon, and Wilson go, and he was not about to take care of Hampton either.

"Well," McCaskey said, "you've been a great player for us and we understand your contributions. But I don't think it would be prudent for us, looking at your situation, to invest in you for next year."

Ditka was incredulous. "So you're not going to give him a contract for next year? So he can come back and play the last four or five games and try to get us turned around and make the playoffs?"

"No," McCaskey said. "I don't think there's any way we can do that."

"That's it," Hampton said, stood up and walked out with Ditka.

OLD GRAY MARE

Regardless, Hampton did come back for the 1990 season, but even with Dent collecting 12 sacks and Trace Armstrong 10, and rookie Mark Carrier interception 10 passes, the run was over. For Hampton, it ended where it all began for the 1985 Bears: against the Raiders, when Hampton found he could in fact be blocked by one man.

The Bears may have gradually lost some of the power to back up the swagger, but they never lost all of the personality.

After Ditka had his heart attack in 1988, Hampton and McMichael got into his office and his best cigars and liquor cabinet. The two went through a number of vintage vices over a period of time. Finally Ditka came back. But that did not deter the two miscreants.

"What are you two doing?!" Ditka challenged when he came back and found the pair in his office puffing on two of his best stogies.

> "They kept pitching the ball and going left and I'd never been 'hooked' in my entire life. And [guard Steve] Wisniewski was hooking me. He got to my shoulder three or four times and drove me off the ball two or three yards, which I'd seen happen to other people, but never to me. It was like sticking a knife in me. I thought, I'm done. . . . I remembered when I first came into the league and Tommy Hart, the great speed rusher, was through, and people were saying, 'The old gray mare ain't what she used to be.' Well, all of a sudden I was the old gray mare."
> —*Dan Hampton*

After a long pull on the Cubans, Hampton and McMichael looked at each other, then at Ditka. "We're saving your life," McMichael answered, taking another long pull.

McDonald's offered rookie Armstrong a commercial in 1989. Hampton and McMichael explained that the outside distraction would slow his progress and hurt the team. Armstrong turned it down. Hampton and McMichael did it instead.

As years went on, the veterans all had master keys to the dorm rooms in Platteville. No one ever admitted how they got them. Receiver Tom Waddle, arriving in the late eighties, went to sleep every night of camp with everything he owned in his room, plus the bed, pushed up against the door so it could not be opened. You simply did not go to sleep before rigging the room's safety shield, Waddle said, because the veterans would unlock doors, come in, and do "awful things to your stuff. Just awful."

There have been reckonings and balancing of some of the scales. Hampton was preparing to do a pregame show with WGN in the late nineties and got a call. It was Singletary, who was newly honored with his own Hall of Fame induction in 1998 and who had pulled out some old game films.

"Dan, I've been watching some film and I have to apologize," Singletary said.

"What do you mean, 'apologize'?" Hampton asked.

"Because when I played I was so wrapped up in this or that that I never appreciated what you and Fridge and Steve did to make me as good a player as I was."

Hampton laughed. "You're just now figuring that out, Samurai? Well, thanks, Mike. Don't think about it."

Hampton, however, did think about it. The call was from the heart, and it touched his.

Ditka eventually would end up years later doing a gig at Casino Magic in Bay St. Louis, Mississippi. He would fly down, spend exactly 24 hours, and get paid $20,000. The host of the event: Buddy Diliberto. The same Diliberto who'd started the "sluts" firestorm at the Super Bowl.

In early October 1989, Ditka was still hot enough that his wife, Diana, was signed as the ad spokeswoman for Hair Performers, a chain of 223 salons through 27 states.

But by early December, *Advertising Age* was headlining a story, "Ditka Down." Midway Airlines, which had used him as its spokesman since 1986, dropped him. That was after Campbell Soup's Chunky Soup and Hanes Corp. had already dumped him. His Bears were 6–7 at the time, but it was over and everybody seemed to know it was never coming back.

The paths followed from Chicago by the '85 Bears led to the most unlikely places. McMichael ended his career with the Packers. After being told at one point in 1993 that he was not welcome to work out at Halas Hall, that he was a negative distraction to the younger players, Dent went on to get another ring with the 49ers, whose quarterbacks he had chased in some of the eighties' most memorable games. Had he played even a couple more years with the 49ers and subsequently been selected for the Hall of Fame, he would have chosen to go in as a 49er.

McMahon went everywhere, starting with the Chargers. He played for the Packers, who had worn towels with his number on their hit lists. He won his second Super Bowl ring as the backup to Brett Favre, the top gun of another era. And he even played for the Vikings, in the same Metrodome where it had all begun for him back in 1985.

Ironically, though the greatness may have been squandered, it never completely left those Bears, at least not some of the magical pixie dust that Chicago and most of America found there. In 2004 Ditka still commanded $30,000 to $50,000 as a keynote speaker.

CHAPTER 18

DA SUPER FANS,
DA BEARS, DA COACH

"It flipped me out because I went back to Chicago later
that year and there were huge billboards for 'da Bears,'
'da Bulls,' even 'Da Paul'. It was unbelievable."

—*Joe Mantegna*

SATURDAY NIGHT LIVE HAD BROUGHT PAYTON to New York to host
the show and eventually would have Ditka as a guest four days after his firing
in 1992. *SNL* would also go on to provide one of the most lasting and creative
reflections of the '85 era.

The Super Fans. A one-set skit in which lovably blowhard, die-hard
Chicago fans toasted and boasted of their heroes, the Super Fans began as a
sketch Robert Smigel had done on stage in 1988 while in Chicago with fellow
SNL writers Conan O'Brien and Bob Odenkirk. Odenkirk grew up in the far-
western suburb of Naperville, Illinois, before making his way to New York
and *SNL* in 1987. Smigel had lived in Chicago from 1982 to 1985, writing
and working with a Second City spin-off.

New Yorker Smigel had noticed the quirks of Chicago's species of fans
during his time there, which overlapped with the time of Ditka's hiring,
McMahon's arrival, and the ascension of the team. Smigel left for *Saturday
Night Live* during the '85 season to begin his tenure with the show, but not
before forming those lasting and humorous impressions of Chicago and its
sports junkies.

Indeed, it almost required an outsider's eye to pick up on what was universal about the type of people who were Chicago fans. So many people, after he

wrote the sketches, would approach him and loudly proclaim, "I *knows* peeepul like daat! D'er *nuts* about da Bearss!" For Smigel, the compliments were nice; the impromptu chance to step into the sketch in real time was priceless. Even after the sketches appeared, people couldn't see themselves in the characters.

The original skit didn't have the odd predictions and hyperbole of the *SNL* sketches, but in some ways was funnier: three guys just sitting on a porch, each convincing the others how the season was going to turn out: "I'll tell ya' one ting dat's gonna happen, my friend. Come January, a certain team from a certain Midwestern town will reign supreme, my friend. And dat team shall be known as . . . *da Bears!*"

And on and on. But ironically, as much fun as it was to conceive and do, Smigel never thought of it as something that could work on *Saturday Night Live*, not for a national TV audience, certainly not one with a New York studio audience.

Then several years later Joe Mantegna, a Chicago guy by way of Los Angeles at that point, was the host of the show. Odenkirk and Smigel started talking about the sketch, and Smigel came up with the notion of the absurdly over-the-top predictions and other declarations.

The Sportswriters was a popular show at the time, a long-running talk show with crusty old scribes sitting around a table, cigars smoldering, talking sports. In the *SNL* sketch, *Sportswriters* legends Bill Gleason, Bill Jauss, Joe Mooshil, and Ben Bentley, and later Rick Telander, were replaced by fans talking sports, all ridiculously biased, with just the *degree* of bias differentiating them.

It was many years after the Super Bowl, but the audience enjoyed seeing a culture replicated, one that hadn't really been done on TV. These weren't New Yorkers or Hollywood types or anything people had seen, just over-the-top Midwestern guys. And it worked; it had an originality about it.

"They came up with this skit and the first time was when I did it," Mantegna said. "The skit was such a smash that the next day, Chicago radio stations ran the entire skit."

The skit was on *SNL* show number 297 and aired January 12, 1991, the day before the Bears would face the Giants. New York was on its way to what would be its memorable Super Bowl escape against Buffalo in the Scott Norwood game. But for the Super Fans, as for many Bears fans, it was still 1985 and would always be.

The Super Fans were surrounded by Polish sausage and bratwurst, sitting at a round table ostensibly inside Ditka's Chicago restaurant. The cast was beyond superstar: Bill Swerski was played by Mantegna, Pat Arnold by Mike Myers, Todd O'Connor by Chris Farley, Carl Wollarski by Smigel, and oddsmaker Danny Sheridan, in a walk-through cameo, was played by Kevin Nealon.

BILL SWERSKI: Alright, we're talking here, live from Ditka's in the heart of Chicago, Illinois. The city of big shoulders, and home, of course, to a certain football team, which has carved out a special place in the pantheon of professional football greats. That team, which is known the world over as . . . da Bears!

SUPER FANS: Da Bears!

BILL SWERSKI: OK, OK, by my watch, we're about 13 minutes from game time. As you are sure aware, da Bears are getting ready for the big playoff game against da New York Giants. Now, let's go around the room for some predictions. Pat?

PAT ARNOLD: Da Bears, 62–3.

BILL SWERSKI: OK. Todd?

TODD O'CONNOR: Bears, 79–zip.

BILL SWERSKI: Oh really? You don't think da Giants will score?

TODD O'CONNOR: No I do *not*! Da Bears' defense is like a wall. You can't go through it.

BILL SWERSKI: Alright. How about you, Carl?

CARL WOLLARSKI: I say, da Bears, 52–14.

PAT ARNOLD: Oh, what? C'mon!

CARL WOLLARSKI: I'm sorry, I'm sorry. I gotta give da Giants credit. I think they'll give da Bears a game!

BILL SWERSKI: Alright, leave him alone, that's his prerogative! As for my prediction, at game's end, uh . . . there will be two teams of contrasting moods heading off da field, my friends. One gloom, one gleeful. The gleeful, of course, will be . . . da Bears!

SUPER FANS: Da Bears!

BILL SWERSKI: Seventy-four to two. I mean, after all, our civic pride is on the line. Because, let's face it, if New York were to somehow beat Chicago, we'd never hear the end of it.

TODD O'CONNOR: Aw, they would *love* it over dare!

BILL SWERSKI: You know, it's absurd really, that we would even have to waste our time comparing ourselves to that crime-ridden *rathole*!

The Super Fans unanimously agree that the Sears Tower is the choice over the Empire State Building. Then on to another issue.

BILL SWERSKI: Alright, alright, let me shift gears here for a moment. What is God's role in this? Obviously he's rooting for da Bears.

PAT ARNOLD: Otherwise he wouldn't have put 'em in Chicago.

CARL WOLLARSKI: That's right.

BILL SWERSKI: That's right. The question is: now, did God create da Bears and *make* them superior to all teams? Or is he a huge fan and *Ditka* made them superior to all other teams?

CARL WOLLARSKI: That's a tough one.

The waitress delivers the bratwurst and the rest of the Super Fans' order. Then . . .

BILL SWERSKI: OK, well, I see now that it's almost time for that foregone conclusion that is today's game.

PAT ARNOLD: Not gonna be pretty!

TODD O'CONNOR: Bears!

SUPER FANS: Bears!

BILL SWERSKI: Now, gentlemen, let me ask you this: what if da Bears were all 14 inches tall, you know, about so high? Now what's your score of today's game?

CARL WOLLARSKI: Against da Giants?

BILL SWERSKI: Yes, give 'em a handicap.

PAT ARNOLD: Yeah, it would be a good game. Mini-Bears 24, Giants 14.

CARL WOLLARSKI: Bears 18, Giants 10. And that would *finally* be a good game.

TODD O'CONNOR: What about da Coach? Would Ditka be mini too?

BILL SWERSKI: No, he would be full grown.

TODD O'CONNOR: Oh, then, uh . . . Mini-Bears 31, Giants 7.

CARL WOLLARSKI: Oh, hold on. Then I can change mine too. I thought it was Mini-Ditka!

BILL SWERSKI: OK, gentlemen, another scenario: da Bears, they don't make it, the plane is delayed . . . and the *only* one who shows up is Ditka. Ditka vs. da Giants. OK, scores?

PAT ARNOLD: Alright, *after* the heart attack, I gotta say Ditka 17, Giants 14. He just barely gets by.

BILL SWERSKI: Alright, that sounds exciting. Perhaps, you know, a late Ditka field goal.

TODD O'CONNOR: Bears!

SUPER FANS: Da Bears!

Danny Sheridan breezes through, is roundly abused after suggesting a point spread of 800 for the mythical Ditka-only vs. Giants matchup, and leaves. The debate returns to celestial heights.

BILL SWERSKI: Alright, now let's get back to our discussion. Bears vs. the Assembled Choir of Angels?

PAT ARNOLD: The whole choir?

BILL SWERSKI: Well, seraphim, cherubim, da whole nine yards.

PAT ARNOLD: Angels.

CARL WOLLARSKI: Angels, but it's close.

TODD O'CONNOR: Bears!

BILL SWERSKI: Alright, Ditka vs. God in a golf match. Now, he's a good golfer.

PAT ARNOLD: Ditka.

TODD O'CONNOR: Dit-ka!

CARL WOLLARSKI: Ditka.

BILL SWERSKI: Well, I see they are setting up the 40-foot screen so I guess it's game time. Now, you enjoy da game, folks, and remember, next week, Bears-Niners.

Then, as the sketch fades, more epic decisions:

BILL SWERSKI: All right now, Bears vs. Stephen Douglas in a debate; what do you think?

SUPER FANS: Da Bears! Da Bears!

The response was immediate and overwhelming. A New York studio audience loved it and so did the national TV audience. In Chicago, Jonathan Brandmeier played the entire skit on his radio show, which launched it in the city that already loved the Bears and was beginning to get its Bulls buzz.

Three months later, for the *SNL* season finale, the decision was made to do a second skit, this time with George Wendt as Mantegna's brother Bob Swerski, but without Mantegna, who they said was recovering from a heart attack. The point was the same.

The skit: Bill Swerski's Super Fans, with George Wendt (Bob Swerski), Chris Farley (Todd O'Connor), Mike Myers (Pat Arnold), and Rob Smigel (Carl Wollarski).

The setting: Ditka's Restaurant, Chicago.

BOB SWERSKI: Now, when we were last privileged to observe da Bears, they were playing the Giants in the postseason. The final score of that game was 31 to 3, and I shan't say who won. Pat, what happened?

PAT ARNOLD: I think it's pretty obvious that coach Ditka had his mind on more important things.

CARL WOLLARSKI: There was a war on, my friend.

TODD O'CONNOR: That's right, our boyss were overseas.

PAT ARNOLD: Yeah, da Coach was probably too busy helpin' Schwarzkopf. . . .

BOB SWERSKI: Now, what if da Bears were to enter the Indianapolis 500? Uh, what would you predict would be the outcome?

TODD O'CONNOR: How would they compete?

BOB SWERSKI: Well, let's say they rode together in a big bus.

CARL WOLLARSKI: Is Ditka drivin'?

BOB SWERSKI: Of course.

CARL WOLLARSKI: Then I like da Bears! . . .

BOB SWERSKI: Now, what if da Bears entered da Preakness?

SUPER FANS: Da Bears!

What then carried the sketch and concept to exponentially greater heights was the rise of the Bulls. The Bears were fading by that time, on their last legs literally and figuratively, as a true entity. They would be clobbered by the Giants in the 1990 postseason not long after the first Super Fans sketch with Mantegna. The Giants were heavily favored, which made the Fans' mania that much more amusing.

In some ways it worked better that the Bears weren't that good anymore. Ditka was a god. Then the Bulls were headed for a world championship, and the interest was escalating. The season-ender had Wendt as Bob Swerski, and "da Bulls" became the next rallying cry for the Fans. The Bulls then truly propelled the sketch even deeper into the consciousness.

Smigel and Odenkirk were invited to Chicago after the Bulls won their championship. They appeared on various sports shows, with Mark Giangreco doing an hour-long special using them as cohosts. Smigel and Wendt came again after the second and third championships, performed, and did a song at the ring ceremony in Grant Park.

The team and Super Fans took a break when Jordan "retired" and then came back for another Grant Park celebration in 1996. Smigel and Wendt came out on stage with Dennis Rodman wigs and tattoos, exploring their feminine sides, and made some comments that didn't endear them to Bulls owner Jerry Reinsdorf. Their charity basket for contributions intended for Reinsdorf "to pay Jordan what he deserves" didn't help.

The fun of the sketch extended beyond the acting for Mantegna and Wendt. For Wendt it was a chance for another identity; he loved that at least once in a while now, people in public were calling, "Da Bears!" to him instead of "Hey, Normy," for his Norm character eternally seated at the end of the bar in the hugely successful *Cheers*. It was his professional second wind.

"For me," Wendt told Mantegna, "I love doing this because it gets people's minds off me as Norm."

Mantegna wasn't as eager to make the role a regular gig, preferring instead to focus on his developing film career. Still, he was pleasantly stunned to fly into Chicago and on his way downtown see billboards along the Kennedy Expressway proclaiming, "Da Bears," "Da Bulls," even "Da Paul." Even DePaul University was having fun with da Bears.

The sketches were tightly written by Smigel and Odenkirk, so there weren't a lot of ad-libs.

The names—Swerski, Wollarski, O'Connor, and such—were chosen because of how they lent themselves to the Chicago speech patterns. Swerski was named after longtime Chicago broadcaster Chuck Swirsky, a fixture at WGN who was his own caricature and someone Odenkirk knew. Eventually, they did an appearance on Swirsky's show.

Smigel had moved to New York and missed the mania of 1985, but sat in New York with his dad for their traditional watching of the Super Bowl. One thing he did remember from watching TV coverage of Chicago's celebration, though, was that there really was someone with a coconut bra and grass skirt on Rush Street, frantically hula-ing, saying nothing, just intent on his art, no doubt thinking, "Bears!" with every spin. Smigel ended up having a Super Fan do the same.

The *SNL* connection did not end with the Super Fans. Payton did a 1987 appearance with Joe Montana, and members of the troupe wondered why McMahon wasn't brought in as well. The deal, however, was to have all-time greats. Payton was quiet and unobtrusive, and *SNL* put together a sketch that had him dancing, knowing that Payton in fact was a former dancer on *Soul Train* with Don Cornelius.

"Seeing Payton in civilian clothes, with the thighs he had, was just unbelievable," Smigel recalled. "It was insane. I never pictured Walter as a muscle monster. But when I saw him . . . amazing."

Smigel wrote a movie for Mantegna, Farley, Wendt, and himself based on the Super Fans. Myers didn't want to do it and was on to his own projects. Smigel wrote the script with Odenkirk after he left *SNL*, which was in a downslide in the midnineties. Unfortunately the network was becoming irritated at the number of movie spin-offs, few of which matched the success of Myers' and Dana Carvey's *Wayne's World*, and NBC was against the film even though Smigel had already written it. And Farley's management was telling him that he shouldn't do a spin-off.

Odenkirk and Smigel also wanted to flesh out the characters, take them beyond the caricatures in the way the *Wayne's World* characters were. The movie parodied what was going on in sports—the baseball strike—and had a whole second thing about how sports were being taken completely away from the average fan and corporate-ized. Wendt's Bob Swerski had Bears season tickets that kept getting worse and worse even though his ticket seniority increased every year. Eventually the Bears were sold to a character who wanted to convert Soldier Field into one big luxury box for about 250 people—with piano bars, clubs, and restaurants but without many fans—and rename it "Soldier Club."

Ironically, the real-life made-over Soldier Field in fact had five thousand fewer seats than the old one. And a bizarre seat-license sale left many long-time season-ticket holders either with nothing or with their poorest preference in seating. It had happened in other cities and eventually happened in Chicago. None other than the venerable Chicago Stadium, scene of Jordan's greatest moments, was razed and the corporate-oriented—right down to its name—United Center was erected as the new home for Da Bulls.

Ditka was on *SNL* the week he was fired in 1992. The Super Fans sent an irate letter to owner Michael McCaskey, declaring that they were returning such things as their sandwiches from Mike Singletary's farewell dinner.

Over the years Smigel did multiple events in Chicago, including with Wendt a roast of Ditka. Wendt and Farley revved up the crowd before the Bears playoff game in 1991, the last playoff game of Ditka's era.

It was all fun, all Bears.

CHAPTER 19

FAREWELL

"This, too, shall pass."

—*Mike Ditka*

THE FINAL YEARS HAD BEEN PAINFUL. The final days, the death throes of Ditka, were agonizing.

The season was marked by Ditka's confrontations with players on the field, fans on the radio, and McCaskey in the front office. After the 1991 season he branded the players "a bunch of overachievers," declaring to the media, "Well, gang, I'm just playing the hand I'm dealt." The implication was that they had gone 11–5 because of superior coaching. Personnel chief Bill Tobin was furious, as were the players.

Ditka was deeply hurt by the publication of *Ditka: Monster of the Midway* by *Sports Illustrated*'s Armen Katayian at the outset of the season, a chronicle of personal and sports details that laid Ditka bare as never before.

Early in 1992, against the Vikings in the "Rollerdome," Harbaugh violated specific Ditka instructions and threw an interception that was returned for a touchdown. Ditka's ensuing sideline tirade directed at Harbaugh was captured by TV, igniting a firestorm of criticism. Ditka blamed Harbaugh for the debacle in Minnesota that led to what McCaskey considered an embarrassment to the franchise on national television. One week later, after what should have been a cooling-off period because of the bye week, Ditka responded to the first question about the Minnesota play by berating the media, saying that out of 400 plays called that season, "You sons of bitches [focus] on one damn play." Peoria *Journal-Star* columnist Phil Theobald then stood up and walked out of the press conference, telling Ditka that he was not about to be called a son of a bitch.

That ended the Monday press conferences. The only early week access then to Ditka was on his weekly radio program on WSCR-AM. Because that was a call-in show, the fuse was lit for confrontation with unhappy fans, and it was not long in coming.

"Neil from Northlake" called and started in on Ditka. Finally Ditka was fed up. He seethed and informed Neil from Northlake, "My office is at 250 Washington Street in Lake Forest, and if you care to come up there, I will kick your ass."

After the December 20 loss to Detroit, Ditka said that it was unlikely he would return in 1993 unless he had greater control over player personnel. The direct threat to Tobin's area was not well received, nor was McCaskey about to transfer any more power to a man he already considered a borderline maniac.

After the season, amid daily speculation and wonderings about the future of the man who had restored the pride of the Bears, albeit with some rough spots along the way, McCaskey simply left town. He went on a family vacation to California as Ditka, his coaches, and the fans twisted. Ditka had dangled McCaskey over a toilet in his ballboy days in training camp. Now Ditka could dangle a little.

Finally McCaskey returned and made known his intentions with indirect talk of "new directions" and a "new era of free agency," with a rationale that players with free choices of where to play would think twice about playing for someone as beyond control as Ditka was.

On January 5, 1993, after a meeting in which Ditka told friends he asked McCaskey to let him keep the job at least through the last year of his contract, McCaskey had what he appeared to want: a prostrate Ditka and reasons enough to fire him. Ditka was told he was out as coach of the Chicago Bears.

The night before, Bears officials secretly contacted the Lake Forest police and arranged to have officers ready for what could be a violent public reaction. Fans in fact gathered near the small Bears headquarters in a form of vigil and to show support for the man many saw as the salvation of the Bears.

A press conference was called. McCaskey went first and gave the news: the Bears would begin their rebuilding process with a new head coach. He did not stay around to answer questions.

Then it was Ditka's turn. There were tears in his eyes and his voice trembled and broke at times:

I will try to do this with class, if I can. The Scriptures tell you that all things shall pass. This too shall pass. Regrets . . . just a few. They are too few to remember. I can't sing it quite as good as he [Sinatra] could. Thirty-two years [in the NFL] . . .

I have a lot of people to thank. I have a lot of coaches that I have worked for over the years, as a player, as an assistant coach. I thank coach Halas.

I guess you have got to thank the players the most because they make it happen. I was blessed. I came here and I inherited a hell of a football team. Man, you've got Walter Payton, you've got a hell of a football team.

We drafted some good kids. We took a run. Pretty good. We did a pretty good job. Players make it happen. I had some great assistant coaches. I respect every one of them. Really loved every one of them I ever had. Disagreements or no disagreements, they have been very vital to my life.

I have had my run-ins with you [media] guys, and I have had a lot of support from you. I appreciate it, and I thank you. I thank the fans of this city.

You know, the Bears will come back. Mike Ditka will survive. I will land on my feet. There is not a problem about that. I don't worry about that. I worry about how this organization is perceived. I believe we will go forward and try to do the things that are necessary to get through the nineties the way it should. I would hope that.

It is hard to erase 17 years. Nothing much else to say but, "Thank you, I appreciate it." But this, too, shall pass.

EPILOGUE

WHERE ARE THEY NOW?

Brad Anderson, wide receiver—Senior vice president at CB Richard Ellis brokerage. Lives in Scottsdale, Arizona.

Tom Andrews, tackle—Played for Seattle before retiring in 1987. Lives in Louisville, Kentucky.

Hub Arkush—Publisher of *Pro Football Weekly*; television and radio personality. Lives in Chicago.

Kurt Becker, guard—Played for L.A. Rams in 1989; returned to Bears in 1990 before retiring.

Todd Bell, safety—Played for the Bears in 1986–1987 after holding out for all of 1985 and finished his career playing for Buddy Ryan in Philadelphia. Went to work at the Ohio State University office of minority affairs before dying of a heart attack in March 2005.

Mark Bortz, guard—Retired after 1993; was the last starter on offense from Super Bowl XX still with the team. Lives in Pardeeville, Wisconsin.

Maury Buford, punter—Retired after 1991. Roofing contractor living in Fort Worth, Texas.

Brian Cabral, linebacker—Lives in Colorado.

Chet Coppock, radio host—Successful raconteur and host of sports talk radio show. Lives in Chicago.

Jim Covert, tackle—Retired in 1991 because of back injuries; executive with HealthSouth. Lives in Chicago.

Richard Dent, defensive end—Super Bowl XX MVP. Left Bears in 1994; played for Philadelphia, San Francisco, and Indianapolis, plus three games with Bears in 1995. Retired after 1997 season with 137.5 sacks, third in NFL history at the time. Successful businessman heading up telecommunications and energy management at RLD Resources LLC. Lives in Chicago.

Buddy Diliberto, New Orleans radio host—Source of the McMahon "sluts" story during Super Bowl week; also poked eyeholes in a paper bag and put it over his head at a New Orleans Saints game in 1980, giving rise to the "bag head" look for frustrated fans everywhere. Died of a heart attack at age 73 in Metairie, Louisiana, in January 2005.

Mike Ditka, coach—Fired by Michael McCaskey in January 1993; coached New Orleans Saints from 1997 to 2000. Radio and television football analyst, weekly show for Chicago sports talk radio, and active in product promotion and charitable work. Lives in Chicago.

Dave Duerson, safety—Won Super Bowl ring with 1990 New York Giants; finished career with Phoenix Cardinals from 1991 to 1993. President of Fair Oaks Farms in Kenosha, Wisconsin, supplier of meat to McDonald's. Former member of Notre Dame board of governors until 2005. Lives in Chicago.

Gary Fencik, safety—Retired after 1987, successful entrepreneur and investor, commercial real estate, asset management with Austin Partners; also a sports radio and television commentator. Lives in Chicago.

Doug Flutie, quarterback—Played for San Diego Chargers in 2004, signed with New England Patriots in 2005.

Leslie Frazier, cornerback—Never played again after his knee injury in Super Bowl XX. Coached at Trinity College in Deerfield, a northern suburb of Chicago, and at the University of Illinois; then held several NFL coaching positions, with the Philadelphia Eagles and Cincinnati Bengals, and was a defensive assistant with the Indianapolis Colts in 2005.

Andy Frederick, tackle—Civil engineer in Texas, designing bridges and large commercial structures. Lives in Dallas, Texas.

Steve Fuller, quarterback—Retired after 1986. Lives in South Carolina.

Willie Gault, receiver—Let go by the Bears in 1988; retired from the Raiders in 1991. Pursued career in acting and producing, appearing in *Thinking Big* (1987) with Fencik, *Night Vision* (1998), and *Lethal Force* (2002) and in TV shows, including *The West Wing*. Lives in Los Angeles, California.

Shaun Gayle, safety—Played for Bears through 1994; retired after spending 1995 with San Diego Chargers. Successful entrepreneur, author, and media commentator. Led organization of 2005 reunion for Bears 20th anniversary of Super Bowl XX. Lives in Chicago.

Dennis Gentry, running back—Retired after 1992. Scout for the Indianapolis Colts.

Forrest Gregg, coach—Fired by Green Bay after 5–9–1 record in 1987; head coach and athletic director at alma mater Southern Methodist University. Voted in 1994 to NFL's 75th anniversary all-time team. Worked for a Detroit-area builder after leaving coaching.

Les Grobstein, radio—Sports talk radio host and radio reporter for national sports outlets. Lives in Chicago.

Dan Hampton, defensive lineman—Part owner of security firm for banking industry. Television and radio football analyst. Voted into the Pro Football Hall of Fame in 2002. Lives in Chicago.

Bryan Harlan, Bears media relations—Left Bears in 2000; partner in Chicago public relations firm representing coaches and players in contract negotiations and business development. Lives in Chicago.

Mike Hartenstine, defensive end—Drafted the round after Walter Payton in 1975; retired after 1986. Successful investor; works for Chicago north shore golf club. Lives in Chicago.

Jay Hilgenberg, center—Traded by the Bears to the Cleveland Browns in 1992; retired from the Cleveland Browns in 1995, an undrafted free agent from Iowa who was voted to seven Pro Bowls. Active in business and charitable promotions; principal in The Club at Strawberry Creek, Kenosha, Wisconsin. Lives in Chicago.

Stefan Humphries, guard—Played for Bears through 1986 and for Denver Broncos from 1987 to 1988. Dentist. Lives in Denver, Colorado.

Tyrone Keys, defensive lineman—Played for Bears through 1985, Tampa Bay from 1986 to 1987, and San Diego in 1988. Lives in Tampa, Florida.

Wayne Larrivee, play-by-play announcer—Left Bears booth to broadcast Green Bay Packers games and college and NBA basketball. Lives in Milwaukee, Wisconsin.

James Maness, tight end—Retired after 1985. Lives in Decatur, Texas.

Wilber Marshall, linebacker—Played for Washington, Houston, and Arizona after leaving Bears in 1988. Plays golf and relaxes. Lives in Florida.

Charles Martin, defensive lineman, Green Bay Packers—Died of kidney failure at age 46 in 2005.

Brian McCaskey—Senior director of Bears business development; active in player relations and working with '85 Bears on commemorative promotions and bridging gap between players and organization. Lives in Chicago.

Michael McCaskey—Removed as Bears president in 1999; remains as chairman of the board. Lives in Chicago.

Bill McGrane—Retired as Bears director of administration in 2004. Lives in Chicago.

Dennis McKinnon, receiver—Worked in television and radio; former assistant football coach for Illinois Benedictine University. Director of sponsor relations for Chicago Bandits national women's fast-pitch softball and other businesses. Lives in Chicago.

Jim McMahon, quarterback—Played for San Diego, Philadelphia, Green Bay, and Minnesota after Bears, won a Super Bowl ring while backing up Brett Favre with the Packers. Private businessman and entrepreneur. Lives in Chicago.

Steve McMichael, defensive tackle—Released by Bears after 1993; finished career with Green Bay Packers in 1994. Former pro wrestler, author, and sports commentator. Lives in Chicago.

Dick Meyer—creator of "The Super Bowl Shuffle," the King of Jock Rock, died of cancer in 1992. His wife, Julia, the "referee" who whistled over any expletives in the video, rereleased "The Super Bowl Shuffle" video, with outtakes and interviews, in 2004.

Emery Moorehead, tight end—Developed real estate business while playing for the Bears; currently with Koenig and Strey Realtors. Lives in Chicago.

Johnny Morris, broadcaster—Former Ditka teammate and wide receiver on sixties Bears; retired. Lives in Chicago.

Jim Morrissey, linebacker—Financial advisor with AXA Equitable. Lives in Chicago.

Keith Ortego, wide receiver—Works for the city of Lake Charles, Louisiana. Lives in Lake Charles.

Alan Page, defensive tackle—Played for Minnesota Vikings from 1967 to 1978, was waived, and signed by Bears for seasons from 1978 to 1981. Elected to Hall of Fame in 1988. Minnesota supreme court justice. Lives in Minneapolis, Minnesota.

Walter Payton, running back—Retired in 1987. Elected to Hall of Fame in 1993. Successful motivational speaker and promoter and involved in auto racing and heavy equipment leasing. Died of bile duct cancer in 1999.

William Perry, defensive tackle—Released by Bears in 1993. Played for Philadelphia Eagles and London Monarchs, as well as having a stint in pro wrestling. When asked what he's doing these days, he replied, "Business, promotional, and personal appearances, product endorsements, and enjoying myself, a whole lotta' fishin.'" Lives in Aiken, South Carolina.

Reggie Phillips, cornerback—With Bears through 1987 and Phoenix in 1988. Lives in Texas.

Mike Richardson, cornerback—With Bears through 1988 and San Francisco in 1989. Lives in California.

Ron Rivera, linebacker—Retired in 1992. Coached with Philadelphia Eagles; current Bears defensive coordinator. Lives in Chicago.

Buddy Ryan, defensive coordinator—Retired after coaching Philadelphia Eagles and Arizona Cardinals and serving as offensive coordinator for Houston Oilers. Raises horses in Kentucky.

Thomas Sanders, running back—With Bears through 1989 and Philadelphia from 1990 to 1991. Works for Forte Industries. Lives in Chicago.

Mike Singletary, linebacker—Successful motivational speaker and businessman; returned to football as linebackers coach for Baltimore Ravens after Bears refused to hire him as an assistant in 2002. Then assistant head coach for San Francisco 49ers. Lives in San Francisco, California, and Chicago.

Dick Stanfel, offensive line coach—Retired from coaching. Lives in Chicago.

Jim Steiner, agent—Continues to represent athletes and public personalities. Lives in St. Louis, Missouri.

Matt Suhey, fullback—Drafted in 1980, scored Bears' first Super Bowl touchdown, and retired in 1990. Successful investor, former trader at Chicago Board of Trade, and has had various successful business ventures. Lives in Chicago.

Ken Taylor, defensive back—Works for Athletes in Action in Oregon. Lives in Portland, Oregon.

Tom Thayer, guard—Released by Bears in 1993; retired from Miami Dolphins after that season. Successful restaurateur and investor, expert surfer during winters, and Bears color commentator during seasons. Lives in Hawaii and Chicago.

Calvin Thomas, running back—Was active with the Teamsters; coaches Little League football. Lives in Chicago.

Cliff Thrift, linebacker—After six seasons with San Diego, played 1985 with Bears and 1986 with Rams. Lives in Oklahoma.

Bill Tobin, personnel director and vice president—Headed football operations for Indianapolis Colts and Detroit Lions. Senior scout for Cincinnati Bengals. Lives in Cincinnati, Ohio, and Florida.

Vince Tobin, defensive coordinator—Head coach of the Arizona Cardinals from 1996 to 2000, Detroit Lions defensive coordinator in 2001, out of football for two seasons, and hired in 2004 as special assistant to Green Bay coach Mike Sherman.

Mike Tomczak, quarterback—Started for Bears in 1989, played for Pittsburgh Steelers, and now college football television analyst for ESPN. Lives in Pittsburgh, Pennsylvania.

Ken Valdiserri—Left Bears in 1999, worked with Vince McMahon on XFL promotion, and now a marketing executive for ESPN in Chicago. Lives in Chicago and Sweden.

Keith Van Horne, tackle—Retired in 1993. Successful restaurateur, investor, and businessman. Lives in Chicago.

Henry Waechter, defensive tackle—Works in fertilizer equipment business, based in Grand Island, Nebraska. Lives in Grand Island.

Otis Wilson, linebacker—Played for Raiders after leaving Bears. Appeared in three feature films, including *The Fugitive* with Harrison Ford and Tommy Lee Jones. Partner in women's fashion design company; now runs 55 Alive, a private foundation that works with Chicago schools and the mayor and governor of Illinois to develop children's nutrition and fitness programs. Lives in Chicago.

Tim Wrightman, tight end—Played 1985–1986 with Bears. Worked in TV, film, and business marketing. Lives in Idaho.

Steve Zucker, agent—Successful agent and attorney; continues limited representation of players. Lives in Chicago.

APPENDIX 1

THE ROSTER

COACHES

Mike Ditka . . . . head coach . . . . hired 1982

Buddy Ryan . . . . defensive coordinator . . . . hired 1978

Ed Hughes . . . . offensive coordinator . . . . hired 1982

OFFENSE

Walter Payton . . . . running back . . . . drafted 1975

Matt Suhey . . . . fullback . . . . drafted 1980

Keith Van Horne . . . . right tackle . . . . drafted 1981

Ken Margerum . . . . wide receiver . . . . drafted 1981

Jay Hilgenberg . . . . center . . . . free agent 1981

Emery Moorehead . . . . tight end . . . . free agent 1981

Jim McMahon . . . . quarterback . . . . drafted 1982

Tim Wrightman . . . . tight end . . . . drafted 1982

Kurt Becker . . . . right guard . . . . drafted 1982

Jim Covert . . . . left tackle . . . . drafted 1983

Willie Gault . . . . wide receiver . . . . drafted 1983

Tom Thayer . . . . right guard . . . . drafted 1985

Mark Bortz . . . . left guard . . . . drafted 1983

Dennis McKinnon . . . . wide receiver . . . . free agent 1983

Stefan Humphries . . . . guard . . . . drafted 1984

Tom Andrews . . . . guard . . . . drafted 1984

Steve Fuller . . . . quarterback . . . . free agent 1984

Thomas Sanders . . . . running back . . . . drafted 1985

Mike Tomczak . . . . quarterback . . . . free agent 1985

Andy Frederick . . . . tackle . . . . free agent 1985

DEFENSE

Mike Hartenstine . . . . left end . . . . drafted 1975

Gary Fencik . . . . safety . . . . free agent 1976

Dan Hampton . . . . left end . . . . drafted 1979

Al Harris . . . . linebacker . . . . drafted 1979

Otis Wilson . . . . left linebacker . . . . drafted 1980

Mike Singletary . . . . middle linebacker . . . . drafted 1981

Todd Bell . . . . safety . . . . drafted 1981

Leslie Frazier . . . . right cornerback . . . . free agent 1981

Steve McMichael . . . . left tackle . . . . free agent 1981

Henry Waechter . . . . tackle . . . . drafted 1982

Mike Richardson . . . . left cornerback . . . . drafted 1983

Dave Duerson . . . . safety . . . . drafted 1983

Richard Dent . . . . right end . . . . drafted 1983

Wilber Marshall . . . . right linebacker . . . . drafted 1984

Ron Rivera . . . . linebacker . . . . drafted 1984

Shaun Gayle . . . . safety . . . . drafted 1984

William Perry . . . . right tackle . . . . drafted 1985

Jim Morrissey . . . . linebacker . . . . drafted 1985

SPECIAL TEAMS

Maury Buford . . . . punter . . . . trade from San Diego 1985

Kevin Butler . . . . kicker . . . . drafted 1985

THE FRONT OFFICE

George Halas . . . . founder . . . . died 1983

Michael McCaskey . . . . president 1983–1999

Bill Tobin . . . . scout, personnel VP 1975–1993

Jerry Vainisi . . . . controller, GM 1972–1986

Bill McGrane . . . . administration . . . . retired 2004

THE STARTERS

OFFENSE

Wide receiver . . . . Willie Gault

Wide receiver . . . . Dennis McKinnon

Tight end . . . . Emery Moorehead

Right tackle . . . . Keith Van Horne

Right guard . . . . Tom Thayer

Center . . . . Jay Hilgenberg

Left guard . . . . Mark Bortz

Left tackle . . . . Jim Covert

Quarterback . . . . Jim McMahon

Running back . . . . Walter Payton

Fullback . . . . Matt Suhey

DEFENSE

Right end . . . . Richard Dent

Right tackle . . . . William Perry

Left tackle . . . . Steve McMichael

Left end . . . . Dan Hampton

Right linebacker . . . . Wilber Marshall

Middle linebacker . . . . Mike Singletary

Left linebacker . . . . Otis Wilson

Right cornerback . . . . Leslie Frazier

Left cornerback . . . . Mike Richardson

Safety . . . . Gary Fencik

Safety . . . . Dave Duerson

SPECIAL TEAMS

Kicker. . . . . Kevin Butler

Punter. . . . . Maury Buford

INDEX

Abitante, Pete, 148
Adidas, 127, 144, 147
Advertising Age, 84, 166, 208
advertising/marketing, sports,
    61–64, 82–86, 118, 127
AIDS epidemic, 2, 87
All-American players, 4, 5, 7,
    33, 48
Allen, George, 14
All-Pro players, 5
Alzado, Lyle, 37, 171
American Bowl, London, Bears
    vs. Cowboys, 165, 171–75
American Express, 167
American Football League
    (AFL), 19
Anderson, Neal, 199
Anderson, O. J., 9
Andre the Giant, 170
Archer, David, 98, 99
Argovitz, Jerry, 13, 62
Arizona State University, 18
Arkush, Hub, 64, 107–8, 119,
    183
Armstrong, Neill, 12
Armstrong, Trace, 204, 205
Associated Press, 146
Atlanta Falcons, 65
    Bears-Falcons game,
    November 24, 1985,
    98–99
Atlanta Journal, 65
Axthelm, Pete, 193

Babcox, Mickey, 117
Baltimore Colts, 21
Becker, Kurt, 60–61
Bee Gees (music group), 173
Bell, Todd, 23, 38, 47, 48, 49,
    162
Belushi, Jim, 169

Bentley, Ben, 210
Berry, Ray, 155
Bias, Len, 171
Bisher, Furman, 65
Blair, Matt, 20
Blue-Gray All-Star Game, 11
Boesky, Ivan, 187–88
Boomer (New Orleans DJ), 145,
    146
Bortz, Mark, 15, 46, 79, 80, 95
Boston Celtics, 171
Boston College, 191
Boston Globe, 139, 148
Boston Red Sox, 45
Bradshaw, Terry, 5, 118
Brandmeier, Jonathan, 118, 214
Brett, George, 141
Brigham Young University, 60,
    149
broadcasters (sportscasters), 20,
    48, 86, 107–8, 118–19,
    144, 158, 162, 189–90
Brock, Dieter, 135, 137
Brown, Jim, 48
Brown, Ray, 78
Brudzinski, Bob, 106
Bryant, Bobby, 2
Buford, Maury, 94, 122
Buoniconti, Nick, 103
Butkus, Dick, 26, 48, 49
Butler, Kevin, 57, 58, 123, 137,
    155, 156, 157, 167

Caito, Fred, 43
Campbell, Earl, 98
Candlestick Park, San Francisco
    Bears-49ers game, January 6,
    1985, 31, 39–41
    Bears-49ers game, October
    13, 1985, 72–75
Carrier, Mark, 204

Carson, Harry, 128
Carter, Anthony, 58
Carvey, Dana, 217
CBS television, 96, 98, 119, 136
Cefalo, Jimmy, 190
Challenger space shuttle, 153,
    165–66
charity
    headbands for, 128, 144, 149
    "Super Bowl Shuffle" and
    charity issue, 98, 110,
    112, 113
Chicago Art Institute, 117
Chicago Bears
    1963 championship team, 20,
    45, 119
    1981 season, 1–2
    and 1982 players strike, 13
    1984 season, 31–41
    1985 playoffs, 127–38
    1985 season, 43–127
    1986 season, 165, 179–92
    and 1987 players strike, 20,
    196
    1987 season, 193, 194–98
    1988 season, 198–203
    1989 season, 203–4, 206
    1990 season, 204
    1991 playoffs, 218
    1991 season, 209–18
    and acupuncture incident,
    140–41
    in American Bowl, London,
    165, 171–75
    as America's Team, 1
    Bears-Buccaneers game,
    September 8, 1985, 49–50
    Bears-Buccaneers game,
    October 6, 1985, 70–72
    Bears-Colts game, December
    8, 1985, 121–23

Bears-Cowboys game,
November 17, 1985,
92–98

Bears-Dolphins game,
December 2, 1985, 103–5

Bears-Falcons game,
November 24, 1985,
98–99

Bears-49ers game, January 6,
1985, 31, 39–41, 47

Bears-49ers game, October
13, 1985, 72–75

Bears-Giants playoffs,
January 5, 1986, 128–32

Bears-Jets game, December
14, 1985, 123–24

Bears-Lions game,
November 10, 1985, 92

Bears-Lions game, December
22, 1985, 124–25

Bears-Packers game, October
21, 1985, 80–81

Bears-Packers game,
November 3, 1985, 89–92

Bears-Packers rivalry, 31,
34–35, 34–36, 36, 77, 81,
89–91

Bears-Patriots game,
September 15, 1985,
51–53

Bears-Raiders game,
November 4, 1984, 31,
36–38

Bears-Rams playoffs,
January 12, 1986, 132–38

Bears-Redskins game,
December 30, 1984,
38–39, 48

Bears-Redskins game,
September 29, 1985,
67–70

Bears-Redskins playoffs,
January 1987, 191

Bears-Vikings game,
September 19, 1985,
56–61

Bears-Vikings game, October
27, 1985, 88–89

"Bermuda Triangle," 88

Big Ben play, 69

book deals, 91, 167–68

in commercials/endorse-
ments, 25, 26, 61, 63–64,
65, 82–86, 87, 91–92,
101–2, 121, 143–44,
166–67, 168–69, 175–76,
181–85, 205

contract disputes, 31–32, 38,
47–48, 49, 129

Ditka on 1992 media guide
cover, 21

downfall of, 165–66

echo alignment, 129

fines, 49, 95, 124, 127, 128,
133, 190

and firing of Ditka, 219–21

Flutie and, 190–91

46 defense, 9, 50–51, 181

"Friday Pump Club," 120

under Halas, 1

headbands, 127, 133–34,
142, 143–44, 149

and Honey Bears cheerleaders, 117

in London, 165, 171–75

and the media, 87, 118–21,
144–48

Monsters of the Midway, 96

quarterback debacles, 27–29

and quarterback McMahon,
55–66

radio shows, 101, 118–19

and relationship with Ditka
after players strike,
196–98

replacement players (Spare
Bears), 20, 193–94, 196,
197

roster, 231–32

Saturday Night Live, Bears
skits on, 209–15, 217

special teams, 24

sports marketing/advertising
of, 61–64, 82–86, 118, 127

in the spotlight, 87–88

starters, 233–34

after the Super Bowl,
159–63, 166–69

"Super Bowl Shuffle"
recording/video, 38, 98,
101, 103, 109–15, 157,
175

during Super Bowl week,
139–51

Super Bowl XX, 153–63

training camp in Platteville,
Wisconsin, 32, 44–47,
179–81, 195, 205

TV shows, 119–20

"Voice of the Bears" television announcer, 48–49

where are they now?, 223–29

woofing, 96, 102, 139

in Wrestlemania II, 169–71

Chicago Blitz (USFL), 14,
19–20

Chicago Bulls, 214, 215–16,
218

Chicago Community Trust, 113

Chicago Cubs, 2

Chicago Stadium, 217–18

Chicago Sun-Times, 81, 139,
183, 202–3

Chicago Symphony Orchestra,
118

Chicago Tribune, 139, 177, 201

Chicago Vocational High
School, 48

Chicago White Sox, 2

Cincinnati Bengals, 26

Clapton, Eric, 12

Clark, Dwight, 128

Clayton, Mark, 106

Clemson University, 53, 78, 199

Cleveland Browns, 181

Cobb, Ty, 50

Coca-Cola, 61, 84, 102, 171

college draft

1961, 17

1975, 2, 88

1979, 4–5

1980, 6, 7, 10

1981, 10–11

1982, 13

1983, 14–16, 69

1984, 32

1986, 199

1988, 199

1989, 199

1990, 199

Collins, Phil, 12, 173

Collinsworth, Cris, 118

computers, 16

Concannon, Jack, 17
Coppock, Chet, 20, 21, 86, 118,
    162, 163, 165, 168–69,
    169, 170–71, 183, 191
Cornelius, Don, 217
County Stadium, Milwaukee, 34
Covert, Jim, 14–15, 40, 41, 68,
    69, 80
    at 1985 training camp, 46
    in Bears-Giants playoffs,
        January 5, 1986, 130, 131,
        132
    in Wrestlemania II, 170
Cox, Ron, 199
Craig, Roger, 40, 72, 128
Cross, Irv, 96
Cross, Randy, 73
Csonka, Larry, 103
Cumby, George, 80, 81, 91

Dahl, Steve, 118
Daily Express (London), 172
Dallas Cowboys, 10, 17, 49,
    134–35, 137
    as "America's Team," 93, 96,
        177
    Bears-Cowboys game,
        November 17, 1985,
        92–98
    in London vs. Bears, 165,
        172, 174, 177
Dangerfield, Rodney, 93
Davis, Wendell, 199
DeBerg, Steve, 49, 50, 70
Dent, Richard, 15–16, 17,
    23–24, 34, 89, 167
    during 1985 season, 46, 49,
        50
    during 1987 season, 196
    during 1988 season, 198,
        199, 200
    in Bears-49ers game,
        October 13, 1985, 74
    in Bears-Cowboys game,
        November 17, 1985, 94,
        95
    in Bears-Dolphins game,
        December 2, 1985, 104,
        105
    in Bears-Giants playoffs,
        January 5, 1986, 129, 130

    in Bears-Jets game,
        December 14, 1985, 123
    in Bears-Rams playoffs,
        January 12, 1986, 137
    contract disputes, 47, 48,
        129, 141, 142
    on Cowboys, 93
    and Ditka, 24, 197–98
    on Flutie, 190
    with 49ers, 206
    and 46 defense, 51
    injuries, 200
    on McMahon, 65
    in Super Bowl, 154, 155, 156
    and "Super Bowl Shuffle"
        recording/video, 109, 113,
        115
    during Super Bowl week,
        143, 145
    as Super Bowl's MVP, 109,
        154
Denver Broncos, 10
DePaul University, 216
Detroit Lions, 1, 37, 38, 191,
    220
    1953 championship team,
        156
    Bears-Lions game,
        November 10, 1985, 92
    Bears-Lions game, December
        22, 1985, 124–25
diabetes campaign, 144
Dickerson, Eric, 127, 134–35,
    136, 137
Dickey, Lynn, 91
Diliberto, Buddy, 145, 146, 148
Ditka, Diana, 177, 206
Ditka, Mike
    at 1985 training camp, 45–46
    during 1986 season, 181–82,
        185–87, 190
    and 1987 players strike, 20,
        196–98
    during 1987 season, 195
    during 1988 season, 200
    during 1989 season, 203–4
    in 1992 media guide, 21
    and Bears-Buccaneers game,
        September 8, 1985, 49
    and Bears-Buccaneers game,
        October 6, 1985, 71, 72

    and Bears-Colts game,
        December 8, 1985, 122
    and Bears-Cowboys game,
        November 17, 1985, 93,
        97
    and Bears-Dolphins game,
        December 2, 1985, 104–7
    and Bears-Falcons game,
        November 24, 1985, 98,
        99
    and Bears-49ers game,
        January 6, 1985, 39–41
    and Bears-49ers game,
        October 13, 1985, 72, 73,
        74, 75
    and Bears-Giants playoffs,
        January 5, 1986, 132
    Bears head coach, 10, 17–29
    and Bears-Lions game,
        December 22, 1985, 124,
        125
    and Bears-Packers game,
        October 21, 1985, 81
    and Bears-Packers rivalry,
        31, 34–36, 77, 81, 90
    and Bears-Rams playoffs,
        January 12, 1986, 133,
        138
    and Bears-Vikings game,
        September 19, 1985, 56,
        58, 60
    beauty-and-the-beast per-
        sona, 24–26
    in commercials/endorse-
        ments, 25, 26, 65, 167,
        181–82, 206
    contract disputes, 31–32, 38
    with Dallas Cowboys, 92–93
    dropped as ad spokesman,
        206
    DUI arrest, 75
    firing of, 28, 209, 218,
        219–21
    flex defense, 10
    "Grabowski Shuffle, The,"
        114
    Gregg-Ditka rivalry, 31,
        34–36, 77, 81
    heart attack, 205
    and McMahon, 21, 27, 28,
        102, 185, 201–2

motivational skills, 23–24
on Payton, 2
and Perry, 77, 79, 80, 81, 88, 89
as a player's coach, 21–23
quarterback debacles, 27–29
radio show, 20, 101
restaurant, 167, 211–15
and rift among Bears players, 185–87
and Ryan, 10, 45, 53, 88
on *Saturday Night Live*, 209, 218
speaker fees, 207
staying power, 26–27
and Super Bowl, 156, 159
after the Super Bowl, 159, 161–62, 163, 167
during Super Bowl week, 141, 142, 146, 147, 149, 150
"Sybil-like" personality, 19–21
TV show, 119, 149, 194
Ditka: Monster of the Midway (Katayian), 219
Dreesen, Tom, 133, 169
Drexel Burnham Lambert (brokerage firm), 84
Duckworth, Bobby, 32
Duerson, Alicia, 162
Duerson, Dave, 3, 14, 70, 71, 96, 101, 162
Dunsmore, Pat, 14, 39

Eason, Tony, 52, 140, 142, 155, 156, 157
Eastwood, Clint, 169
echo alignment, 129
Edwards, LaVell, 60
Eller, Carl, 51
Emrich, Clyde, 37
Enberg, Dick, 144, 158
equipment, sports, endorsements for, 127
Erhardt, Ron, Bears coach, 6
Esiason, Boomer, 118
Evans, Vince, 19
Ewbank, Weeb, 9

Farley, Chris, 217, 218
in *Saturday Night Live* skit, 211–15

Fencik, Gary, 1, 10, 12–13, 23, 32, 41, 101, 166, 183
in Bears-Rams playoffs, January 12, 1986, 136
in Bears-Redskins game, December 30, 1984, 39
on Ditka, 18
in London, 172, 173, 177
and the Super Bowl, 140, 167
Ferguson, Joe, 124, 128
Finks, Jim, Bears general manager, 2, 7, 11, 14, 15–16, 18, 47, 55
Fisdale, Rick, 61, 62
Flaxman, Barry, 172
flex defense, 10
Florida State University, 199
Flutie, Doug, 27–28, 166–67, 185, 190–91, 200
Flynt, Larry, 61
46 defense, 9, 50–51, 181
Franz, Dennis, 133
Frazier, Leslie, 35, 39, 50
in Bears-Cowboys game, November 17, 1985, 95
in Bears-Dolphins game, December 2, 1985, 104
in Bears-49ers game, October 13, 1985, 73
in Bears-Vikings game, September 19, 1985, 58
in Super Bowl, 156–57
Frederick, Andy, 68
"Friday Pump Club," 120
Friedman, Mitch, 181
Fuller, Steve, 27, 39, 40, 58, 92, 94, 98, 105, 106, 133, 185

Gastineau, Mark, 123
Gault, Willie, 14, 39, 43, 68–69, 124, 137
and acupuncture incident, 140
in Bears-Buccaneers game, October 6, 1985, 71
in Bears-Giants playoffs, January 5, 1986, 132
in Bears-Redskins game, September 29, 1985, 68

in Bears-Vikings game, September 19, 1985, 59, 60
in Super Bowl, 155, 157–58
and "Super Bowl Shuffle" recording/video, 109, 110, 111
traded to Raiders, 198, 202
Gayle, Shaun, 23, 32, 43, 47
in Bears-Giants playoffs, January 5, 1986, 130, 131
in Bears-Redskins game, September 29, 1985, 68
on Ditka, 19, 24
Payton and, 122–23
in Super Bowl, 153
after the Super Bowl, 168–69
Geiger, Kenny, 197
Gentry, Dennis, 68, 131
Giangreco, Mark, 146, 215
Gibbs, Joe, 67
Gifford, Frank, 191
Gleason, Bill, 210
Gorbachev, Mikhail, 139
"Grabowski Shuffle, The," 114
Grange, Red, 171
Grant, Bud, 56
Green Bay Packers, 21–22, 32, 49, 77
Bears' 1986 season and, 188
Bears-Packers game, October 21, 1985, 80–81
Bears-Packers game, November 3, 1985, 89–92
Bears-Packers rivalry, 31, 34–35, 36, 43
McMahon with, 207
McMichael with, 206
Green, Darrell, 39
Greene, "Mean" Joe, 51
Greenwood, L. C., 51
Gregg, Forrest, 31, 34–35, 36, 77, 81
Grier, Rosey, 51
Grobstein, Les, 119–20, 137, 139, 144–48
Grogan, Steve, 157
Gulf War, 79–80
Guy, Ray, 36

Haeger, Gary, 149
Hahn, Robert, 125

Hair Performers (salons), 206
Halas, George, 1, 137
  death of, 16, 32
  and Ditka, 17, 18, 28
  grandsons, 16, 140
  and McMahon's contract, 13,
    14, 62
  and "Ryan" letter, 13
Hampton, Dan, 3, 4–6, 7, 34,
  67, 72, 88, 89, 109, 193,
  196, 198
  at 1985 training camp, 45, 46
  on 1988 season, 199
  in Bears-Cowboys game,
    November 17, 1985, 94,
    96, 97
  in Bears-Dolphins game,
    December 2, 1985, 106,
    107
  and Bears-49ers game,
    October 13, 1985, 74
  and Bears-Packers rivalry, 90
  in Bears-Rams playoffs,
    January 12, 1986, 136
  in Bears-Vikings game,
    September 19, 1985, 58
  on Bortz, 15
  departure from Bears, 204,
    205
  Ditka and, 19, 32
  and 46 defense, 51
  injuries, 203–4
  and McMahon, 65, 201
  on Payton, 120
  on Perry, 78, 83
  and rift among Bears players,
    186–87
  on Ryan, 10, 150
  and Singletary, 206
  in Super Bowl, 153, 155–56
  after the Super Bowl, 159,
    184–85
  and "Super Bowl Shuffle"
    recording/video, 114
  during Super Bowl week,
    140, 142, 151
Hannah, John, 156
Harbaugh, Jim, 28, 185, 201,
  219
Harlan, Bryan, 91, 174
Harper, Roland, 10

Harris, Al, 33, 47, 48, 49, 162
Harrison, George, 12, 173
Hart, Gary, 196
Hart, Jim, 48, 49
Hartenstine, Mike, 2, 34, 51,
  88–89
  on Bears-Dolphins game,
    December 2, 1985, 107–8
  Ditka and, 19
  on Flutie, 191
  on Payton and Super Bowl,
    159
  and "Super Bowl Shuffle"
    recording/video, 114
Hartigan, Neal, 113
headbanding, 127, 133–34, 142,
  143–44, 149
Heisman Trophy winner, 166
Herron, Bruce, 8
Hiaasen, Carl, 104
Hilgenberg, Jay, 1, 10–11, 22,
  33–34, 37, 122
  at 1985 training camp, 46
  in Bears-Cowboys game,
    November 17, 1985, 95
  in Bears-Dolphins game,
    December 2, 1985, 106–7
  in Bears-Vikings game,
    September 19, 1985, 59
  on Ditka, 102
  on Perry, 78
  and rift among Bears players,
    187
  and "Super Bowl Shuffle"
    recording/video, 114
Hogeboom, Gary, 94–95
Holloway, Brian, 155
Holmes, Bud, 112
Holmgren, Mike, 60
Honey Bears cheerleaders, 117
Hope, Bob, 91
Houston Gamblers (USFL), 62
Houston Oilers (AFL), 19
Hubert H. Humphrey
  Metrodome, Minneapolis,
  20, 24–25, 28, 37
  Bears-Vikings game,
    September 19, 1985,
    56–61
Hudson, Rock, 87
Hughes, Ed, 60, 131, 191

Hulk Hogan, 70, 171
Humm, David, 36
Humphries, Stefan, 168–69

Illinois Acupuncture
  Association, 141
Illinois attorney general, office
  of, 113
Indianapolis Colts, 49
  Bears-Colts game, December
    8, 1985, 121–23
Iranian hostage crisis, 1, 2
Iraq, 79–80
Iron Sheik, 171

Jackson Five, 133
Jackson, Michael, 14, 38, 115,
  153
Jackson, Noah, 19
Jackson State University, 3
Jackson, Tom, 118
James, Craig, 52, 135, 156
Jauss, Bill, 210
Jaworski, Ron, 118
Jefferson, John, 35
Jeter, Gary, 135
Jimmy the Greek, 136
Jobe, Frank, 189
Johns, Katherine, 145
Johnson, Don, 104, 153
Johnson, Jimmy, 96
Johnson, Lanny, 203
Johnson, Louise, 81
Jones, Charlie, 189–90
Jones, Ed "Too Tall," 95, 135,
  174
Jones, Jerry, 96
Jordan, Michael, 216, 217–18
Juvenile Diabetes Foundation,
  144, 169

Kansas City Chiefs, 21, 48
Katayian, Armen, 219
Kelly-Springfield Tire
  Company, 184
Khan, Chaka, 173
Kiick, Jim, 103
King Kong Bundy, 171
King Tonga, 170
"Kingfish Shuffle, The"
  (recording), 110

Klecko, Joe, 123
Koch, Greg, 90
Kramer, Tommy, 23, 58, 60, 88
Kuechenberg, Bob, 103

Lambeau Field, Wisconsin,
    Bears-Packers game,
    November 3, 1985, 89–92
Landecker, John, 119
Landeta, Sean, 130–31
Landeta Whiff, 130–31
Landry, Tom, 10, 17–18, 92–93,
    95, 96
Larrivee, Wayne, 44, 48–49,
    179, 189
Lee, Mark, 90, 188
Lennon, John, 1–2
Leo Burnett (ad agency), 61
Lincoln, Keith, 135
Lippett, Ronnie, 140
Lipps, Louis, 189
Lisch, Rusty, 27
Lombardi, Vince, 34
London Monarchs, 86, 175–76
Long, Howie, 11, 12, 31, 36, 37,
    118
Los Angeles Raiders
    Bears-Raiders game,
    November 4, 1984, 31,
    36–38
    Gault traded to, 198, 202
Los Angeles Rams, 51, 96, 191
    Bears-Rams playoffs,
    January 12, 1986, 132–38
    "Fearsome Foursome" of the
    sixties, 51
Luckman, Sid, 55
Lundy, Lamar, 51
Luther, Ed, 32

Madden, John, 98, 133, 136,
    171
    '85 All-Madden team, 149
Maguire, Paul, 177
Mancini, Boom Boom, 171
Manley, Dexter, 68
Manning, Archie, 37
Mantegna, Joe, 81, 110, 155,
    209, 210, 216, 217
    in *Saturday Night Live* skit,
    211–15

Margerum, Ken, 44, 173
Marino, Dan, 14–15, 72, 104–5
marketing/advertising, sports,
    61–64, 82–86, 118, 127
Marshall Fields (department
    store), 127
Marshall, Jim, 51
Marshall, Leonard, 130
Marshall, Wilber, 32–34, 74
    at 1985 training camp, 46
    in Bears-Dolphins game,
    December 2, 1985, 104,
    105, 106
    in Bears-Giants playoffs,
    January 5, 1986, 130
    in Bears-Lions game,
    December 22, 1985, 124
    in Bears-Rams playoffs,
    January 12, 1986, 137
    in the "Bermuda Triangle,"
    88
    fines, 124, 128
    and 46 defense, 50, 51
    with Redskins, 198
    in Super Bowl, 155
Martin, Charles, 35, 188
Matthews, Kevin, 118
Matuszak, John, 11
Maxwell, Dick, 148
McAuliffe, Christa, 153, 165
McCaskey, Ed, 148
McCaskey, Michael, 129, 177,
    188
    during 1986 season, 182–83
    contract disputes, 47
    and Ditka, 197, 202, 218
    and Ditka's contract, 31–32,
    38
    and firing of Ditka, 28,
    219–21
    and Honey Bears decision,
    117
    and McMahon, 141, 148
    and player departures,
    198–99, 204
    president of Chicago Bears,
    16
    after the Super Bowl,
    159–60, 168
McCaskey, Pat, 140, 154
McConnell, Joe, 48

McDonald's, 82–83, 84, 85,
    121, 124, 205
McEnroe, John, 133
McGinnis, Dave, 177
McGrane, Bill, 4–5, 64, 148,
    161
McIlvanney, Hugh, 173
McIntyre, Guy, 40, 75
McKinnon, Dennis, 40, 60, 70,
    132
McMahon, Jim, 9, 13–14, 18,
    35, 39, 41, 55, 87, 125,
    133
    during 1985 season, 45
    during 1987 season, 193, 195
    and acupuncture incident,
    140–41
    in Bears-Buccaneers game,
    October 6, 1985, 70–71
    in Bears-Colts game,
    December 8, 1985, 122
    and Bears-Dolphins game,
    December 2, 1985, 105,
    106
    in Bears-49ers game,
    October 13, 1985, 75
    in Bears-Giants playoffs,
    January 5, 1986, 132
    in Bears-Packers game,
    October 21, 1985, 80
    in Bears-Packers game,
    November 3, 1985, 90, 91
    in Bears-Patriots game,
    September 15, 1985, 52
    in Bears-Raiders game,
    November 4, 1984, 36–37
    in Bears-Rams playoffs,
    January 12, 1986, 137
    in Bears-Redskins game,
    September 29, 1985,
    67–68, 70
    in Bears-Vikings game,
    September 19, 1985,
    56–61
    with Chargers, 200–202, 207
    charities, 128, 144
    in commercials/endorse-
    ments, 61, 63–64, 65, 84,
    127, 143–44, 166–67,
    169, 182
    contracts, 61, 62

Ditka and, 21, 27, 28, 102,
185, 201–2
Flutie replaces, 190
and the "Friday Pump Club,"
120
headbands, 127, 133–34,
142, 143–44, 149
injuries, 21, 28, 57, 92,
140–41, 186, 187,
188–89, 200
in London, 172, 176
"Mac appeal," 64–66
marketing of, 61–64, 82, 84
with Packers, 207
and rift among Bears players,
186–87
roast at Caesar's Palace for,
171
Ryan and, 9–10, 55
and "sluts" incident, 144–48
in Super Bowl, 154, 155,
156, 157–58, 159
after the Super Bowl,
161–62, 166–67, 168,
169, 171, 185
and "Super Bowl Shuffle"
recording/video, 112–13,
114
during Super Bowl week,
140–41, 142, 143–48, 149
with Vikings, 207
McMahon, Nancy, 62, 102, 182
McMahon, Vince, 169–71
McMichael, Debra, 179, 184
McMichael, Steve, 4, 6–7, 9, 89,
114, 151, 205
during 1985 season, 44–45,
46, 51
in Bears-Buccaneers game,
October 6, 1985, 71, 74
in Bears-Cowboys game,
November 17, 1985, 95,
97
in Bears-Dolphins game,
December 2, 1985, 107
in Bears-49ers game,
October 13, 1985, 73
and Bears-Packers rivalry, 91
in Bears-Rams playoffs,
January 12, 1986, 136
Ditka and, 19

with Packers, 206
in Super Bowl, 156
after the Super Bowl, 159,
166, 183, 185
Me and Mrs. P's (restaurant), 19
Meadowlands, Bears-Jets game,
December 14, 1985,
123–24
media
Bears and British, 172,
173–75
Bears and the, 87, 118–21
Ditka and the, 25–26, 40
McMahon and "sluts" inci-
dent, 144–48
McMahon's relationship with
the, 64–65
during Super Bowl week,
139, 140, 141, 142,
144–48
Metrodome, Minneapolis. See
Hubert H. Humphrey
Metrodome
Meyer, Richard, 110, 115
Miami Dolphins, 4, 12, 15, 72,
97
Bears-Dolphins game,
December 2, 1985, 103–5
Miami Herald, 103, 104
Miami Vice (TV show), 104,
182
Minnesota Supreme Court, 4
Minnesota Vikings, 4, 20, 23,
24–25, 37, 51, 219
Bears' 1986 season and, 185
Bears-Vikings game,
September 19, 1985,
56–61
Bears-Vikings game, October
27, 1985, 88–89
McMahon with, 207
"Purple People Eaters" of the
seventies, 51
Mitchum, Marty, 5
Monday Night Football (ABC
television), 27, 56, 79,
80–81, 82, 87, 104–5, 195
Montana, Joe, 40, 55, 63, 72,
73, 128, 149, 200
Moore, Mary Tyler, 144
Moore, Nat, 104, 105, 106

Moorehead, Emery, 10, 21, 37,
47, 60, 65, 71, 156,
168–69, 191–92
Mooshil, Joe, 146, 210
Morris, Desmond, 174
Morris, Jeannie, 40, 149
Morris, Joe, 129–30
Morris, Johnny, 119, 146, 149
Mr. T, 70
Muckensturm, Jerry, 33
Murray, Bill, 133
Musburger, Brent, 96
Myers, Mike, 217
in Saturday Night Live skit,
211–15

Namath, Joe, 9, 57, 110
national events of eighties, 1–2,
31, 43, 44, 51, 87, 153,
165, 169, 171, 187–88,
193–94
National Football Conference
(NFC) Central Division
Bears' 1984 division title,
38
Bears' 1985 win, 137
Bears in 1984 NFC
Championship game, 72
Bears in 1988 NFC
Championship game, 200
National Football League (NFL)
1982 defensive player of the
year, 4
1982 Most Valuable Player, 4
1985 Executive of the Year,
16
1985 Most Valuable Player,
109, 154
commissioner, 81, 133–34
endorsements and, 127
first international game,
American Bowl, 165,
171–75
46 defense, 50–51
founding of Minnesota
Vikings franchise, 56
"McMahon Rule," 143
NFL Europe, 86, 175
NFL Properties, 84
players strikes, 1982, 1987,
13, 20, 196

Rozelle and headband
  incident, 133–34
  and unauthorized apparel,
    133–34, 143–44
USFL and, 33
NBC television, 144, 190
Neal, Dan, 1, 11, 33
Nealon, Kevin, 211
Never Die Easy (Payton), 3
New England Patriots, 6–7, 28,
  56, 107, 133, 200
  Bears-Patriots game,
    September 15, 1985,
    51–53
  during Super Bowl week,
    139, 140, 143
  in Super Bowl XX, 154–59
New Jersey Generals (USFL),
  166
New Orleans Saints, 11, 193
New York Giants, 162
  Bears' 1987 season and, 194,
    195–96
  Bears-Giants playoffs,
    January 5, 1986, 128–32
New York Jets, 5, 9, 103
  Bears-Jets game, December
    14, 1985, 123–24
Newsweek magazine, 63, 193
Nixon, Richard, 124
Norman, Greg, 133
North, Oliver, 188
Northwest National Bank,
  Chicago, 125

Oakland Raiders, 11, 12
O'Bradovich, Ed, 45
O'Brien, Conan, 209
O'Brien, Ken, 123
Observer, The (London), 173
O'Connor, Fred, 2
Odenkirk, Bob, 209, 210, 217
Olsen, Merlin, 36, 51, 144, 158
Olympics, 1980, 1984, 1, 31
Omni magazine, 91
Orange Bowl, Bears-Dolphins
  game, December 2, 1985,
  103–5
Osborne, Jim, 34
Osbourne, Ozzy, 170–71
Owens, Dennis, 156

Page, Alan, 4, 13, 19, 51
Pagel, Mike, 122
Palmer, Brad "the Professor,"
  48, 179–80
Pappas, Gus, 120
Parcells, Bill, 128, 132, 195
Pardee, Jack, 93
Parsons, Bob, 19–20
Payton, Connie, 102
Payton, Walter, 2–3, 4, 20, 40,
  55, 88, 127
  during 1985 season, 48, 50
  at 1986 training camp, 179
  autobiography, 3
  in Bears-Buccaneers game,
    October 6, 1985, 71
  in Bears-Colts game,
    December 8, 1985, 122,
    122–23
  in Bears-Cowboys game,
    November 17, 1985, 94
  in Bears-Dolphins game,
    December 2, 1985, 105,
    106
  in Bears-Falcons game,
    November 24, 1985, 98
  in Bears-49ers game,
    October 13, 1985, 74, 75
  in Bears-Jets game,
    December 14, 1985, 123
  in Bears-Lions game,
    November 10, 1985, 92
  in Bears-Packers game,
    October 21, 1985, 80, 81
  in Bears-Packers game,
    November 3, 1985, 91
  in Bears-Patriots game,
    September 15, 1985, 52
  in Bears-Redskins game,
    December 30, 1984, 39
  in Bears-Redskins game,
    September 29, 1985,
    67–68, 70
  in Bears-Vikings game,
    September 19, 1985, 59,
    60
  death of, 3, 227
  and Jim Brown's rushing
    record, 48
  last game, 195
  in London, 172, 177

  retirement, 198
  on *Saturday Night Live*, 209,
    217
  in Super Bowl, 155, 159
  after the Super Bowl,
    160–62, 167
  and "Super Bowl Shuffle"
    recording/video, 112–13
  during Super Bowl week,
    149–50
  TV commentaries, 120
Pennsylvania State University,
  2
Peoria *Journal-Star*, 219
Perry, Sherry, 85, 112, 173, 179,
  183, 184, 195
Perry, William "the
  Refrigerator," 31, 40, 51,
  53, 72–73, 78–80, 127
  at 1985 training camp, 45
  in Bears-Cowboys game,
    November 17, 1985, 94
  in Bears-Dolphins game,
    December 2, 1985, 104,
    107
  in Bears-49ers game,
    October 13, 1985, 74, 75
  in Bears-Lions game,
    November 10, 1985, 92
  in Bears-Packers game,
    October 21, 1985, 80–81
  in Bears-Packers game,
    November 3, 1985, 91
  in Bears-Rams playoffs,
    January 12, 1986, 137
  in commercials/endorse-
    ments, 61, 65, 82–86, 87,
    91–92, 175–76, 182, 184,
    185
  "Fridge Mania," 77, 79,
    81–86, 91
  in London, 172, 173, 174,
    177
  marketing of, 82–86
  popularity after Super Bowl,
    175–76
  in Super Bowl, 156, 158, 159
  after the Super Bowl, 159,
    167, 168
  and "Super Bowl Shuffle"
    recording/video, 112

during Super Bowl week,
142, 149
weight problems, 195, 198
in Wrestlemania II, 170
Philadelphia Eagles, 12, 17, 86,
151, 167, 176
Bears' 1986 season and, 181
Ryan as coach for, 150–51,
167, 181, 196, 200
Phipps, Mike, 19
Pickel, Bill, 37
Pierson, Don, 201
Pittsburgh Steelers, 5, 51, 74,
157, 189
Plank, Doug, 50
Plater, Danny, 149
Platteville, Wisconsin, Bears
training camp in, 32,
44–47, 179–81, 195, 205
Players Association, 13, 196
Pontiac Silverdome, Bears-
Lions game, December
22, 1985, 124–25
Pope, Edwin, 103
Powell, Marvin, 5
Pro Bowls, 1, 3, 9, 15, 34, 35,
46, 50, 56, 162, 165, 199
Pro Football Hall of Fame
Butkus in, 48
Singletary in, 206
Pro Football Weekly, 4, 64
Pyle, Mike, 20, 119

radio
Bears players with radio
shows, 101, 118–19
Ditka's radio show, 20, 101,
220
Miami radio stations on
Bears-Dolphins, 103
"Super Bowl Shuffle"
recording, 103, 111
WGN-AM, Chicago, 44,
118–19
WLS-AM, New Orleans,
144–45
WMAQ-AM radio, Chicago,
20
Rains, Dan, 70
Reagan, Ronald, 1, 2, 3, 43,
139, 153, 169

Red Label Records, 110
Reinsdorf, Jerry, 216
replacement players, 20,
193–94, 196, 197
Retton, Mary Lou, 31
RFK Stadium, Washington DC,
Bears-Redskins game,
December 30, 1984,
38–39
Rice, Donna, 194
Rice, Jerry, 72, 200
Richards, Keith, 11, 133
Richardson, Mike, 10, 14, 23,
73, 94, 95, 97
Riggins, John, 39, 70
Riggs, Gerald, 98
Rivera, Ron, 32
Robinson, John, 136
Rodman, Dennis, 216
Rolling Stone magazine, 63, 143
Rose, Jim, 146
Rose, Pete, 50
Rowdy Roddy Piper, 171
Rozelle, Pete, 81, 133–34
Ryan, Buddy (defensive coordi-
nator), 4, 5–6, 8–10, 12,
13, 23, 72, 123
during 1984 season, 32, 33,
35
during 1985 season, 45, 50
and Bears-Dolphins game,
December 2, 1985, 104–7
and Bears-49ers game,
October 13, 1985, 74
and Bears-Patriots game,
September 15, 1985, 52
and Bears-Redskins game,
September 29, 1985, 67
as coach for Philadelphia
Eagles, 150–51, 167, 181,
196, 200
departure from Bears,
150–51, 159
Ditka and, 10, 45, 53, 88
and 46 defense, 9, 50–51,
181
and Giants offense, 130
and Perry, 77, 78, 79
and Super Bowl, 157
after the Super Bowl, 162
Rypien, Mark, 203

Sadat, Anwar, 2
Saldi, Jay, 16
Salisbury, Sean, 118
San Diego Chargers, 27, 32,
135, 201, 207
San Diego Padres, 2
San Francisco 49ers, 103, 128,
129
1988 NFC Championship
win over Bears, 200
Bears-49ers game, January 6,
1985, 31, 39–41, 47
Bears-49ers game, October
13, 1985, 72–75
Dent with, 206
Sanders, "Neon" Deion, 118
Saturday Night Live, January 12,
1991 (TV show), Bears
skit on, 209–15, 217
Savage, Macho Man Randy, 171
Schafer, Michael, 189
Sharpe, Sterling, 118
Shearer, Brad, 7
Sheridan, Danny, 211, 213
Shiriashi, Hiroshi, 140, 141
Shula, Don, 12, 104, 106
Shurmur, Fritz, 6–7, 136
Simms, Phil, 128, 129, 130,
131, 195, 196
Simpson, O. J., 98
Singletary, Kim, 47, 52, 56
Singletary, Mike, 8–9, 11, 33,
41, 70, 74, 124
in Bears-Cowboys game,
November 17, 1985, 96
in Bears-Patriots game,
September 15, 1985, 52
in Bears-Rams playoffs,
January 12, 1986, 137
in Bears-Vikings game,
September 19, 1985, 56
in the "Bermuda Triangle," 88
contract disputes, 47–48, 49
on Dent, 129
and Hampton, 206
in Super Bowl, 155, 156
after the Super Bowl, 167–68
Smigel, Robert, 209, 210, 216,
217, 218
in Saturday Night Live skit,
211–15

Smith, Emmitt, 2
Snyder, Jimmy "the Greek," 136
soccer, 173–74, 175, 176, 177
Soldier Field, Chicago, 25, 217
  Bears-Buccaneers game,
    September 8, 1985, 49–50
  Bears-Colts game, December
    8, 1985, 121–23
  Bears-Falcons game,
    November 24, 1985,
    98–99
  Bears-Giants playoffs,
    January 5, 1986, 128–32
  Bears-Lions game,
    November 10, 1985, 92
  Bears-Packers game, October
    21, 1985, 80–81
  Bears-Patriots game,
    September 15, 1985,
    51–53
  Bears-Raiders game,
    November 4, 1984, 31,
    36–38
  Bears-Rams playoffs,
    January 12, 1986, 132–38
  Bears-Redskins game,
    September 29, 1985,
    67–70
  Bears-Redskins playoffs,
    January 1987, 191
  Bears-Vikings game, October
    27, 1985, 88–89
Solti, Sir Georg, 118
Sons, Ray, 81
Sorey, Revie, 1, 5
Soul Train (TV show), 217
Southern Illinois University, 48
Southern Methodist University,
  135
"Spare Bears" (replacement
  players), 20, 193–94, 196,
  197
Sports Illustrated magazine, 63,
  219
sportscasters, 20, 48, 86, 107–8,
  118–19, 144, 158, 162,
  189–90
sportswriters, 65, 81, 103, 104,
  172, 173–75, 201, 202–3
Sportswriters, The (TV show),
  210

Stallone, Sylvester, 87
Stanfel, Dick, 15, 22, 61, 156
Starr, Bart, 34
Starr, Ringo, 12, 173
Staubach, Roger, 93
Steiner, Jim, 81–82, 83–84, 86,
  184, 185
Stenerud, Jan, 57
Stephenson, Dwight, 106, 107
Stewart, Rod, 12, 173
Stills, Ken, 90
Studd, Big John, 170
Studwell, Scott, 59
Suhey, Matt, 7, 10, 90, 92, 132,
  156, 173, 179
Summerall, Pat, 98
Sun Devil Stadium, at Arizona
  State, 18
Sun (London), 174–75
Sunday Express (London), 176
Sunday Times (London), 172
Super Bowl III, 9
"Super Bowl Shuffle, The"
  (recording/video), 38, 98,
  101, 103, 109–17, 157,
  175
Super Bowl XX
  aftermath, 159–63, 166–69
  January 26, 1985, 154–63
  pregame preparations,
    153–54
  Super Bowl rings, 168
  Super Bowl week, 139–51
  ticket sales for, 125
  20ᵗʰ anniversary of, 29
Superdome, New Orleans, 143
Super Bowl XX, Bears vs.
  Patriots at, 154–59
Swirsky, Chuck, 49, 216
Sybil (book/movie), 19

Tagliabue, Paul, 148
Tampa Bay Buccaneers, 35
  Bears-Buccaneers game,
    September 8, 1985, 49–50
  Bears-Buccaneers game,
    October 6, 1985, 70–72
Tate, David, 24
Taylor, Lawrence, 70, 109, 128,
  130, 131–32
Telander, Rick, 210

television
  ABC's Bears telecasts, 27,
    56–58, 79, 80–81, 82, 87,
    104–5, 195
  Bears' Chicago broadcasts,
    48–49, 179
  CBS' Bears telecasts, 96, 98,
    136
  David Letterman's show, 91
  Ditka and the media, 25–26,
    40, 119
  Ditka's TV show, 119, 149,
    194
  McMahon's relationship with
    the media, 64
  Miami TV station on Bears-
    Dolphins, 103–4
  NBC's Super Bowl broad-
    cast, 144, 158
  viewing audience for Super
    Bowl XX, 139
  WBBM, Chicago, 179
  WGN, Chicago, 48–49,
    107–8, 179, 205, 216
Tennessee State University, 15
Texas Stadium, Bears-Cowboys
  game, November 17,
  1985, 92–98
Thayer, Tom, 14, 142, 200
  at 1985 training camp, 45, 46
  in Bears-Cowboys game,
    November 17, 1985, 95
  on Bears-Dolphins game,
    December 2, 1985, 104
  in Bears-Vikings game,
    September 19, 1985, 61
  on McMahon, 57
  after the Super Bowl, 167
Theismann, Joe, 39, 67, 69–70
Theobald, Phil, 219
Thomas, Bob, 123
Time magazine, 16
Tobin, Bill, 177, 219
  Bears scout, 2, 15, 16, 53, 81
Tobin, Vince, 181
Tomczak, Mike, 27, 98, 167,
  185, 201
Tossell, David, 175, 176
Tufo, Rich, 110
Tyler, Wendell, 40
Tyson, Mike, 8

United States Football League
(USFL)
Chicago Blitz, 14, 19–20
Houston Gamblers, 62
New Jersey Generals, 166
NFL and, 33
United Way, 149
University of Arkansas, 4
University of California, 32
University of Colorado, 24
University of Florida, 32, 33
University of Illinois, 48
University of Iowa, 10, 33
University of Louisville, 7, 8
University of Notre Dame, 4,
45, 70, 82
University of Pittsburgh, 14–15
University of Southern
California, 5, 12, 64
University of Tennessee, 68
University of Texas, 7, 62

Vainisi, Jerry, Bears general
manager, 47, 141, 147,
185
Valdiserri, Ken, 39–40, 75, 91,
121, 140, 148, 161, 173
Van Brocklin, Norm, 65
Van Horne, Keith, 5, 11–12, 14,
21–22, 31, 36
during 1985 season, 46, 50
and Bears-Buccaneers game,
October 6, 1985, 71
in Bears-Cowboys game,
November 17, 1985, 95
in Bears-Giants playoffs,
January 5, 1986, 130
in Bears-Packers game,
October 21, 1985, 80
and Flutie, 190, 191
in London, 172, 173
in Super Bowl, 156
after the Super Bowl, 162
Vasilopolous, Bobby, 40,
149–50
Veterans Stadium, Philadelphia,
196

video, "Super Bowl Shuffle,"
111–13

Waddle, Tom, 205
Waechter, Henry, 98
Walker, Herschel, 33
Walsh, Bill, 26–27, 39–40, 60,
72, 73, 75, 132
Wannstedt, Dave, 86, 96
Warhol, Andy, 194
Washington, Harold, 110, 162
Washington, Joe, 38
Washington Redskins, 16, 36,
43, 49, 194
Bears-Redskins game,
December 30, 1984,
38–39, 48
Bears-Redskins game,
September 29, 1985,
67–70
Bears-Redskins playoffs,
January 1987, 191
Marshall with, 198
Watts, Rickey, 19
Wayne's World (movie), 217
Wendt, George, 214–16, 217, 218
West Coast offense, 60, 72
White, Danny, 94
White, Dwight, 51
White, Randy, 95, 135
White, Reggie, 12
White, Vanna, 153
Wilder, James, 50
Willis, Bruce, 171
Willis, Peter Tom, 199
Willsmer, Russell, 177
Wilson, Marc, 36, 37
Wilson, Otis, 7–8, 9, 33, 38, 43,
52, 74, 87, 148
at 1985 training camp, 46
in Bears-Buccaneers game,
October 6, 1985, 71
in Bears-Cowboys game,
November 17, 1985,
94–95, 96, 97
in Bears-Falcons game,
November 24, 1985, 99

in Bears-Giants playoffs,
January 5, 1986, 130, 131
in Bears-Packers game,
October 21, 1985, 81
in Bears-Packers game,
November 3, 1985,
90–91
in Bears-Rams playoffs,
January 12, 1986, 137
in Bears-Redskins game,
December 30, 1984, 38
in the "Bermuda Triangle,"
88
contract dispute, 202–3
departure from Bears, 203
on Dickerson, 136
and 46 defense, 50, 51
injuries, 202–3
and Louis Lipp incident,
189–90
and Perry, 85, 174
on Ryan, 8
in Super Bowl, 154, 155, 156
after the Super Bowl, 159,
184
and "Super Bowl Shuffle"
recording/video, 109, 110,
111, 112
during Super Bowl week, 42,
139
in Wrestlemania II, 171
Winston, Fred, 145
Woolford, Donnell, 199, 203
Wooten, Ron, 142, 157
Wrestlemania, 86
Wrestlemania II, 169–71
Wrigley Field, Chicago, 50

Yale University, 12
Yarno, George, 49–50
Young, Steve, 33

Zorn, Jim, 81
Zucker, Shelley, 62
Zucker, Steve, 61–64, 82, 112,
134, 144, 147, 182, 188,
189, 193, 201–2